D1384558

FROM NEWTON'S SLEEP

FROM

NEWTON'S

SLEEP

Joseph Vining

PRINCETON UNIVERSITY PRESS

PRINCETON, NEW JERSEY

COPYRIGHT © 1995 BY PRINCETON UNIVERSITY PRESS

PUBLISHED BY PRINCETON UNIVERSITY PRESS, 41 WILLIAM STREET,

PRINCETON, NEW JERSEY 08540

IN THE UNITED KINGDOM: PRINCETON UNIVERSITY PRESS, CHICHESTER, WEST SUSSEX

ALL RIGHTS RESERVED

LIBRARY OF CONGRESS CATALOGING-IN-PUBLICATION DATA

VINING, JOSEPH

P. CM.

FROM NEWTON'S SLEEP / JOSEPH VINING.

INCLUDES BIBLIOGRAPHICAL REFERENCES AND INDEX.

ISBN 0-691-03487-7 (CLOTH)

I. LAW—PHILOSOPHY. I. TITLE.

K230.V56F76 1994   304'.1—DC20   94-16619 CIP

FRONTISPIECE: DETAIL OF WILLIAM BLAKE'S COLOR PRINT, NEWTON (1795), COURTESY OF
THE TATE GALLERY, LONDON.

THE LINES FROM "MONET'S 'WATERLILIES'" ARE REPRINTED FROM COLLECTED POEMS OF
ROBERT HAYDEN, EDITED BY FREDERICK GLAYSHER, BY PERMISSION OF LIVERIGHT
PUBLISHING CORPORATION. COPYRIGHT © 1985 BY ERMA HAYDEN.

THE LINES FROM "WIDOW" AND "THE MAHARAJAH'S WELL" ARE REPRINTED FROM DAVID
SUTTON, SETTLEMENTS, BY PERMISSION OF PETERLOO POETS. COPYRIGHT © 1991
BY DAVID SUTTON.

THIS BOOK HAS BEEN COMPOSED IN ADOBE TRUMP MEDIAEVAL

DESIGNED BY FRANK MAHOOD

PRINCETON UNIVERSITY PRESS BOOKS ARE PRINTED ON ACID-FREE PAPER AND MEET THE
GUIDELINES FOR PERMANENCE AND DURABILITY OF THE COMMITTEE ON PRODUCTION
GUIDELINES FOR BOOK LONGEVITY OF THE COUNCIL ON LIBRARY RESOURCES

PRINTED IN THE UNITED STATES OF AMERICA

10 9 8 7 6 5 4 3 2 1

ꙮ NEWTON'S SLEEP

"Newton's Sleep" is from William Blake's imagination, as the state that comes when the mind is wholly occupied by the form of thought of which Newton is celebrated as the great source. "May God us keep / From Single vision & Newton's sleep!" are the memorable lines, the close of "With happiness stretch'd across the hills" (1802). They are quoted still in sober secular disputes as Blake's "Jerusalem" is sung still by excited secular utopians. Before the exclamation and appeal Blake has summoned the qualities of human vision and what human vision is vision of, by number (not surrendering even number to Newton), from "twofold Always," the "inward eye," and rising on.

Blake's vision of Newton's Sleep is unaffected by the custom today of describing cosmological argument and speculation in this century as post-Newtonian. Indeed, neither the Newtonian nor the post-Newtonian is actually Newtonian. Newton himself in his nights' sleep dreamed beyond a world of single vision, and in his life and person declined to bind himself to the form of thought he systematized and make it the form of thought itself.

Against Newton's Sleep, keeping us from it, is the presence of law in the human mind. Newton's Sleep can steal over us only as law withdraws.

Contents ⚘ _____

Contents of Sections 🐦

xiv CONTENTS

SECTION ❦ I

Introductory

1.1 ❧ Radical Law

Breathing air is so natural that air's presence does not rise
to consciousness. It is taken for granted. The ambient love
of a parent, even of husband or wife, can pass unnoticed
also. Breathing man and beloved reflecting on the nature
of things are both fully capable of omitting air and love
from their articulated conceptions and, when challenged,
denying they are necessary, with comic or tragic effect. "I
do not need them, no one needs them, they do not exist,"
says someone breathing, assuming, and depending, to others who are breathing, assuming, and depending. And they
may say, "How true." Myths and tales are full of the possibility and the consequence.

Law is like these. Much discussion of the nature of
things omits it entirely, taking it for granted, supposing,
without thinking about it, that it is there and always will
be. If its claims press a bit on a reflective consciousness,
which has built a structure of propositions that does not
take it into account, the same comic or tragic posture can
be seen, denial that it is necessary, or that it exists, by
beings breathing it, assuming it, and depending upon it.
Literary and philosophic schools that find in a phrase of
Rimbaud or Wallace Stevens or a cry of Nietzsche or
Kierkegaard the turning point in Western thought give no
thought to law. Physicists who see now only a tiny gap
between their symbolic systems and a Theory of Everything, biologists who place man among the fossils, economists who plan the future, give no thought to law.

Law is the great overlooked fact in modern thought. Its
true acknowledgment would threaten radical change,
even among those whose articulated visions attempt to
compete with both positivism, on the one hand, and

positivism's enemy, historicism, on the other. With law enters personification, in the large and in the small, substance that does not ultimately become form or process, responsibility that goes beyond the existence of things that consciousness reflects upon. Musical, mathematical, evolutionary visions of the ultimate ground of what is, become only partial visions, insufficient. Human language, still conceived as only in part metaphorical and personal even by those who resist a universal sway for mathematical form, is pulled away from the very notion of the literal. The meanings of those who speak of the nature of things, ultimate and proximate, expand to the wholes of what they express in all they say.

Law will not be acknowledged soon by the articulate. The shifts in the structures of propositions now entertained would be too large. But the legal form of thought is engaged in daily by innumerable thousands of the less articulate, quite as much as the mathematical form of thought; the legal form of thought is not about to die from disuse. And if law itself should begin to disappear, then, like air, its absence might press its necessity into consciousness.

I.2   ฿   *Law as Evidence*

Law, philosophy of mind, and metaphysics are interwoven. They are dependent, not independent of one another. Which of them is evidence, which conclusion? You can say thus and so is the view of mind to be entertained and such and such is the consequence for law. But if there is law, in practice and thought, proceeding at large in the world, and if authority is asserted and accepted, it is equally true that there is a consequence for views of mind. Such is the connection between law, mind, and cosmology that they are aspects of the same, and when we ask what our situation actually is as an empiric matter, what views of mind are actually entertained, what larger beliefs actually are in the world, it is too often overlooked that law is evidence of view and belief far stronger than academic statement or introspection can provide.

1.3 ✌ *Partial Insight*

"Not a lawyer," observed Flaubert, playing with the connection between poetry and law and resisting its strength, "but carries within him the debris of a poet."

1.4 ✌ *Texts and Obedience*

The question for a lawyer facing a text is always why respond to it, why (to use the word) *obey*? Why entertain the thought of obedience? If something in you pushes you in another direction, why pay attention if there is no concrete threat or threat that you cannot avoid through imaginativeness, cleverness, application, and luck?

Against that which from without or within pushes you in some direction, there are only those small shapes on a page—unless something is being said to you.

1.5   *The Dailiness of Law*

The ordinary legal text stands somewhere between piece of journalism and sacred text or studied work of art. Legal method holds it there.

Journalism does not last. It is not read closely, reread— there is hardly time to do so. It is replaced. It cannot be reread, read closely, if it does not last, and if it is not re-read, it does not last. It disappears.

The legal text, like a piece of journalism, also is re-placed. But it is read closely in course of writing the new statement of law that replaces it. Legal method, close reading, makes a legal text last at least long enough to be read closely, and pulling back from the rush of journalism, and looking to the studied work of art, demands devotion of the time and care to writing that will support close reading.

1.6   *The Legal Order*

"*I say* to *you* in the *name* of the *law*." Except (perhaps) for some of the articles and prepositions, "the" and "to" and "of," each word in this sentence is a mystery. The *I*, the *you*, the *name* of the law, the *law* itself, the *saying*: none has a common meaning that does not disappear into a winding way.

Someone speaking the sentence might mean "I want you to do this." But that is not the sentence spoken. The sen-tence spoken is used as if the speaker meant to say something other than something about his wants. What does he mean if we take seriously each word of what he says?

I.7   *Person and Substance*

A gifted computer programmer wished to have his computer "talk endlessly and in perfect English about nothing" because "the output generated by such programming can be fascinating, humorous, even aesthetically pleasing." He created Racter (a contraction of Raconteur), which conjugated both regular and irregular verbs, remembered the gender of nouns, and, most important, could assign a "variable status" to "randomly chosen 'things,'" which might be "individual words, clause or sentence forms, paragraph structures, indeed whole story forms." He believed he had achieved a program in which "the programmer is removed to a very great extent from the specific form of the system's output." What Racter forms "is dependent upon what it finds in its files, and what it can find is an extremely wide range of words that are categorized in a specific fashion and what might be called 'syntax directives,' which tell the computer how to string the words together. An important faculty of the program is its ability to direct the computer to maintain certain randomly chosen variables (words or phrases), which will then appear and reappear as a given block of prose is generated." He concludes, "This seems to spin a thread of what might initially pass for coherent thinking throughout the computer-generated copy so that once the program is run, its output is not only new and unknowable, it is apparently thoughtful."

Describing what he has done, the programmer uses quotation marks around some of his own words, such as "things" in referring to words, clauses, or story forms, and he uses explicitly the language of *appearance* and *reality* to which uses of quotation marks point—"what might initially pass," "apparently thoughtful." But he does not put quotation marks around the fascinating, the humorous, and the aesthetically pleasing he finds in the program's output. Therein lies a question that nonlawyers must face as they look at and respond to natural forms or as they think occasionally about their own connection with nature. But for the lawyer, that underlying question must be faced as he goes about his work. Will he read such a text? Will he allow it to inform his judgment as he forms his own statement of what others ought to do?

Given the word "love" and instructed to write an "essay," Racter generated this output:

> We will commence with a question: does steak love lettuce? This question is implacably hard and inevitably difficult to answer. Here is a question: does an electron love a proton, or does it love a neutron? Here is a question: does a man love a woman or, to be specific and to be precise, does Bill love Diane? The interesting and critical response to this question is: no! He is obsessed and infatuated with her. He is loony and crazy about her. That is not the love of steak and lettuce, of electron and proton and neutron. This dissertation will show that the love of a man and a woman is not the love of steak and lettuce. Love is interesting to me and fascinating to you but it is painful to Bill and Diane. That is love!

Are these words and sentences, as the programmer says, "about nothing"? The "seeming," the "passing for," have as their implicit contrast (from which they themselves draw their meaning) substance, even reality—neither of them with quotes about them—which is what a person's words, sentences, and paragraphs are about. Seeming and only seeming, and the absence of aboutness, are inextricably connected in our experience, and both are in turn inextricably connected to the presence or absence of a speaking person who is alive to the mind.

For the nonlawyer this may be a curiosity to be reflected upon, until time for reflection runs out and there is a turn to other matters. For the lawyer these connections are critical. They start, and they stop, his work. For following upon his work is action, or restraint, intervention in the world, by the lawyer himself or by those listening to the lawyer, with consequences helping or harming what all actually care about.

1.8 ✒ *Demonology*

A turn that is not made so long as one remains in legal discourse is that which is made at the beginning of much modern social science, the elimination of the entity in discourse by reducing or dissolving it ("it," after the terms "him," "her," or "them" have been cast aside) into a point which is the focus of forces operating. The forces operating then become the real objects of interest, like the demons of primitive exclamation.

Such a turn is not made in legal discourse because, if it were made, the very object of inquiry would be lost. In legal discourse there is search for responsibility or authority, neither of which a force can have, or to use the old word, a demon immune to human appeal.

1.9 ❧ *Law as Heresy*

Legal thought is the representative form now of that larger movement of thought which accompanied and found form in art, literature, dance, and music before they began to be about themselves. Cartesian orthodoxy, the learning in schools that thought must begin with clear and distinct ideas, has gradually limited to law an experience of thought that openly assumes and seeks meaning—hardly limiting it, of course, for law is pervasive, daily and deep in the thought of all—but limiting it to law (where it cannot be given up, any more than law can be given up) until what is taught in schools gradually changes again.

Beginning with clear and distinct ideas, and building on them: how wrong this is, though "objectivity" is conceived now to be based upon it. The error in it is twofold.

Ideas, clear and distinct, are to be captured, tied down linguistically or otherwise—they do not themselves lead on to other ideas or beyond themselves, and they do not themselves lead one on. But the what of an idea escapes, always escapes. It leads on, unfolds, is not captured, and cannot be made into a unit, a bit, a package, nor even represented by a word or symbol by itself and outside the context of all words and symbols thrown out, painted, drawn, used, selected and put together again and again by the person thinking.

The whatness of an idea cannot be confined so or made so static, for the what is not separate from the person thinking—this is the second fold of the fundamental error, the separation of self from ideas, distinct from them, clear of them, as they are distinct among themselves and clear of one another. The *love, fear,* and *envy* treated in psychology are a person's love, fear, and envy, and always escape (and anyone can see they escape) the definitions proposed to capture them so that those using and building on the definitions can, through a mere shake of the head, be seen not to be speaking of or thinking about *love*, *fear*, or *envy*. So too with the *individual*, the *dignity*, or the *office* of political theory, the *altruism* or the *deception* of evolutionary biology, the *language* or the *mind* of cognitive science. Ideas reached for to make them clear and distinct escape the grasp. The what of the idea pursued in thinking, what it is, leads on and takes the self with it.

I.10 ☙ *Belief*

There are two separable places for belief or the absence of it, two kinds of belief. One place, one kind, is ontological, belief with respect to the existence of some particular event in history, or belief in mind or in supraindividual entity or in spirit. This is what is usually in mind when referring to someone (or to a lawyer *qua* lawyer) as a "believer."

The other kind of belief is belief in what one says, that it is one's own, that one is in what one says, that it comes from within and is access to what is within one. This is what is spoken of usually when speaking of authenticity.

But the two come together, so much so that they may not be separable, when one uses language as evidence of belief and as evidence even of one's own belief, as when one asks oneself, "What do I actually believe?" and notes the mind, the spirit, the concrete historical truth, the supraindividual entities, to which sentences one has spoken refer, or which are presupposed by one's use of the language (one's method or analytic actions in coming to and out with the language one speaks). If, as a lawyer, one believes that what one says to be the law is indeed the law, if one stands behind it (not merely in the sense of being willing to accept the risk of monetary liability), and if one then looks at what one says, one is faced with the question of belief in that to which one ostensibly refers or in that which is presupposed by what one has done in coming to what one says.

There is nothing literal about the language one uses. What one means in saying "court," for instance, or "the law," is not fixed by rule or dictionary. There is no absolutely necessary answer to the question what one means or someone else means (though much in law turns on the answer). But what is always discovered is that pushing on the metaphors of one's usage pushes one beyond the here and now of the individual's situation, pushes more toward transcendence than toward an uninformed and isolated particular. The connection of the two kinds of belief also poses again the question of the objectivity of language that in its benign form (the form in which the lawyer Owen Barfield pursued it in *Poetic Diction*) is the question whether word or language carries something and can tell us something in addition to what is contingently scratched on our blank slates.

I.11   *Thinking in Categories*

In thinking about human affairs are we confined to two basic categories of phenomena? The biological, which is a given, and the social construct, wholly changeable and with no necessity whatever to it?

There is a third. Call it the spiritually determined, to give away nothing to the biological in dignity and force. In it is that of experience which is necessary to meaning. Any part of it is changeable, escapable. But if meaningless-ness is the consequence of change, of the living-with or the living-without that change brings, there is pressure, a pressure of the spirit, to change again until the part fits again and what was lived-without is restored or what was lived-with at the cost of life is left behind. Active partici-pation in its being, by us affected by it, makes the spiritu-ally determined different at beginning and end from the biologically determined. But the spiritually determined is equally different from the malleable constrictions, called socially constructed, that happen to have been served up by a process operating over time and that may or may not advance what we imagine to be our independently chosen purposes.

I.12 ❧ *Appearance and Action*

An actress appears in a movie musical. Another singer's voice is substituted for hers on the soundtrack. She is a composite. Her singing is the appearance of singing. Why should this be any different from the facades of the town in the movie, which are composites and mere appearances ("mere," since verisimilitude has been the coin of the photographic medium)? But it is. There is a fundamental difference where a person is conceived.

Everything, including another person, may be coming to be seen as a composite. Such a vision of the world may be relative to the times, and ultimately perhaps no one will want to say that the composites perceived are less true or real than the reality experienced by an earlier gen-eration, the "reality" against which "mere appearance" stood in contrast. But there is something not relative, which runs from generation to generation, that what one perceives as a composite one would not mind torturing. In fact, what one did to it would not be called torture.

I.13 & *Playing in Prison*

We are given lines to learn, in a play; lines to speak to ourselves, in a novel or poem; lines to say with others, in a liturgy. The lines spoken are not us speaking. They are quotations, the words of another, mouthed. But, as can be so clear in learning and speaking a part in a play, they can open the unrealized self. For the deprived, depraved, and brutalized, in possession only of the language of sex and anger, lines so spoken can be escape, a channel opening for dammed aspiration. To those not so deprived, they can be a channel for greater aspiration. Admiration proceeds from wonder, imitation from admiration: there seems a reverse flow too, admiration proceeding from imitation, wonder from admiration. There is identification with what is *in* the words, that frees the speaker to go on.

But the speaker rarely goes on to anything that is fully and absolutely her own. A play learned within a prison is an image of life itself; partial, though, because the glory of the world does not figure in it.

What sets apart the learning and speaking of quotations that are from the materials of law is that they never were speech of an individual author, but were speech rather of a person identified with all. What pulls the two instances together is that in the words of the play, poem, or liturgy which act as a rung for the speaker to pull up on, there is actually little that is the property only of the individual author of them. What that is which is beyond the individual author few today wish to articulate with a name. Reductionists who speak of "language itself speaking through the individual" may with averted eyes be timidly reaching to touch it.

1.14 ❦ *Texts among the Nonlegal*

Science is experimental, but general apprehension of scientific propositions about the world is not a product of scientific method. All but a tiny number of persons who ask themselves what they believe, and who must make decisions on the basis of it, know virtually nothing of the mathematics or substance of the scientific disciplines out of which claims are made about the nature of life and the world. They have been taught, by figures of authority in schools, who have said, "Believe this, this is the truth." "Why believe it?" something in every student asks at some time. "Because the teacher says so" is always part of the real answer. If challenged the teacher will adduce texts in support of what he or she is instructing students to believe and take as ground for their belief about themselves and what they should do. Most teachers and most authors of the texts pointed to by teachers have never themselves engaged in experimental science except at a rudimentary level. Nor could they check empirically the basis of what they teach. There is faith, that if an almost inconceivable amount of time and resources were devoted to repeating the experience of generations that is summed up in the texts, the repetition would yield texts much the same as these to which they point. There is faith in the wisdom of the texts. There is faith in the fidelity of the teacher. Conviction when and if it arises in this context, about what is true and what is not true, what is possible and what is not possible, is not rooted differently from conviction arising out of other disciplines that also teach from texts.

1.15 ❧ *The Dependent Theorist*

Law is not a natural object. Theorists of law and critics of law require judges, lawyers—they have to have law—before they can say anything at all, be who they purport to be, critics, theorists. If they have no notion what a lawyer is to be other than what a lawyer is, then the continuation of the lawyer's life as the lawyer lives it is essential to their work—even though the activity of the lawyer proceeds on premises they reject.

1.16 ❧ *Science*

An old lady does eggs. She enjoys the bit of money that comes in, but she does eggs mostly because she wants to see people every day.

She picks up an egg in the daily round and for the first time feels its shape and warmth, pauses and notices it. She puts a mark on time. A satisfaction courses through her.

Science has nothing to say about any of this, nothing whatever.

1.17 ✍ *Historicism*

Would you live your life over again, the same life, making again the choices you made? A common question, some-times put hungrily to a celebrity, sometimes put to oneself.

This one of us answers, How meaningless a question, how foolish to ask it. I, *I*, would not be standing here to listen had I not made the choices I made. I am the product of my choices, the present outcome of my history, dissolv-ing, dissolving each fraction of an instant, as you who made those meaningless sounds in the air just now are dissolving before my eyes. I could not go back and do oth-erwise without destroying myself: I had to make the choices I did, else it would not have been me who made them. All is process, you know, all just is.

But another of us says, I understand your question. I do not deny that you have asked it. It is not beyond my un-derstanding that you could have asked such a question, and the choice I make now, to wonder whether I would live my life again as I have, is not different from the choices I make in the living of life today looking to what I might be, or the choices I routinely make to correct or redirect a choice just after I have made it and it has slipped into the past. In fact, that I understand you is something of a choice. It is the choice to exist. But that I do understand you also tells me that I exist, and that you exist, and that we no more dissolve into and over decades than we dis-solve this instant, this infinite fraction of an instant, in which we face one another. I am the product of my choices, true, but all is not process, I am more than my choices, and what exists does not just exist.

1.18 ❧ *The Evidence of Beauty*

Among things in general some things are beautiful. More things are beautiful than we think, as more people are good (or have their own beauty) if justly perceived. But a thing is not to be assumed beautiful, nor a person good or beautiful, just because it or he or she exists in the world, with the fault only in our perception or the confining mold of our culture.

Some things are beautiful, some things just are. Why is the natural shape of a certain mountain among the things that are beautiful? How does returning to its presence restore us as beautiful things do? Why might we even love a mountain (the claim of love is heard) or respond to it with art?

The mountain as a nest of owls, chipmunks, foxes, and deer we might love as a stand-in for them. But one who loves the mountain itself responds to it for its form, not its life's glances. To say we are wired, as in sexual attraction, or acculturated, is to say we respond because we do—that there is no answer to the question. The very capacity to ask the question suggests that the answer there is no answer is suspect. It is as suspect as saying there is no beauty, that perception of beauty is what happens to neurons within and nothing more—most unscientific because it ignores the evidence, the beauty.

The question is not whether you think or believe or act as if a mountain is beautiful; the question for you yourself is whether it is beautiful. You would not examine a mountain or other thing closely, trying to perceive it justly, looking at it over and over to see its beauty, unless you thought it might really be beautiful. Your attention would shift to something else. The mountain is not a swinging pocket watch on which you concentrate for the purpose of inducing a state within yourself. Nor would you undertake to persuade another it was beautiful if you did not think it really was beautiful. Any persuasion along such lines in which you did engage would have another purpose.

True, beauty is both in the object and in the observer. Both are necessary. In a world where life and time pass, the observer must act and must construct the beauty the observer sees. But she does so on the presupposition that it is there. She seeks to transcend herself. She gives herself life as she gives it life; it gives her life she does not have without it. It cannot be reduced to her and her circumstances.

Are you pressed on the reality of beauty only if you must do something to another or act on your view, only if a moral question is raised? But you *must* act, even in the absence of another, even in deepest privacy, to look and to pay attention. You must decide to do so. It does not just happen. Images do not flit across our fixed eyeballs, or stop for a while before them; and even if they did, there must be decision in looking at one thing or another within the image.

1.19 ✿ *Justification in Law and Justification in Science*

Sociobiology justifies what we like least about ourselves. Economics has served the same purpose. All science may be justificatory, inevitably so, avoiding justificatory effect only to the extent its mode of thought is breached. Science seeks reasons for what is. It starts with what is, not what might have been and what might yet be. If a situation in which manual laborers receive the least and the idle rich the most is the situation that presents itself, then any science will find reasons for the distributional difference. The reasons found will tend to show that the situation must be so, for science explains. It is not open to the scientist to say the principal reason is human will, which might change the situation if persuaded to do so. And there is no explanation, in the scientific sense, in saying that in the nineteenth century children worked eighteen-hour days six days a week in the coal mines because those in power were cruel and greedy and developed ways of avoiding seeing or taking responsibility for what they were doing to children. That is instead an argument for change. That is a moral argument, with a hint of eschatology to it, precisely the mode of thought the scientist is seeking to escape. Why does the pigeon peck the button that turns on the light? Not because the one who connected the button to the light argued to the pigeon that it should.

I.20   ❧   *Various Impossibilities*

If either the speaker we hear, or what is said, consists of an arrangement of constant and identical or replaceable units, the individuality of which arrangement is the probabilistic unlikeliness of an identical arrangement because of the large number of possible arrangements of such units; and if either the speaker or what is said, being such an object, interacts with other such objects according to what are called "rules," which may change but which are ultimately translatable from words into mathematical notations and into the causal postulates of the physical world; then I might say the experience of Shakespeare is or would be impossible.

"So what?" someone, or you, might say. "Not a loss to make us pause in our construction of a way of thinking about ourselves and the world; a minor cultural disappearance, from a small island and a distant time. Abandoned temples do disappear into dust. Whole languages become unreadable. So what that Shakespeare will be no more, will be impossible if this way of thinking is true? We go on."

Then I might say art is or would be impossible. "So what?" again someone might say. "Art is museums that hold on to the past. Art is a pleasure for spare time or fills time for those who don't have to make a living, like sports. Art impossible? That is no reason for us to take our eyes off what we are doing or step back from pressing on to understand how things work, including ourselves, and to convince ourselves of the truth of our understanding." Someone else might add, "What is art anyway, but a reflection of the way things work?"

Then I would say law is impossible and must be abandoned. "No," everyone would say. They might ignore me as I say it, this fragment of speech. But they would not say, "So what?"

"Law impossible? That is unthinkable." Someone might go further and say, "Besides, rules are like law and law is rules, producing the particular interactions of the systems we call 'ourselves' with each other and with the rest of our environment. Look at Genesis if you want; look at the way your Blackstone begins on your 'common law,' his 'Of the Nature of Laws in General': 'Law, in its most general and comprehensive sense, signifies a rule of action, and is applied indiscriminately to all kinds of action, whether animate or inanimate, rational or irrational.

Thus we say, the laws of motion, of gravitation, of optics, or mechanics, as well as the laws of nature and of nations. And it is that rule of action, which is prescribed by some superior, and which the inferior is bound to obey.' Sure, we can't abandon law. That is an impossibility. But we are not abandoning law."

And with this might begin the inquiry and discussion that accompanies the shedding of indifference and a sitting up from a lounging back. And I would continue my part by saying in turn, "You go to a lawyer as a client. You ask for a statement of law, and you listen carefully. You are careful in another way, not necessarily taking the statement you are hearing as stating the law. There is no reason to be any less careful when you hear a lawyer talk about law, including me of course. In fact you must be especially empirical there, looking as much to what lawyers say and do when they make statements of law to you as to what they say about what they have said and done, if you are seriously concerned with what human law is and whether it must be lost or abandoned if the vision you are working toward contains the world—and you believe, as good scientists do, that impossibilities work in two directions."

I.21 ᛒ *Lawyers' Weaknesses*

Lawyers have great difficulty with the materials of their work. Lawyers seem to want the static, the reduced, the confined, the possessed, and they seem to want to ignore time rolling on. They like the status quo. They like property.

But a value is not static. However it is stated or defined, innumerable tasks are left open for one who must state or define it; and then it itself seems to change as time goes on.

Moreover, a value is nothing for those who oppose one another. It can command no assent from the unwilling. It can be sought only jointly in good faith—and jointness is not the stance of lawyers who want something from outside that will impose itself on two adversaries. A value does not impose itself from the outside.

Lawyers' weaknesses are only our weaknesses, presented back to us and seen because lawyers work within an articulated discipline where all is enlarged, sharpened.

I.22 ᵰ *Seriousness*

Justice, eschatology, heresy, canonicity, hierarchy, legislation, office—the possible connections between law and theology that might be explored make a long list. One connection apparent to any observer is a common seriousness. There is in law a special and uneasy relation between thought and action, that has always set law as a subject matter apart from most other branches of secular learning. Humor is necessary to getting through a day of the practice of law. But as to conclusions of law, there is no more playing around than there is horsing about in a warehouse of bombs. The literary quality in legal analysis stops short of merger of the literary and the legal. There remains the difference that belles lettres can have much fun with a warehouse of bombs, at a safe distance, but lawyers are always inside it. And lawyers might discover, if only as a curious fact, that theologians find themselves in the same situation.

1.23 ❧ *Useful Heresy*

"Postmodernism" and "cultural relativism" in legal thought are born of charity and humility. Those who promote the advantages of "postmodernism" are full of commitment and substantive belief. They are, one might think, firmly in the Western religious tradition, not at all secular, and insofar as there is an attempt by them to place postmodernism at the center of thought, as a vision of the world, their vision can be viewed as simply a heresy in that tradition, and a useful one.

Postmodernism (on the one side of law) is much like economic analysis of law on the other, which emphasizes what is too often forgotten, that strategic behavior produces unanticipated outcomes and that there is more self-interest in talk and action than most would like to think. Both postmodernism and economic analysis are warnings, on the one side to be more humble and less sure, on the other side to be aware of the play of strategic behavior and selfishness in human activity. But neither postmodernism nor economic analysis can come to the center of thought. Both abstract away critical parts of experience. Both silently assume authority, both, in their admirable egalitarianism, silently accept and assume the source of human equality, which is spiritual. Were either to come in from the edges of thought to thought's center and be joined to responsible action, there could no longer be denial in them, as there is, of that upon which they entirely depend. They would be no longer what they are now, but, like the mind of an individual becoming a lawyer, inevitably transformed by a claim of authority.

1.24 ❧ *Ritual in Youth and Age*

Is the distinctively legal in fact not related to actual decision making, but formal observance instead? The legal
has its purposes, but its purposes are those of formal
observance?

A function of law may well be simply holding ourselves
together. The motions and the talk in law may help maintain sanity. Polite discourse masks the most terrible cruelty and psychological assault—the very stuff of the nov-
elist's observation—yet all might agree that no people
could do without polite discourse or social form because
they would disintegrate in worse explosions, inconsistent
feeling let loose, passions of the moment. So legal talk,
though unconnected to particular outcomes, serves as a
damping force, a lid, order to cling to; and that, it may be
said, is all it is.

But if that is all the legal is, how can lawyers who are
aware of what they are doing continue to do it, valuable
though they may think it to be? They do it thus, comes
the reply. We know we can operate for a time by habit.
Polite talk, small talk, is a craft. Because we are taught to
do it and to do it well before we wake up to what it is we
are doing, we find ourselves capable of continuing for a
time even while awake. During that time we teach the
young to do it, carefully refraining from telling them
while we teach. By the time they awake later in their lives
they too will be capable of performing the formalities au-
tomatically, long enough to teach their successors.

But test the thesis by predicting from it. We should find
the practice of law mostly in the hands of the young.

1.25 ❧ *Conventional Trivialization*

John Stuart Mill wrote Florence Nightingale that he was not convinced by her proof of the existence of God. A law, she had argued, implies a lawgiver. The universe is full of laws, hence it follows that the universe has a lawgiver. Mill did not explain to Nightingale why he was unconvinced, but Lytton Strachey leapt in to do so. "Clearly," Strachey said, "if we are to trust the analogy of human institutions, we must remember that laws are, as a matter of fact, not dispensed by lawgivers, but passed by Act of Parliament." Strachey is quite wrong, neat, but wrong. The piece of writing that emerges from Parliament is not the law. It is evidence of the law, which is used in the course of arriving at a statement of law. Whatever else one may think of Nightingale's proof, Strachey's conventional trivialization of the law leaves her claim untouched.

1.26 ❧ *Explaining Confucianism: An Exercise in the Identification of the Nonlegal*

The Confucian *Spring and Autumn Annals* are at once legal, literary, and religious texts. They have been read, interpreted, commented upon, and translated for more than two thousand years. Their age is ten times the age of Western lawyers' central texts.

A distinguished scholar of Chinese, an American political scientist, presented to an American group interested in problems of interpretation a text from the *Annals* titled "The First Year of Duke Yin." The text was six Chinese characters that, translated character by character, what some call literally, into six English words, read "Initial year spring king inaugural month." Translated into an English sentence they read, "It was the duke's first year, the spring, the king's first month." That was all there was to the text, and that produced a smile in everyone in the audience but the lawyers, many of whom were fresh from arguing about the nine or ten words of the First Amendment.

The speaker then went through some of the voluminous commentary on this text. Commentary was often cast in question-and-answer form for teaching purposes. The so-called "Gongyang Commentary," for example, read thus:

Question: Why does the text first give "king" and then "first month"?

Answer: *[To show that] it was the king's first month.*

Question: Why does it so mention the king's first month?

Answer: *To magnify the union of the kingdom.*

Question: Why is it not said that the duke came to the [vacant] seat?

Answer: *To give full expression to the duke's mind.*

Question: In what way does it give full expression to the duke's mind?

Answer: *The duke intended to bring the State to order and then restore it to Hwan.*

Question: What is meant by restoring it to Hwan?

The political scientist's own discussion of the text— and here he was, two thousand years later, talking about this text and not some other—began by joining the general amusement that so much had been drawn from and such an amount of commentary had piled up on such a small number of words placed in a certain order, "Initial year spring king inaugural month." He went on to say that in fact there were inadequate grounds for thinking Confucius was author or even editor of the *Spring and Autumn Annals*. He suggested Confucius had been made the author or editor of the *Annals* to give them authority. Then he argued that the readings of the *Annals* set out in the successive commentaries were dictated by the particular political and social needs of the particular epoch in which the words were read—in the example of the Gongyang Commentary, a particular need for unity. Chinese work with the text was behavior produced by socioeconomic forces and explainable by reference to them. The conclusion of his presentation distinguished the Chinese mentality that had existed for millennia, up to the twentieth century, from the modern mentality, including presumably the speaker's own and that of his audience.

Then came a question, from a Muslim. Did the Chinese themselves during those thousands of years think what they were doing was ever so slightly ridiculous? The phenomenon being explained, this reading, interpretation, translation, restatement, commentary, was not quite yet understandable. It was therefore not quite yet explained, "inexplicable" as we say when we are in a puzzle.

The answer came back that, no, up to the end of the nineteenth century Chinese actually believed Confucius had been the editor and what they were doing was meaningful. They did not think of it as ridiculous, they were not doing it in that spirit.

"Spirit," mused the Muslim. "The Koran is of course very different from this six-word text," she said. "The Koran is so full of fine detail and apparently mutually contradictory remarks. But for that reason too one has to look for the spirit of it." The speaker, puzzled, repeated, "That reason too?" "Yes," replied the Muslim. "Whether the text is spare like the Chinese, or complex like the Koran, one must look for the spirit of it—look in the spirit, look for the spirit." The scholar fell silent. The modern mentality had confronted a contemporary interpreter, seriousness, the not-ridiculous.

The Chinese could not have thought that what they were doing was only engaging in practices or conventional behavior. That is not what they were doing. We cannot assert that we understand at all what they were doing for those thousands of years up to our own little century if we do not acknowledge the phenomenon for what it is. We cannot do that if we do not, in fact, have some sympathy with it because we engage or can imagine ourselves engaging in the same search for spirit—being in the spirit of the thing. Reduction of the reading of the *Spring and Autumn Annals* to the historical product of socioeconomic forces eliminates the very phenomenon that is sought to be understood and that was the attraction to the task of understanding. If that is all it is, the product of forces, like a stone as we tend to want to view a stone, our own interest in it needs explanation. What the Chinese were doing must call to us with a voice, that has a sound different from the sound of a dead mechanism.

The Chinese text is indeed curious. It does have to be explained or interpreted, with its reference to the "king's first month" and the "duke's first year." But as soon as this is said, it will be thought at some level that the text really does not have to be explained. It need not be paid any attention at all, certainly not such lavish attention. It should not be paid attention, unless it is thought there is something of importance to be drawn from it. There must be some reason other than convention to continue struggling with texts, reason in its large and unconstricted sense as that which makes behavior not foolish to the person behaving. (Only in the authoritarian setting of a school, in which a text can be assigned and attention to it coerced, would reading be undertaken on any other supposition: adult readers would not dwell upon its words, there being always beckoning and pressing some less foolish use of time.)

What is the ground for wanting to deny such reason to the Confucian? In the end we pull back from denying it, but what is the ground for wanting to do so? Putting aside the question whether it was Confucius who touched the words, we must ask how the historian of interpretation can be so very certain that the maker of the little text did not see what was wrought from it in commentaries. If we draw back and look at ourselves, we can see an assumption, a position a priori, that the maker could not have meant what was later drawn out, or even—we toy with the thought—meant much of anything. This is our ground, the resting place of our minds, this assumption, this a priori position.

Such an assumption is not only what is methodologically necessary to useful science, an elimination of spirit so that one can see what there might be without it: in these fields parallel to lawyers' work such an assumption is part of the mentality that is thought to have begun with historical consciousness and a turn to system and process. But it is an assumption diametrically the opposite of the reader's assumption when reading, as we still say, in good faith. And it is an assumption inconsistent with the creation or existence of legitimacy or authority, in which the *Spring and Autumn Annals* played their part in China. Viewing what was going on as merely a process erases the authority the Chinese experienced. If such a view is pulled into our own time, it eliminates authority for us. If we are not willing to take such a view of ourselves, we must ask why we are justified in taking such a view of those who came before us—the past of our culture—or of those of other cultures, their past or their present. Translation is writing, restatement, a comment about something, the what, the substance of the statement translated. Reading is translation. Like translation it presumes mind, whether reading is across time, across cultures, or face to face within a culture within the span of time we call the present.

Meaning exists *now*, it is said. That is true. Readers, it is said, create meaning by their own active work and are not vessels into whom meaning is poured through a text, proteins organized by being plugged into the surface of a code. That is true. But discovery of meaning behind a text, it is also said or implied, would, even if it were possible, be discovery only of a historical fact, a person bound to time and place, an "is," not a voice with a claim upon our attention. That is not true. That is expression only of an assumption against transcendence of time and place, an assumption that persons and the personal, acknowledgment of whom is a half-turn away from science, must be in history, in process; reflection also of the assumption that to say is only to do, that saying something is only doing something. Doing, acting, can be put into process, its pattern into system or form: it is not beyond process, system, form. To acknowledge that beyond is to take a full turn away from science.

That is the full turn taken by law, and that turn is the reason law is the loose thread in thinking that is distinctively modern or postmodern, confidently positivist, or confidently historicist. Law pulls constantly away from science, because it is the companion of responsible action in which suffering is brought and responsibility taken for it, and suffering is experienced if action is not taken. Orders are given in law, and the order given is searched for in the materials of law, the texts, statements of law. The two senses of an order, an order which is form and an order which is a thrust to do or to think, are most certainly connected. One searches for form in the texts in the course of one's work with them. But though connected the two senses of an order do not merge, because an order in the sense of form is not enough to produce an order to do or think. Form merely is. If it *says* anything at all, it says no more than I am, what the ultimate form evoked in the old phrase the music of the spheres may be thought to say.

Thus, law may part from art as well as nature as science conceives nature. Just how complete the turn from natural science must be, how deep the difference might be down to a vision of the very nature of the universe itself, is in the one word care. For law, mind is caring mind. Mind that does not care is no mind to seek, no mind to take into oneself, no mind to obey: it has no authority.

I.27 ℬ *Sanity and Sight*

The authoritarian is the "avoidance of love," in Stanley Cavell's phrase summing up his reading of *King Lear*. But the blindness and madness that follow Lear's avoidance of love, like sight and sanity that glow on the other side, are at the dramatic extreme of the notion. There are degrees of dreariness and melancholy in between. Dreariness and melancholy are everyday experiences that attend the fading of the authoritative in daily life, its replacement by the authoritarian. Keats, sometimes called the healthiest poet, knew the melancholy fit that can fall at any time on one who realizes how truly time and process are part of him, joy's hand "ever at his lips bidding adieu."

Keats's remedy is to look into another's eyes.

1.28 🦢 *Law and Religion*

The real connection between law and religion lies in pre-suppositions which make life and work in each go forward. Religion is pervasive, reaching the end of every aspect of the life of the religious. But so, in its way, is law pervasive. There is no discussion of justice or social policy that is not law-laden. This is obviously true of anything economic. Any reference to contracting, to property, or to the institutional structure of commerce leads rapidly to law. If the terms of such discourse are pressed at all, if the discussion they inhabit is not shallow, rootless, inconsequential, masquerading, they lead to legal texts, to legal method, and to lawyers. Anything jurisdictional, any talk of remedy, any argument about crime does so immediately. Even such a question as the "abstract justice" of abortion must lead to family law, to husbands and wives, to parents, to the community and the place of the child in it.

When the law-laden terms of discourse in secular life do give themselves over to law, what they are giving themselves over to is not some pronouncement by some individual or some identifiable set of individuals, or even to some single text or finite number of texts whose words have a meaning given from without. Upon explicit entry into law there is a focus upon legal texts—focus is part of any engaged discourse. But the focus is on all legal texts. There is no single text, not on abortion, not on corporations purchasing their own stock, not on the implications of the word "injunction," which is or could be the end of the search. Disciplined pursuit of law-laden questions leads to legal texts but then through them and out again, as light is seen narrowing down to go through a lens or prism and then expanding beyond. Legal work on the texts is not a means of tracing out what the texts say, but of hearing the law. The law lives—exists—when it is heard, and it is heard through legal work.

And here the connection with religion, the work to make law heard proceeds only on presuppositions. If it does not proceed on those presuppositions, it does not produce anything to which there is any sense of obligation. That which evokes no sense of obligation is not law. It is only an appearance of law, the legalistic, the authoritarian, not sovereign but an enemy. Principal among the presuppositions of legal work are that a person speaks through the texts; that there is mind; that mind is caring mind. These are the links between the experience of law and religious experience.

There is the possibility that the presuppositions which must be entertained to do legal work need only be working presuppositions, and that one can remain agnostic as to them to the end of one's life. This would distinguish them and the experience of law from religious experience in a fundamental way. What is the religious faith? In the West (and in the English language) the religious faith is that there is spirit and that life has meaning—or, as is sometimes said, that life is not existence only but is good, is a good. One can wonder whether there can be such faith or any faith without belief. Faith may be a more beleaguered state of mind than belief, but there is not much difference between them. Both are engaged, both involve an identification of oneself with that which is brought forth for belief *in* or faith *in*. One is oneself inside the believed, and faith (if faith is different) connects one also to that in which one has faith; as in marriage, as in what is always hoped for between parent and child—most different from the working presupposition that remains outside.

In law the possibility of conscious illusion, the living to the end of one's life with only working assumptions, cannot be absolutely denied. Economics operates with a working assumption of economic man, physics works with particles, waves and other units of thought and discourse that are only working assumptions. But, on the other hand, economics and physics are not so pervasive in life. The door is closed on economics and physics at 5:00 or 10:00 in the evening and the whole person returns home, or goes out to search for home. Actual belief in that which is presupposed in law may be necessary, in the largest sense, necessary beyond the necessities of logic that cannot even begin without definition of entities. Belief may be necessary to actual and actually experienced obligation and authority, to actual persistence in legal work that can lead to actual obligation and authority.

But belief is also an empirical question, empirical again in the largest sense. When one asks, "What do I believe?" one does not have any very special access to one's belief. That one does not have any very special access is why one asks the question "What do I believe?"—one's own puzzlement, the absence of any direct, conclusive answer coming from within one. One looks at the evidence of what one says and does, at which others beyond one can also look. The world of belief is a somewhat public one, in law as in religion. And when one looks to what one does and says, and how one acts in one's whole life, a conclusion something to the effect that one actually believes, and that one is not proceeding in law any more than in religion merely on a working presupposition, becomes the more inescapable the more one looks seriously at, takes seriously, *faces* the evidence being so continuously laid out and left in one's own trail.

I.29 ☙ *A Temptation to Universalism*

How like authority in law is authority in Buddhism as Luis Gómez envisions and paints it.

His, or Buddhism's, *circles* of authority: they mirror the circling back that is seen in law, the creation of authority by the person seeking authority, through work with faith that meaning is there to be found, and then, after the search and construction, the merging of the person seeking with what is found—so that authority lives in the present in the particularities of the individual person in whom authority speaks.

In both law and Buddhism, perception and inference are the sources of knowledge, but texts are an avenue to perception, perhaps the avenue to perception for all but the mysteriously inspired. Authority does not reside in the texts but beyond them; it is nonetheless virtually unreachable without them.

In both it is a person who is heard and on whom one models one's action—modeling, imitating, conforming, identifying are perhaps what "obedience" is, but only the meaningful is to be obeyed—the Buddha on the one hand, the law or the partial speaker of the law on the other.

In both, faith or trust is a prerequisite to the achievement of that which gives to you a sense of certainty, will, and therefore power—a self, authority yourself—and which gives to others the same, if they are engaged in the same way with the texts and with you. In both, the very purpose and effect of authority is the maintenance of a sense of self against death or loss of self in the endless and meaningless processes of the world.

In both, community is necessary to authority, community knit together by texts, presupposed—and made possible—by language itself.

Even the ultimate perception in Buddhism, the foundation of authority in Buddhism that is paradoxically the perception there is no foundation, may be similar. The paradox of such a foundation lies only in the difficulty of using a language, our language, that consists largely of materialist metaphors. In law too there is no foundation because the self is not absorbed into whatever might be proposed as foundational—there is no foundation in the sense presupposed by science or even history. The emphasis of the statement of the Buddhist faith or hope or perception, that "there is no self," should be upon the *is*. The self *is* not, the perception being acknowledgment of freedom, and of oneself never captured or transformed into material or processes that merely are.

1.30 ❧ *Cosmology: An Exercise in the Identification of the Nonlegal*

The scientist betrays science when he speaks of any of man's ultimate interests, or his own. Consider a distinguished physicist, Freeman Dyson, literate, reflective, reaching out to theology to speak of last things and of the place of life in the universe as cosmology now conceives it. Dyson may be taken as exemplar and not just example, worthy of the respect of close reading of the kind lawyers give to opinions and other legal texts. His text to be read is his Gifford Lectures, *Infinite in All Directions* (1988), delivered from the same podium from which William James's *Varieties of Religious Experience* (1902) and Michael Polanyi's *Personal Knowledge* (1958) were heard.

Dyson undertakes to set out reason for cosmic optimism, ultimate hope. He begins by being troubled by

Steven Weinberg's conclusion to an account of the origin of the universe, *The First Three Minutes* (1977), that "'the more the universe seems comprehensible, the more it also seems pointless.'" He explicitly rejects the positivism of Jacques Monod, summed up in Monod's aphorism "'Any mingling of knowledge with values is unlawful, forbidden'" (but Monod invokes law, and thus trips upon himself). Dyson's object is to reintroduce value and purpose into scientific thought by showing rigorously how the existence of life might affect the future of the universe. This he does in three steps.

First, escaping from the body, he outlines his "fundamental assumption concerning the nature of life," that

> *life resides* in organization rather than in substance. *I* am assuming that my *consciousness* is inherent in the way the molecules in *my* head are organized, not in the substance of the molecules themselves. If this assumption is true, that life *is* organization rather than substance, then it *makes sense* to *imagine* life detached from flesh and blood and embodied in networks of superconducting circuitry or in interstellar dust clouds.

Dyson's thought is graspable enough—there is a familiar gnosticism to it—but those words of his to which emphasis has been added here, "life," "resides," "makes sense," "I," "my," "imagine," even "consciousness," all point away from the thought.

Dyson's second step is to quantify life so that he can work with it rigorously, to make eschatology, the study of the end of the universe, "a respectable scientific discipline and not merely a branch of theology." This he does using information theory (which addresses the reading and speaking that are the material of law) and drawing on notions of entropy from the physics of energy. "Every *living* creature," he proposes, is *characterized* by a number Q which is a measure of the *complexity* of the creature. To measure Q, *we* do not need to know anything about the internal structure of the creature. Q can be measured by observing from the *outside* the *behavior* of the creature and *its* interaction with its environment. Q is simply the *quantity* of entropy produced by the creature's metabolism during the time it takes to perform an elementary response to a stimulus. . . . By an elementary response, I mean a simple *action* such as moving when poked or *yelling* when *hurt*. When the quantity of entropy is expressed in bits of *information*, . . . the quantity Q becomes a pure number. . . . It measures the number of *bits* of information that must be *processed* to keep a *person alive* long enough to *say*, "*Cogito, ergo sum.*"

Again, we may grasp the picture of life and humanity proposed by the words, the vision of a system "processing" "bits" of "information," and grasp the "characterization" of life, a characterization viewed as complete, achieved by "observing from the outside the behavior of the creature." But then there are those words "yelling" and "hurt." What are we to suppose that Dyson himself means by them? "Yelling," "hurt," they do not appear in the language of entropy or information theory. And there are the little quiet words, "we," "person," "say." Staying strictly on the "outside," observing what a creature "does," he uses as an example of a creature *doing* something a creature *saying* something, and the something the creature says is "Cogito, ergo sum." We may ask what Dyson thinks "Cogito, ergo sum" means, why he uses the phrase, whether he really thinks the phrase is only a "bit" of "information" to be processed by a system. In this passage, as in the previous passage, there is on the one hand the most arbitrary reductionism, echoing what can be heard in the air around, and on the other hand betrayal of lack of belief, on Dyson's own part, in that reduction.

Third, Dyson moves from what he calls his "hypothesis of abstraction"—the transformation of a living creature into a "pure number"—to his "hypothesis of adaptability," which is this:

> Suppose that we have two environments A and B. . . . If a creature of complexity Q can exist in A, then an *equivalent creature* with the same complexity Q can exist in B. The word "equivalent" means that the creature in B has the same *behavior patterns* as the creature in A. If one is *intelligent*, the other is *equally intelligent*. If one is *conscious*, the other is also conscious. If one of them can talk to its *friends* about the content of its consciousness, the other will describe in an *equivalent language* a *subjectively* identical consciousness.

"Equivalent language" should raise the eyebrow of anyone who attends to the problems of translation, but raising the eyebrow more should be the appearance of "consciousness," the "subjective," and "friends." Neither the "subjective" nor "friends" has a place in this that he is developing, above all not friends. The crack in it shows in his jump from "behavior patterns," responses to stimuli, measurable from the outside, to subjectivity and talk with friends. What do friends talk about really? The mark of love is that there need be no talk at all.

The end of Dyson's demonstration is that by genetically engineering complex organization into new substances and sending it off away from this dying sun to diversify and adapt, complex organization can survive, expand, and ultimately fill the whole universe however attenuated the energy situation in the universe as a whole becomes. "The mistakes which we shall inevitably make in our initial plantings," he says, "will in time be *rectified* as their offspring diversify and spread through the cosmos." If one world dies, there will be another to take its place. The prediction, the ultimate hope, the cause for cosmic optimism, is that complex organization, life, that which we are, will not die. The final suggestion is that as complex organization fills the universe it reveals that it is God, and that we are the beginning of God to be.

All in this view of the world and ourselves flows from the reduction of all to process and pattern, the first step in scientific thinking, and from the associated reduction of saying to doing. Everything depends upon these two assumptions, that the person or self can be collapsed into pattern and process, and that saying can be equated to doing or "behavior," permitting observation from the outside. If either assumption cannot be made, nothing of the rest follows. But no evidence is given for these assumptions. None is ever given by those who build on them. The evidence of our experience points against them, our experience of the phenomena of the world, our experience of love. As evidence, our very words point against these assumptions or assertions, our use of *we*, or *friend*, or *pointless* that pushes off from the opposite of pointlessness.

There are two Dysons. One of them does seem to see the end or the ultimate as a circle of friends sitting around talking, albeit in relationships "calculated from the laws of physics and information theory." For this second Dyson, invoking friends sitting around seems to be invoking something real, not merely an atavistic reversion to an Olympian image of heaven out of his childhood books— heaven as gods reclining on billowy clouds scattered about. He personifies mind, which "waited for 3 billion years on this planet before composing its first string quartet." While staunchly maintaining that his own mind is "a million butterfly brains working together in a human skull" and insisting confidently that though "still totally mysterious" this mind of his works "by natural processes," he observes that his own mind has "the power to *dream*, to calculate, to *see* and to *hear*, to *speak* and to *listen*, to *translate* thoughts and feelings into marks on paper which other brains can *interpret*." Very quickly in this same passage Dyson moves to transform "mind," remembering perhaps that it must be a product of biological evolution, into a "force," and he moves then from "force" to "control." He darts back across the divide to a world more comfortable to him, the world of forces and patterns and survival and domination, still so very late nineteenth century, still so very, in a way, World-War-I-German-General-Staff. But those words "speak," "listen," and "dream" remain there peeping out. There is even a vision of "our last poets" "*singing*" at the end of the implosion of a finite universe, which says as much about Dyson as does his number Q.

How are we to read these answers this exemplar of late twentieth-century thought gives to last questions? Two Dysons, a Dyson speaking only to then speak against himself—with what are we left after we read? We must either ignore the whole, as we are used to doing with madmen on boxes, or we must choose.

In choosing the second Dyson—if that is the reading—it does help to have an explanation or theory, from the outside, of the first Dyson, of Dyson's *behavior* in this regard. It helps because we are after all children of the twentieth century. There is the pattern of psychological adolescence, a recognizable conjunction of curiosity and domination, an interest in getting large and an interest in novelty sufficient and consuming in themselves, in Dyson's immediate answer to that first question "Why survive?" which must be answered before last questions can be asked and answered—"What will happen if we do seek to survive?" Superficial adolescence may be the explanation. We use it with friends and family. The second Dyson is to be glimpsed through the first, and whatever is behind or beneath is center or base. But treating the first Dyson as superficial like a net on a face and dismissing it as such is too easy and too Panglossian. Threads of the first Dyson run through the modern soul; the first Dyson is the Dyson that Dyson wants us to hear. We need the help of another explanation.

What of simple self-destruction, destruction of the self? We know that is possible. The free can destroy themselves because they are free.

That gives us also an explanation of law.

I.31 ❧ *Ceremonial Litigation*

Trial by oath, trial by ordeal, trial by augury and battle may have reflected belief that through particular ceremony and certain acts man could compel the intervention of the divine, to reveal what to do—or, as was sometimes said, to reveal the truth, truth from which some decision or chosen action must follow.

We may wonder how different is much of modern litigation, civil or criminal—not just in characteristics that can be seen from without, such as the fact that it is often an ordeal with uncertain outcome, but in our very conception of it that at the deepest level maintains our continued participation in it and acceptance of its outcome, vindicating the innocent, condemning the guilty, allocating money and material goods to rightful possession. How could vindications, condemnations, allocations that are accepted, be so accepted, be defended so stoutly against the skeptic, be protected so against reconsideration, if it were not thought that what is *done* arouses the attention of Truth and Justice, and compels Truth and Justice to touch, not any one of the participants dancing, but what emerges from all their twists and turns and speeches and silences as they tumble to the conclusion of the ceremonies they perform within their columned temples?

We may wonder but must reject the thought. We know this is not how Truth and Justice appear. They do not touch the outcome. They do not act. We act, and if they touch us it is through what may be said to us that we attend to and understand.

1.32 ❧ *Understanding Law*

Why does one *want* to understand law? Curiosity? Mere curiosity? Would that drive all the ins and outs of analysis and speculation, all the labor going forward on the detail of its form, the argument one hears, the often angry mutual criticism and recriminations of those who say they are seeking to understand it? There are surely experiences that reward curiosity with more delight.

Is it power? Over the law? What one understands one can manipulate, as one can manipulate natural phenomena when they are understood? But understanding the law would give one no power over it, of the kind one might have over a system whose secret one knows. Law is beyond the individual, and perhaps the collective too. And if some few who understood it got together to manipulate it, what they would be manipulating would turn out (for that reason) not to be law.

Is it freedom, from the law? What one understands is explained and what is explained is reduced, from what it seems to be, to something else by which one may be less affected or from which one can better separate oneself? But the law, if it is the law, is not an experience or phenomenon one seeks to separate oneself from. One might as well say one seeks freedom from oneself when one is seeking oneself.

One *wants* to understand law for the same reason one *wants* to understand what someone says. One is motivated, driven, pulled, not by curiosity, nor by desire or lust for power, nor by yearning for freedom from bonds, but by thirst for meaning and recoil from the senseless, the mad, the empty. One wants to understand law to achieve law.

I.33 ✑ *The Kafkaesque*

"Kafkaesque," like "legalistic," is a pejorative in legal writing drawn largely from Kafka's phantasmagoric picture of an authoritarian world in *The Trial*. The overlapping absences and presences of the authoritarian are all there to be seen—the reverse of each of which marks law's presence.

The absence of persons. At the end of *The Trial*, "a human figure, faint and insubstantial . . . , leaned abruptly far forward and stretched both arms still farther. Who was it? A friend? A good man? Someone who sympathized? Someone who wanted to help? . . . Where was the Judge whom he had never seen? Where was the High Court, to which he had never penetrated?"

With the absence of persons, the absence of caring.

Voices, and individuals, are without identity, not being persons. The interrogators in the beginning of *The Trial* are in casual dress. The pair who are executioners in the end appear in frock coats "with top-hats that were apparently uncollapsible." None will and none can declare himself, who he is. They cannot because there can be no pure self-identification, but there can be no identification without authenticity and here there is no authenticity. Even smiles are not intentional.

And so reality is absent. The Interrogation Commission is "not a real Interrogation Commission." As the situation develops the whole seems more and more "a joke, a rude joke." Or "theatre": voices make statements "not really meaning them."

The voices and actions of others than the sufferer are hardly even forces with that reality force can claim. What they cause is not destruction, but self-destruction. This is the presence in the authoritarian world. But it is a presence that consumes itself, to leave nothing in the end. Executioners do plunge the knife and the knife that kills does come from beneath one of their twin frock coats. But they expect the sufferer to plunge the knife himself. And the sufferer's refusal—his only refusal—is in the end only the act of an animal, the animal in him to which he has been reduced. "He died like a dog" is his epitaph. It is he who steers the way to a place of execution, leading his executioners in lock step with him on either side. They seem to take no direction of their own—of course, for they have no human purpose without identity, not being persons.

What is also present in this world, beyond the self moving to destroy itself, and the knife in the end, is madness. Madness is linked with death, the "lifeless elements," which is presence also but a presence on the edge of absence. The dress, from which the first-heard seeming voice emerges, "one could not quite tell what actual purpose it served." The mad inconsistency of statements, the "senselessness" of them, drives the sufferer caught in this world mad as well, without sense, inconsistent himself in his own statements and actions.

And there is also present what appears to be a chain of command ending in "humble subordinates" who have "no standing" and who themselves are senselessly punished.

Madness, self-destruction, death, and senseless command: against these is set the authority of law; these set law's ultimate undertaking and function in the world. Throughout *The Trial* there is appeal to the Law. Had it been answered, had law appeared, what was absent would be present: identity; reality; persons.

The young sing out to the rising sun,
Before school,
What the old whisper to the setting;
The old sing to the young
To trouble them

❧ THE CIRCLE

There is the truth of pathos,
The fallacy of fact.
Should not the setting sun
Take the ebb of life
And blunt its edge?
But, no, we're told,
We must not look
To West for comfort,
Not whisper twice
Our own's the sun,
The sun's our own,
Though this is what sustains us
And makes the fact a fact,
This world which is our own,
Our own which is this world.
We are not exiled from this round
This nesting home for fact.

SECTION ❧ II

The Life of Forms

On the Language of

Legal Thought

II.1 🎘 *The Direction of the Flow of Evidence*

Law's words are not a system. They have not been made a system despite all the force of interest in making them so that has been brought to bear for ages. If there were ever words that power, attention, ingenuity, and time could forge into a certain system, a form that could be held out, grasped all around, and known, they would be law's words. That this has not happened in law should be taken as saying something, not about the defects and failings of law and lawyers, but about the nature of language itself. Is human language convention only? Pure form ultimately? Ask whether law is convention only, pure form: if it is not, there is reason to look beyond form in thinking of language.

II.2 🎘 *Mathematics*

Mathematics haunts law. It is the temptation of the century past. "Be me," it says, like the temptor in the old tales. "You, who are written in your human language, write yourself in mine."

But mathematics cannot be a model of human language, for two reasons that stand before all others. The first is that human language is about the substantive. Mathematics is tautological. The second reason, associated with this difference between being about something in the human world and being tautological, is that there is usually in mathematics an assumption made of the unvarying identity of the unit of reference (at its simplest the x or the 2). In human discourse the question what one is talking about, what one's unit of reference is to be, is perpetual—what a human being is, what a father is, what a corporation is, even what a tree or a wolf is that tree or wolf can be conceived as something other than an aspect of the mountain where it lives.

This indeed is why mathematics is so tempting. It promises stability. For the weary it is promise of rest. Translated to physics now speaking boldly of its Theory of Everything, it promises an end to uncertainty: the qualitative that human discourse is about is illusion. What we are really is stable basic entities merely rearranging themselves quantitatively, their reality being exactly equivalent to their stability contrasting so with the transience of the qualitative, that epiphenomenon playing on the surface.

II.3 ❧ *Law in Space*

Might a diagram express the law on a matter as well as a verbal formulation—what is often called a "rule"? It might, if diagrams were as many and as quick to draw as the rules tumbling from the lips of legal analysts closing in on their own statements of law—if their drawing were like the signing of the deaf, spatial language, so that one determining the law would see a diagram here and a diagram there merging into and replaced by further diagrams all offered by others similarly engaged in determining and expressing the law.

Otherwise the diagram would stand between the analyst and what the analyst seeks. Presented as an alternative to "the rule," it would imply that its alternative existed, a system of words that everyone would acknowledge as the singular expression of the law and not simply one among many texts any legal analyst faces and uses in making decisions and formulating one more expression of law. Drawing on mathematical thought in which entities are defined in terms of one another and maintain their identities within a system, it would divert the analyst's attention to itself and, to that extent, silence law.

II.4 ❧ *Writing*

The way we talk, taken as a whole, is access to the way we think, but the two are not the same. Certainly the way we talk, taken in part, may not be the way we think. Our object is always to try to pull the two together, the part with the whole, talk with thought. That is what *writing* is, including legal writing.

II.5 ❧ *Speaking Generally and Listening to Detail*

Ruminating on the place of close reading in their own work, the legally trained note that they do not include the details of what judges say. Their own statements of law are put in a rather general way. But though they do not work the details of what judges say into the fabric of what they themselves say, they do not fail to pay close attention to those details. They still engage in close reading. They speak in a general way, but they do not read any legal text to discover what its author is saying in a general way only. In reading a text as a whole they look to tiny evidences. They must attend closely to the details of what each is saying to determine what is being said. In the same way, anyone listening to the legally trained stating in a general way his or her conclusions of law will attend to the details of the statement in order to determine what those conclusions are. Speakers speak generally; listeners attend to detail; each of us is both speaker and listener.

II.6   🐾   *Dictionaries*

Lawyers and judges cite the dictionary in arguments about the meanings of words in statements of law. But a dictionary does not give either the meanings of words or rules for the use of words. It offers empirical descriptions of usage of a probabilistic kind, which any poet can confound and the poet in each of us does confound. The only possible rule to be drawn from them is a pragmatic one—if you want to be more quickly understood, you might try using this word in these ways. Even then it is still *you* who is understood, not the word. And any pragmatic if-then rule is questionably pragmatic, because an attention to statistical usage presumes speakers who are equal and interchangeable within a set of speakers, and listeners who are equal and interchangeable within a set of listeners, a presumption at war with the way speakers and listeners in fact approach one another.

A good dictionary also calls to conscious mind some of the history of metaphorical expression that the word's

parts, its spelling, and its sound represent. This too is on
a statistical basis, though survival of metaphor may not be
reflection of frequency of usage itself but rather of the
depth of breakthrough to what there is to be expressed.

II.7 ❧ *Rules and Repetition*

When you speak or write, how do you know that you are
repeating yourself? How does a listener know? The question is *what* you are saying.

A statement of law, particularly one that includes quotation of formulations of law designated by the speaker as
"rules," may be presented as a form of repetition. You
know no more that it is repetition, even when you identify quotations or recognize embedded patterns of words,
than you know that you are just repeating yourself or your
friend is just repeating himself. When you suspect you
may be repeating yourself, are you really? The question is
what you are saying.

II.8 ❧ *Saying One Thing and*
Meaning Another

Lawyers working with what they call "legal fictions"
(which they know, because they call them fictions, are
not fictions at all but the truth of the matter as much as
truth appears through the use of any words) understand
easily that the exclamation "You are saying one thing but

you mean another" can never be a charge against a person. If the exclaiming listener is so confident he knows what the speaker means, then the speaker has made her meaning plain and, for this listener, has said what she means. At most the exclamation is an observation on a proposed concept of language, or perhaps a wish (if the wish were true) that language might be more like mathematics. There may be a complaint also implied, that the listener has had to do some work, but a conclusion so expressed might equally be an involuntary tribute to the admirable vividness of the expression the speaker used, the way it has succeeded as a whole in rewarding the listener's work (which work was itself a tribute to the speaker).

The related remark "Oh, you're just saying that" is part of the listener's working. Often made to a speaker on a matter of particular importance to the listener, it is an invitation to enlarge the whole that is being read. "Oh, you're just saying that" may ultimately ripen into a charge, of lack of connection between the speaker and her words. The "that" in the remark is an expression of and by the listener, what he wishes he could read in the speaker. And the "just saying" is part of the running observation about language that users of language can be constantly heard to make, that words divorced from person—what is sometimes called the literal—are no more than sounds of leaves rustling and branches clicking.

II.9 ❧ *The* Objet Trouvé *and the Meaning of Interpretation*

Think of the entwined branches of a tree, the patterns they make against the sky. How often have you lain on your back studying them? But you bring your meaning to them. You do not read them, translate them, interpret them. You can interpret another's painting or photograph of them—but not the branches themselves, at least not as natural phenomena are currently generally conceived.

Words and sentences on paper are as such no different from the branches of a tree. They are tracings, marks, contrasts of light and dark. If, as when you lie staring up beneath a tree, you bring your meaning to these shapes and you do not take your meaning from them because you have concluded there was no meaning put in them in their making and so there is none there to be taken, then you are not interpreting them in saying what you say about them. You are using them as you might use any other device, including indeed the device of a word whose use in the situation would not be suggested by its dictionary definition (what is then called a metaphor), to say what you are otherwise moved to say. You are saying what you want to say, not what you hear a voice beyond your immediate voice saying.

So it is with any *objet trouvé*. There is said to be an outline of the human brain to be perceived around the figure of God reaching to give life to Adam on the Sistine Chapel ceiling. That shape is an *objet trouvé* if it is assumed that its appearance there was no part of Michelangelo's design, conscious, semiconscious, or unconscious. And there is nothing whatever to be drawn from it, however intriguing its appearance is as an imitation of an outline of the human brain. It is a meaningless coincidence, produced by the hand of Michelangelo, to be sure, but like the configuration of shells thrown up on a beach in the shape of a word—"love," for instance—that is the product of the systems and processes we call natural.

But the matter, of course, is more complicated than this. When an *objet trouvé* is found in the forms we call painting or sentences, the conclusion that it is an *objet trouvé* is a decision, a decision based on evidence. The more or less absolute presumption of the modern mind about natural forms—that they are mindless—is not available as it is with stones that might be sculpture, branches that might be drawings, arrangements of shells left behind by waves on a beach that might be words, patterns of fissures on a rock that might be petroglyphs. And the result of a reading which is undertaken on the contrary presupposition—that what is read is the meaning of an author—is itself taken as evidence that the presupposition obtains in fact.

What stands in the way of then moving from presupposition to belief (belief in that which before is only supposed) is some extrinsic factor that keeps the author separate (separate, in the mind of the reader poised to believe) from the meaning perceived. There are many such extrinsic factors, but important among them today is limitation of the author to time and place, conceiving the author from the first as situated in history, part of the system within which he or she breathed and ate. For something of an analogy in physical perception, do we think Michelangelo could have known the shape of the human brain in cross section, him, in his century? If we do not think so, then we will not interpret his marks as an image of the brain or go on to ask what might be meant by that choice of form, the question *why* that goes beyond the questions *what* or *how*. Our eyes will pass on to other features. But if we do continue, on that presupposition which supports the work of close reading or looking, and we do work with the shape in all its detail, noting with the doctor's eye, for instance, that here is the vertebral artery, that this cherub's foot is the shape of the pituitary gland in the brain and is in just the right place, and that, furthermore, while other feet have five toes this same cherub's foot is bifed—the very shape of the pituitary gland's two lobes—we may begin to be less confident of our conclusion about what Michelangelo could not have known. Open to evidence, we may doubt that what we see is merely an *objet trouvé*, on the basis of the evidence that is the result of our work. And to the extent we steal back to look, or keep casting interpretive glances at the shape on the ceiling, we reveal to ourselves and others what we actually think of Michelangelo's knowledge and mind, whatever we may say about that as historian, biographer, neurologist, or cognitive scientist.

Closer to the situation of the lawyer—less involved with physical perception on the part of the author and having more to do with the observer's perception of form in art (since the shape of the brain would be like the appearance of a word in a painting rather than a salient curve or contrast in it)—we can ask whether Michelangelo could have known or experienced the modern agonies which a reader today can trace in his images, and for which the reader emerges with greater appreciation after an hour in communion with his work. What would make us say Michelangelo did not see what we see in his text? It may be convention. The extrinsic factor may be only a conventional limitation we impose on the mind of speakers in the past, a circle we, not they, draw around what they can have heard before they spoke—artificial, a peculiar artifact of our time, and a convention not taken up even in our time in the thought and practice of giving and receiving orders in law. The artificiality of such limitations, their conventional quality, is kept before us as a constant possibility by the thought and the practice everywhere of giving and receiving a legitimate order: daily thought, daily practice always pressing beyond such limitations, ignoring them, quite evidently not observing them.

II.10 ✍ *Linguistic Paradoxes*

When you are presented with the statement "Everything I say is a lie," you are meant to be puzzled by it (another such is the statement on the trick card, which reads, "The statement on the other side is true," the statement on the other side being "The statement on the other side is false"). But your puzzlement—if you are in fact puzzled— would be in part a consequence of restricting yourself to that statement alone. Your puzzlement would be a consequence of forgetting that it is a person who speaks, and that to understand what is said you look to the person, who exists over time and says many things and whose meaning is understood by reference to all the person says. This is true for mere statements, and true of statements you are asked to obey and follow.

Various paradoxes fun to play with—"Please ignore this sign," "This sentence is false," "Never say never"—assume a different character when you attend to them seriously. For then you do not puzzle over the statement but over the meaning of the person who says it. *It* does not say anything, any more than would such words in the same sequence typed out by mice running over a keyboard. The person who says it perforce says many things and the person's meaning is understood by reference to all he says. If taking all in all the listener can make no sense, she may suspect madness, and ignore the speaker and turn her attention elsewhere.

Bafflement and restricting oneself to a single statement and forgetting that it is a person who speaks are connected. Of course and always there are difficulties met when one moves from words to person and seeks to understand and one does not treat as mad all that one cannot (yet) understand; but one's puzzlement then, if one is in fact puzzled but still attentive, is of a different order.

II.11 ❦ Obedience as a Special Context for Interpretation

When one is asked to "follow" a statement, one is asked to follow its meaning. The first thing an order giver may be expected to say when things do not go as he expects is "You fool! I didn't mean that. I meant this. You were wrong. You made a mistake." If a farmer were to order his man, "Buy me four sacks of oats for the cattle" and the man were to reply, "Oats? Don't you mean barley?" the farmer would angrily say, "Yes, of course I mean barley for cattle. Oats would make them sick." If the man did not raise a question, or had no chance to question, and there were sanctions for disobedience, would he face sanctions for buying oats or for buying barley?

II.12 ❧ *Evasion*

A written or spoken form of words is evaded only if the form is fixed in the focus of attention, and its sounds or the shapes of its marks are held constant. If form is not held constant, there is nothing there to be properly evaded: there is only a question about what is there. If a fixed form is no longer attended to, it is rather ignored than evaded.

Forms may stay fixed in Torah faithfully copied in the smallest detail, or in an unamended constitution; but in either, and in any large and complex text, the centrality in attention of any of the myriad forms in the composition may come and go. Neither fixity of form nor fixity in attention is often found or found for long, and finding them both together at once is even rarer—attention to and use of a form is as much threatened by time as fixity in the form itself is threatened.

Evasion of something that is given written or spoken form is another matter.

II.13 ❧ *Reading Gestures*

Meaning is not a matter of observation and evidence only, however widely netted the evidence; there are presumptions involved, presumptions that are tied to taking action in the world and to the consequences of taking action.

Compare word with gesture, for example the gesture of putting your hand on the arm of someone in consolation. One pushing your hand away in another country might be respected: you may conclude not to put your hand on him again. The gesture is known differently there. But pushing off a consoling hand in the United States may not be respected: it may be doubted that he really never wants to be touched thus again. And so the gesture is made again, and perhaps again and again, until you are fully convinced that his reading of it is different from yours.

(You may of course conclude that he does not want consolation itself, really does not want it. You would, however, be long in coming to that conclusion of substance: much would flow from it in your treatment of him in other situations. And it would not, in any event, absolutely determine whether you continued making gestures of consolation when he was distressed.)

II.14 ✍ *Action and Person*

In law an act is an actualization, whether the act is a court's or an individual's. It is read, together with words, for meaning. Words may be judged inconsistent with action, and, equally, action may be judged inconsistent with words.

The use of a word, the speaking of it, is an action also. It actualizes also, and a word uttered, in speech or writing, is not the same as a word contemplated. Signing a name is the signal example; notes and bills of exchange, which are the taking on of obligations, are "uttered" in legal usage.

Saying out loud "I love you," rather than thinking it and being thought to think it, may change the world; so is there a change when the word "divorce" is uttered even as a possibility. (And the irrevocability of change is countered by persuasion that—as heard so often after a blow, a touching in anger—"it was not I, not me really" or "it was I, but I was out of my mind" who did or said that.)

Words of law especially are inseparable from effect in the world, not perhaps as much as the Hebrew *dabar*, the word of God that brings about what it says, but showing their theological connections in being pointed always toward action and having force other words do not. Words, even words of law, can of course be impotent—words as such are only puffs in the air—but then an act can be impotent or countered also, and not much sustained physical action in the presence of others is possible without words of law. Not much is possible to achieve, even physically, without either the acts of others or their forbearance and deference.

But though the utterance of words is action and action is actualization (as words are actualization) of mind and meaning, there seems still a difference between action and the utterance of words. Hypocrisy is a stronger charge than inconsistency. The meaning of a precedent of a court is judged in light of the action the court orders, which, if there is resistance to it, will ultimately be physical action. The ancient common law distinction between "dictum" and "holding" in a court opinion (a statement of law at large and a statement necessary to what the court orders), notoriously difficult though the distinction may be to carry through, does give physical action a special place in the determination of meaning that is involved in the creation of authority, which in turn gives words of law such force in the world as they have.

Why is physical action given a special place? Action is not determinative of meaning. Action cannot trump words, because behavior itself, of court or official, or of individuals, is not law. Meaning must be given to action, as indeed to a word. In itself action has none. Like words, action is only potential evidence of meaning. But as actualization of meaning in a material world of givens and physical consequences, action is special evidence of belief, of the authenticity of the statement being heard and read, of the connection of the speaker to it. Action taken on stated belief is a demonstration of the authenticity of the belief—or is initially seen as such and continues to be seen so unless the whole, statement and action, is seen to be manipulative, staged, unreal, or the action and the stated belief are seen to be unconnected, the one not founded on the other but having independent origins (the action often then being designated as the symptom of illness). Though not determinative, action is particularly strong, in the sense of the strength of evidence, and it makes equally strong demands upon the actor.

The extreme form of the demonstration is martyrdom. Heightened authenticity heightens attention, and attention is an index of authority. The whole, statement and action, receives the longer and the closer reading. Action taken in law, and the consequences attending action, press those responsible, for the action and for the consequences, toward exploration of authentic belief; the exploration of the authenticity of that belief by others, those further in the chain and web of implementation, and by those affected by and bearing the consequences, produces the field of force of the action, granting or contracting the connection of the action to authority, and thus, coming full circle back to the physical, its effectiveness and effects.

But action may be inconsistent with words, as a person's words may be inconsistent with one another. A person says he gives, but he takes. A person loves, and says she does not love. A person says he is helping, and he hurts. A charge of hypocrisy is grounded on the difference, if the action is taken as authentic—that to which the speaker is connected. Easy charges of hypocrisy are a mark of literalism, an assumption of knowledge without the work of understanding, knowledge of not just what words mean but what an action means, its purpose and origins. Without purpose or origin in responsible mind, action (or in law what is the close equivalent, failure to act) is not *action*; it is merely an event in the world, the appearance of blood, the snapping of a bone, money present in hand one moment and not in that hand the next moment—nothing more. Without purpose and origin, "love," "giving," "taking," "hurting," "helping" are merely motions, movement of objects, just occurrences that inevitably occur somewhere sometime, or (if an omission) that never happened. A charge of hypocrisy made by the reader, the analyst, is thus necessarily a claim of knowledge of purpose and the origin of action, whether the charge is made with the confident ease of the authoritarian, or after the struggle that accompanies the possibility of deference.

Before a charge of hypocrisy is reached and all that flows from it in withdrawal of respect (from an individual, who is then opened to sanctions; or from an official, who may then be ignored or defied), there is only a difference, between the apparent meaning of words and the apparent meaning of action. And it is possible, despite the presumptions that commonly characterize actions, to conclude that action is not what it appears to be. It is a mistake, a stupidity about means and ends, that does not have its own origin in irresponsibility. Or it is read in light of words: hurt it did, but it was not meant to hurt; or, on reflection, what seemed a taking was indeed a giving as the accompanying words would have it. These conclusions are the result of an inquiry that, where individuals rather than courts or officials are being read, is frequently given the name *mens rea* ("the mind of the accused") in analysis that might lead to criminal condemnation, or *scienter* ("awareness") in analysis that leads to allocation or reallocation of material wealth. Generically, the conclusion is a disconnection of the person whose meaning is being constructed from the action as it has been presumptively characterized—the absence of *mens rea* or *scienter* is the absence of mind, the absence of mind is the severing of connection between person and action and the reduction of action to brute occurrence without meaning—or, in the alternative, the conclusion is recharacterization of the action in establishing a connection between it and responsible mind. Neither disconnection nor reconnection is done without recourse and reference to words uttered. The extreme of the disconnection of the person from action, in legal analysis, is a conclusion of insanity, as the extreme of infusion of the person into action, outside legal analysis, is martyrdom.

II.15 ✍ *Novelty and Error*

How can a person be understood when he uses a word in a new way? Words do *have* meanings, do they not? A claim will lie, will it not, that he is simply wrong in his usage?

We can imagine that a word *has* meanings even though they cannot be made equivalent to the meanings of other words or of other sets of words. But the meanings a word *has*, to which a person is introduced in life, include rich and deep associations that echo and reverberate until they are too faint to hear in any conscious way. If any one person uses a word and means that use from the depths of his being, no one attending to and seeking to understand what he is saying is equipped to declare that the word is being given a meaning it did not have before, or that its use is wrong.

II.16 ✍ *The Metaphorical Word*

In close reading, one has to imagine another using a word and imagine why another used that word. Reading is a constant calling upon the imagination. There is a running question "why" in the reading mind, asked over and over.

But the question "why" is not asked out of ignorance, doubt, or challenge. And it is answered by oneself. It is actually hardly a question at all, more the inchoate and preliminary form of identification, of placing oneself with the writer, heads together as it were, and looking at the choosing and choice of the word through his or her eyes.

II.17 ᴇ *Metaphor and Deceit*

"But God did not put his finger on the tablets of stone to
write the Ten Commandments, yet Moses said he did!"
Did Moses really mean the people to believe God put finger on stone? Was that the meaning of what he said?

As in the law of deceit, meaning is everything and
meaning cannot be determined without mind. Action to
be taken as a consequence of words, and blame, and
blame's mirror-image praise, all turn to mind like the pho-
totropic to a source of light.

But then the individual who speaks in metaphor, even
including Moses, does perhaps want his listener actually
to believe, if only part way, as a child may be both skepti-
cal and believing at the same time, *seeing* Mole and Rat
sitting in overstuffed armchairs inside a hollow tree in a
forest, *knowing* they are not to be found there. The deceit
is benign, it is play, it is fantasy in which everyone is to
join with good to come of it in the end, a residue of understanding left behind as if understanding were precipitated
out of good drink and then washed down with it.

There may be no deceit at all when the meaning is ex-
amined; or if there is, it may make no difference and be all
to the good.

II.18 ☞ *Systems and Lying*

You come up to a vending machine and put in some money. Sounds come out of it:

> Hi. I'm a *talking* vending machine. *You* need to put in more money. *Please* make *your* selection. *Thank you* for using this machine.

Which words are lies?

II.19 ☞ *The Duality of Everyday Language*

Writing wholly unconverted about religious conversion is not quite writing about *it*, religious conversion. Yet if converted one must have at least one foot on the outside in order to write about it. Language itself puts us in that stance. We do not have to struggle to assume the position of being both inside and outside. The instant one says something one is detached from it and critical of it, able to ask whether it is what one really thinks, and yet one is sufficiently behind it to say it and knows it is not someone else who is saying it.

A similar intersection between the inside and the outside, where we stand, is that between the ought and the is. When one asks why a person does a thing or behaves in a certain way, the question can be taken as an inquiry into cause, an aspect of the is. The answer might be that a person does a thing because she should, because she has good reasons. If we were to say, "No, not any of that: she does a thing because she *thinks* she should," we would step entirely outside. But then we have no explanation why, for then we do not understand her behavior. The goodness of the reasons, which moves her, the reason in the reasons as reasons, is not yet perceptible to us, and therefore though we may have moved toward the "how," the "why" is still missing. Moreover, we do not know whether she really thinks she should. We may not even have the "how" in hand. For both perception of the ought and reality of the is, we must step inside.

II.20 ❧ *Knowability*

The ancient and continuing claim of the radical unknowability of another—the perennial great doubt, the constant shaking of faith—is equally a claim about language, that proceeds today as it always has from the temptation of the mathematical. The claim of radical unknowability, whether made to ourselves in private thought or aloud and abroad, is a change of allegiance, to the literal. The negation in the claim is the denial of the metaphorical and of spirit the condition and twin of the metaphorical.

Venturing the smaller claim, of the unknowability of other cultures, or the unknowability of the past, leads equally to radical isolation, ultimate aloneness, a falling from all sides in and down to Euclidian point. For there is no line at which to stop, between other cultures and the subcultures of our own culture, or between the subcultures of our own culture and the cultures of each individual in it; then, even within ourselves, we are not to be knowable to ourselves, over time or across our conflicts.

But we come out of our isolation. Mathematics is not the model, and there is no literal language, and all is metaphorical even including the denial of the metaphorical. We uncover the premise—there is no need to exclaim over it loudly, which tends to raise doubt—on which the metaphorical proceeds, that there is a unity and spirit. Without spirit there is nothing in law, no reason to read or listen closely, to defer, to be deferred to. There is no authority and no responsibility for action to advance, protect, intervene, allow. And in fact there we are, reading and listening closely, deferring, being deferred to, granting and accepting responsibility.

II.21 ❧ *The Evolution of Art*

If biologists and sociobiologists say the thrill of music is a tingling of the nerve ends and what they are doing is proposing a coherent new explanation of that tingling, and go on to lay a charge of closed-mindedness against those who refuse to acknowledge the strength of that coherent view of the world, the response of the accused should be to note what biologists do to language.

That to which *our* word "thrill" refers is not that to which the word refers in *their* sentences. They reveal indeed that they have not the slightest inkling what the word "music" is used to mean or of what the "thrill of music" is or of what the phrase refers to—or rather that they have not the slightest inkling when they are thinking in their capacity as biologists. Words for them become ciphers whose content is determined by their method and which no longer reflect the experience they purport to explain. So too with opera or drama explained sociobiologically as "scenario building": confronted with such an explanation, anyone of musical or theatrical sensibility cannot get much beyond an initial response that the commentator is not talking about opera or drama, or that he has a tin ear and does not know the first thing about opera or drama. No question of respect for his position has time to develop. Sociobiological discussion of art is not far different from sociobiological discussion of the human experience of depression. If depression is explained sociobiologically as a form of energy conservation, one is led not just to suspect but to know that the theorist is not talking about either clinical or religious depression. His words and sentences are simply not referring to the experience those words have been used to express.

The sociobiologists' problem in discussing any feature of human experience is that they are outside the tautologies of mathematics or quasi-mathematical talk and are using human language. Talked about the way they wish to talk about it, what they are talking about inevitably slips away from them.

II.22 ❧ *The Purely Legal*

Lawyers do not have nice specifications of what evidence can be looked to when inquiring what the law is on a matter. There is a technique, which is to focus upon a canon of texts and, if they are available, upon central texts generated by an institutional arrangement that is usually hierarchical in form. But in reading those texts, reading them seriously to understand them, lawyers do not "exclude evidence" (as a litigating lawyer would say), close their eyes to evidence of meaning (or lack of meaning). Some of that evidence is of the form we call sociological. All the evidence is about the life of the aspirations and ways of thinking with which lawyers work. "Formalism" pretends that evidence of the way a term or notion works in the world is not relevant to what the term or notion may be or may mean in law, and that law is a closed system— formalism pretends and only pretends, because there are no decisions so obviously for ulterior reasons as those emerging from decision making that boasts its formality and self-contained nature, its exclusivity.

There is as a consequence no notion of the "purely legal." Legal discourse is not a closed system. The meaning of texts is a real meaning. To the degree it is not, what is put forward is a species of tyranny. Lawyers' work and the way the world works may be in tension. They are never detached. Legal discourse looks to discourse that is not identified as legal, just as nonlegal discourse looks to law and is law-laden, itself always permeated with law and legal reference.

II.23 ♛ *Words and Music*

Lawyers asked to search whether law really is convention and no more than convention may independently ask whether human language is convention and no more than convention. If language is not convention only, then law may not be; if language is convention only, then there is a question how law could be anything other—with much at stake in the answer.

Listen to sung words not knowing the language—a Bach Passion or a Schubert song cycle in German if you do not know German—or imagine such listening. You are not then attending to pure music, however music and the nature of purity in music may be conceived. The soloists or chorus are saying something. Their voices are not instruments only furnishing notes as flutes furnish notes. And what it is they are saying can be entered into somewhat without knowing the language. The what that is being said is not in the words—one does not know them—but is through the words. The experience would not be at all the same if only notes were being struck. Would there be this emphasis you hear, or that falling away, this or that turning and twisting of the sounds? Would you attend to it? The reason for this that you do hear and the reason you attend to it is that the sounds are speech. You are, as it were, at the second of three levels of all or any speech: the first, in which words are known and there is attention to them as words; the second, the level that can be experienced separately in this way, in which words affect the form and force of sound and what is being said through words are reasons for forms and forces to which one attends; and the third, sometimes called musical in itself, beyond molding by words.

Only at the first level is language susceptible to reduction to the words themselves and then, by further paring, to the literal or the definitional. Only at the third level are its regularities, its rhythms, counterpoints, harmonies and associated dissonances, which are like those of music without words, susceptible to approach as pure form. Only at the first and third levels can language be seen as convention by those seeking to see it so, as something that simply happens.

But language escapes. All speech is like song, with not just a second but innumerable levels between its words and whatever in it might be severed from expression and confined to a world of form. Levels each giving way to a next, innumerable, they deny the dichotomies that allow us to abstract the personal from our experience. Because they deny dichotomies, upon which logic itself depends, they may hide from our conscious thought and require special circumstances to perceive. But the prevalence of song throughout the world should alert us to the limitations of the generalizations about language we are tempted to make and, for that matter, our generalizations about music. The prevalance of song throughout the world speaks even to our generalizations about that part of the experienced world we call law.

II.24   *Music and Linguistics*

What is the information conveyed by an ascending chord? Not, surely, that it is ascending. Such news would command no attention.

What is the logic of an ascending chord? That there is a note beyond the scale.

Language is not very different. Its logic, and the information it conveys, are not much easier to put into words.

II.25 ✿ *Live Performance*

The conductor of the amateur performance of the operetta, keeping the tempo up and taut, reaches over the orchestra and pulls with his hand the tenor and soprano
line, above and in front of the chorus and orchestra. Tenor
and soprano respond. The chorus gambols, there is wit
and fling, its dance has energy. The ensemble swells and
comes to an end, newly heard, as good as ever heard, better, memories may say, than any performance seen. But it
ends, and vanishes into the memories of the audience and
the performers. There is applause, the louder and more
heartfelt the greater the regret that it has ended and van-
ished. Applause is a dirge, clapping the hands together a
funereal gesture, the time for applause and the curtain
calls a service of farewell to what was brought to life.

How foolish applause would be directed at a machine
when a recording comes to its end. A recording is a system, fixed though subject to decay, maintaining over and
over a precise repetition of electronic signals and sounds
in sequence and combination. Sometimes applause erupts
in a movie house from an audience enthusiastic about the
movie. It dies away, clappers embarrassed, the foolishness
of it apparent. There is no farewell—the record is rewind-
ing to run again. The clappers are applauding themselves,
their own imaginations, by which they put themselves in
the position of seeming to see a performance that is alive
and that therefore must die away (and that therefore must
be heard and seen with all the attention the mind can
summon up).

Why do the performers extend themselves so, reach, respond to the hand that pulls the line out and over to make
the shape that the ear hears as it has never heard before?

Not just for the anonymous audience in the dark, though energy can be pulled from them. Not, these amateurs, out of ambition to rise in a professional hierarchy, a hope that a scout is in the audience. Not out of fear of dismissal if performance does not reach some unspecified standard. There is response because there is a mutual energy drawn one from another that spirals up. There is the reality of this performance, that this is not a practice performance that can be corrected, the putting of oneself into it held back and postponed. But there is above all the work itself, its life (or were this not an operetta, its depth), an extending of self for the work which lives and lives again if self is extended.

So does the law live and live again in restatement if there is a person present restating the law in extension of self.

II.26 ❧ *Presuppositions of Reading*

A student came in to see me about his seminar paper. He had wanted to apply some of the comments of a difficult author to problems in law. He was discouraged. Every time he had felt he had grasped something, he found when he went back and looked at the texts again that his previous understanding was inadequate. Furthermore, all he had now was some sixty pages of thoughts, which were themselves difficult.

He ought not to have been discouraged. He was a lawyer, or becoming one. Reading his difficult author was like reading law, or poetry. One read him with faith. Of course, faith in your author is not, I said, entirely based upon "au-

thorities" explicating him who tell us, not least by the use
of their own lives, that it is worth reading him. Even with
Hegel—the student brought up Hegel—you can read the
text yourself and obtain enough encouragement to keep
going, rather more perhaps than with your author, but
your author speaks directly also and not only through exe-
getes. Differences here are only of degree: one must proceed a bit more on faith, on the presupposition that the
work and effort will have been worth it.

But by the same token, because one proceeds on this
presupposition rather more, it is also true that what one
determines to be the meaning of the author, and what one
therefore takes away from the text, is very much a product of one's own work, made possible by one's presupposition. If what we take away changes as we go back to the
text again and again, the reason may be that there has
been a change in us, our resources, our understanding of
life. That we have not discovered its final meaning (because we discover that it means something new to us each
time, and have no reason to think that readings have come
to an end) is as much a tribute to us as it is an indication
of the difficulty of the author. It is a sign of adequacy in us,
not inadequacy. The meaning we take away from the text
becomes more easily seen to be attributable to us as well
as to the author. And the *us*, to which there is such attribution—who we are, what our mind is, what its limits are,
what speaks through us and listens in us—will remain a
question. It also has not been captured. It is no given, any
more than the author is a given.

When the text does not break down, we have a sign of
the greatness of the text; but on the other hand, we continue with the text, before the breakdown that does not
come, because of the strength of our presupposition. That
faith we bring to the text, and without it the text would
not have or give up a meaning. Pressed to answer whether

the meaning we take away is the author's meaning, we should say yes, if conceived as joined with ours (and ours with meaning that is not possessed by us alone), because the author's meaning is itself forward-pointing, to whatever a person with ultimate faith would be able to do with an artifact produced. There is less difference than we might think between the author's meaning and the meaning the text has for us as a consequence of what we bring to it, bringing, as we do, both our strength of inclination to work at reading and our personal experience of existence in the world to which he too is addressing himself.

Writing generally has a theme, a thread, to carry the reader along. But the more universal the work, the more contingent the thread is: *War and Peace*, it might appear, need not be about nineteenth-century Russia at all, but it is the narrative and characterization in *War and Peace* that attract us to read it and take away from it what of the universal we do take away. Such ease is missing in legal writing, though the stories in the cases help; but the form of legal writing is not unique to law, and there is a prick of urgency in reading law that helps a person in traversing a hard path to arrive at a place that cannot be reached otherwise.

II.27 ✣ *The Turing Test*

The Turing Test for machine intelligence proposes discourse with—with what? With some*thing*? No; with some*one*? No—such that one (who believes himself not to be a machine) cannot tell whether the other is machine or human. But why would one engage in such discourse?

Why would one listen and analyze in the first place? One begins with a presumption that one's interlocutor is intelligent. One does not lead up to it. The presumption that we would be interested at all in engaging in the Turing Test presumes we are machines. The conclusion tested is implicit in the premises.

II.28 ❧ *Candor and Joint Writing*

If one coauthor, working on a jointly authored piece of writing, suggests a change or insertion in a sentence or paragraph without fully disclosing such of his intentions and reasons as another coauthor might want to know, and the other accepts the change in ignorance, then to that extent there is no joint mind behind the writing. And arguments about the meaning of the writing are then necessarily limited in how far they can go. The mind and the meaning are to that degree vitiated by the manipulativeness and the secrecy of the one who put himself thereby outside. To that degree the listener thereafter must also remain outside, for with respect to that aspect of the text there is no inside for him to come into. Manipulativeness, secrecy, and being outside—these are three aspects of the same. The listener, being outside, must remain manipulative, if not wholly so, and the text will to that degree not have authority.

Of course the use of a word or the change of a word can have intentions and consequences on many levels, and fullness of disclosure cannot be judged by a single measure. Indeed, fullness of disclosure cannot be quantitative, except in a manner of speaking, for it is measured by what the other would want to know. Moreover, disclosure itself proceeds by words, the intended meaning of which must be determined (and a record of statistical usage, such as is summed up in a dictionary, is only an initial tool, some evidence). To the extent the matter can be imagined quantitatively, it is never clear that "small" changes do not have "enormous" consequences. That is indeed a reason for wanting the original of anything rather than a copy, and even in the physical world it is one of the truths of causation that great events turn upon small details.

It may be wondered why the other does not ask for disclosure if there is silence. But assumptions of *caveat emptor* can hardly apply. Words are not things that can be inspected, and in any event nondisclosure occurs as much through noise as silence. There is trust or always the appearance of trust between coauthors, and the presence of trust is some reason (or explanation) for the other's not persistently asking the one's intention (assuming he would know what to ask about). The principal reason, however, is time, for actually we never give up some vigilance: we know our best friends are not always their best selves. The other does not persist long in inquiry, principally for want of time. By the same token, the one may fail to disclose purely for want of time, and not in secrecy and manipulation. But lack of time does not supply mind. The consequence remains. And since there is not ever enough time, the listener always has his work to do even when all is said and not said, done and not done with the best of wills.

II.29 ❧ *Literal Meaning and the Agreed-Upon*

A literal meaning of a word is merely a possible meaning. Only agreement between speakers could conceivably produce a literal meaning that was anything more than a possible meaning. There is no legislative power in some majority of speakers that could make a possible meaning into the actual meaning.

Agreement between speakers each time before speaking does not occur. Speakers are (of course) not always face to face. They also do not know what words they will use. Besides, no one is in much of a position to set about agreeing. There may not be words in which to agree; nor is it clear that one can oneself say what one means by a word that has appeared in a series of words one has uttered. The word has been used to say what one has said. One might have used other words if those had come closer to saying it: in turning to use other words, one may be turning away from what one has said.

II.30 ❧ *Literal Meaning and Disagreement*

Collectively bargained agreements between management and labor typically contain an arbitration provision withdrawing from courts and the legal reading of texts. An arbitrator rather than a judge will decide disputes under the agreement.

The arbitrator presents this, as a case not infrequently seen: in the course of bargaining the parties put to each other clauses worded alike but reveal, each to the other, that what each means to express by the words is different and in conflict. The clause is included in the agreement nonetheless, each signs the one string of words, and each takes the chance that in a future dispute an arbitrator will rule against it. The arbitrator knows this was the situation at signing.

In view of the equal positions of the parties and the absence of any obligation (in arbitration) to make a statement of law generally applicable, there is difficulty in adopting the "tort mode" of contract analysis, that is, the approach to contract designated as the objective approach—visiting a publicly determined consequence of using a sign upon an actor in the same way the consequence of any nonverbal act might be visited on him. But the arbitrator cannot fall back upon intent either. His position is not even that of a legislator seeking to define words, whose words have no force except as they are read. His position is that of a primal force, but one that will be felt only by those before him.

II.31 ❧ *Hermeneutics*

The very essence of hermeneutics is the securing of the correct text—not correct in the sense of conventionally established, but correct in the sense that it is a text that makes possible close reading, as no text can be that is a net of adventitious omissions and interpolations stitched in without communion. Reading *is* interpretation, which *is* translation, which *is* rewriting, which *is* writing; but reading begins with a text that is an expression, not a linguistic phenomenon.

The essence of hermeneutics is still with us. No fight over the recovery or transmission of an ancient text was more passionate than the fight produced by a proposed change of words in Joyce's *Ulysses*.

II.32 ❧ *Present Meaning*

Give up the notion that an author's meaning is apart from our creation of it. Shy away from phrases such as "recovering" an author's meaning from a text. "Recreate" would be a better word than "recover" in describing what we do. In the simplest case we can experience, which is speaking directly to and being spoken to by an author of speech, intent or meaning is not *in* history, not a historical thing.

If the meaning of the author speaking were such a thing in history, the evidence of the text would be of what was, what exists in the past only. But an author lives, and exists in the present—always in the present. His meaning must be in the present also. Otherwise it is not *his* meaning.

When someone before us says something and we try to catch what he says, that something is immediately in the past. Yet we read what he said after we have caught it, to determine the meaning of the person with us in the present. The text is evidence of what was said—we seek an accurate text—and what was said is evidence of what is meant. The situation does not change as the text recedes into the past.

And if the author dies? But this death of which we speak is a very human notion. Without spirit there is no *death*. There is only a transformation of matter. He must be still with us, or the meaning we draw is not his meaning. Meaning must live if it is to be meaning, and so must he if it is to live. Thus are we pushed to think an individual speaking in space and time speaks always for another, that other (at the least) being a little longer-lived than the individual whose life is rounded by a sleep, or (at the most) transcending time altogether.

In fact, we do not cease to think an individual present, in understanding his meaning, if he goes off to sleep. Civilization has been on earth so short a time it is not impossible to think of all the dead who have thought and spoken as off taking a rest.

II.33   ☞   *The Quality of Legal Language*

Any lawyer, any judge, is a listener as well as a speaker. He or she listens to appeals being made—appeals that what another is doing is not justified by what the law says, what another is saying is not what the law says—and listens then to claims, by those who are thus challenged, that they do speak the law and what they do in the world is justified by the law. The lawyer as listener may also be directed, by these voices challenging or these voices in defense (both voices seeking some particular application of force beyond the strength of an individual's arm), to others who purport to speak the law, other lawyers, other courts, the legislature. All these voices are speaking "to the merits" of a legal case and are arguments "on the merits."

The question that, in one formulation or another, begins every such listening "on the merits" is "Who are these people speaking?"—one common formulation of it is "Why are these people here?" A successful answer by challengers or defenders, on their own behalf or with respect to others to whose remarks they direct attention, is the construction of a recognizable identity that has some elements of the authentic in it, and is living, in the non-biological sense of living.

Yet the listener, to whom an appeal to hear or to be heard is made, has a part in constructing that identity. The person who is perceived is perceived as a result of that person's work but also of work on the listener's part. The person who is another is never completely other; but the person constructed by the listener—created—is not constructed solipsistically.

This fact, that a person appearing to a lawyer is not a given but is nonetheless and at the same time essential to understanding and essential indeed to the will to do the work of understanding, flows from the very nature of legal language, and perhaps all human language except the mathematical. All legal language is metaphorical in the sense that its meaning is not a given but is constructed, as is the meaning of a person, through the work of under-standing. Metaphor is not the use of the name of one thing for the name of something else. That would be a literalism once removed. In metaphor the word or pattern of words disattached from a previous object of understanding is not reattached to another previous object of understanding, but is used to express something new—or alive, which is the same—and that something new is meaning itself, the meaning of what is being said. Metaphor is the result actually of a search for precision, an attempt to speak the new which is in mind beyond language and of which language is only evidence.

The highlighting in law of this aspect of human language, its metaphorical quality, rises from the evident claim a statement of law must make on action. Interven-

tion or self-restraint, making choices with real consequences for what one cares about, is what law at once
speaks to. And if it is to affect action by anything other
than force and evoke anything but evasive maneuver, it
must actually speak to the person to whom its words and
sounds are directed, have force in and of itself, lay claim
on the mind. One does not *obey* what one does not approach in that attitude of mind which in law is called
"good faith" and which people outside law call simply
"faith." *Systems* of sounds and shapes are used as machines are used—the attitude of mind a machine or system calls forth, when it is seen as such, as machine or
system, is strategic, manipulative.

How can meaning be "beyond language"? "Beyond"
has been well crafted by its users, though like so many old
metaphors its roots are in the physical and the geographi-
cal. Its resonances help it convey how it itself can be used,
how its use—the use of the word "beyond"—is the very
denial of the silence to which "meaning beyond language" might be thought to relegate anyone who thinks of
attempting to speak. Is "what is beyond" beyond the
grasp? It is, if the grasp is physical. That "what is beyond"
is beyond the physical—beyond the marks, the sounds—is
precisely what leads to the reaching and maintains the
hard effort of reaching.

And what is "beyond" something is not identical with
it, or reducible to it, or a reflection of it. But as long as any
of us is not that something either, or any *thing*, what is
beyond and not identical with it is not, on that account,
beyond one of us reaching, nor never identical with one of
us reaching.

And "beyond" always has a temporal sense—space and
time have long been connected. To be beyond is to be
"ahead," as in a race. But living meaning is ahead of language, in the present, where we are also, where the lis-

tener is, the one reaching. What is living is always in the present, and what is in the present is always in a way and in a sense "new," as what is behind is in some way and in some sense "old" and dead in the past. Language is evidence, and all evidence is in the past. As anyone working with texts transmitted, reproduced, restored, and maintained soon learns, what is momentarily at hand is itself only evidence of that evidence, the more so with each moment that passes.

Certainly "beyond" and its resonances are not enough to argue and evoke the quality of legal language—music is not made of a single chord. The present in which the person lives, for instance, is not a present only of the here and now. And experience in life and recorded experience does suggest there may be a last line that language alone and by itself does not cross, a residual mystery which is in part the consequence of the irreducibility of meaning to the linguistic phenomena of the material world, and which striving through language and the passing on of striving through language will not itself bring to any level of consciousness.

But, nonetheless, the "beyondness" of meaning can indicate the quality of legal language that makes what is to occur in law, translation between cultures and individuals and across time, at all possible, and, with translation, makes at all possible any reading for understanding, or any speaking that is worthwhile undertaking (as speaking to, really *to*, a pile of stones would not be worthwhile). The words and patterns of words of one language—and of one individual's way of talking—have developed historically and in contexts that are different from those of other languages or other individuals' ways of talking. That in itself does not make inevitable that the meanings conveyed (through one language and through another) cannot be the "same" or "identical" at the only point at which meaning does exist, the present. We ask, thinking of possible difference, "Are our meanings the same?" Their possible merging is in the "our" which is so hard to banish from speech and which serves to mark that most implicit and silent decision we make that another creature is a human being. The evidence of our meanings may be different. Our meanings need not be different for that reason alone. If there is translation at all, there is a presumption of mind on each side. Translation is a restatement of the spirit of what is said, not a reproduction of a thing. This is what any person reaches for when he or she speaks, the mind. If it were not the meaning rather than the language that is being translated—or read for understanding and restated—there would be no thrust to do the detailed work of translation (or reading) that must be done. There would be no captivation by the texts in the first place. No one afterward would be interested in or listen to what one had to say about the textual evidence to which one had devoted one's time. Whether there *is* translation in the end depends wholly upon the attitude of approach—as does action in response depend upon the attitude of approach.

The Detail and the Whole

On the Logic of Legal Thought

III.1 🐦 *The Empiricism of*
Legal Method

Legal method is the close reading of fragments, to reach the actuality of what is, and legal method is the putting together of fragments, to reach the actuality beyond what merely is.

What is closely read is always only evidence, twofold evidence, or threefold: evidence of the fragment itself, which is always receding in the past; evidence of what makes the fragment fragmentary, of the reason for seeking to read it in the evidence of it, the reason for preserving evidence of it to be read. And the reading of any fragment must itself be maintained in evidence, to be read closely later as evidence of the reading, while present attention turns to the close reading of another fragment and the forming of evidence of that reading.

Ultimately these readings merge. The fragments, and the fragments of fragments, are put together. In the merging of these readings is the intimation of meaning—the source of will, what draws and drives the effort.

III.2 🎋 *Writing the Text*

Reading a volume of David Sutton's poetry, his fourth, I come upon these lines in *Widow*:

> I listen to the worries of the old:
>
> .   .   .
>
> The genteel expectations one by one
> Fall from you life. I listen to it all.
> I counsel: . . .

Later, in *The Maharajah's Well*, I read

> It was Ishree, Maharajah of Benares,
> That wrote to Edward Reade, Lieutenant Governor,
> Born is the Ipsden country, friend to Benares
> Through years of famine and mutiny, missing always
> A far-off hamlet lost among the beechwoods,
>
> .   .   .

What am I to do with the "you" I see in the first poem or the "is" later? Sutton is alive. I might ask him. But I am a stranger to him. He is in another country. I must find him, introduce myself to him, press myself on him asking for his time (and trust) in asking him even to listen to my question. And it is only a matter of small chance that our individual lives overlap and that the David Sutton who wrote this text is a David Sutton who might be asked. What do I do? I change the "you" to "your," the "is" to "in," and read on. I may be hardly conscious that I do so.

This is the beginning of legal method. It is the beginning of scholarship itself.

III.3 ॐ *The Problems and the Possibilities*

If you or I learn that a part of a sentence in an essay by a well-loved author whom we treat most seriously is the addition of an editor, that part is flagged for us. How closely, something in us asks, did our author scrutinize the addition? We are moved toward the possible opening of the text to our own interpolations and additions.

And how, something deeper within us will ask, was it possible for our author to adopt the words of that part at all? The words did not initially come to him. The words flagged for us are the words of another that came to another, are a quotation, but this is not a quotation that came to our author's mind. We are taken to the question of the origin of words, within us, or within any whom we read.

We need not in the end always put aside the part added. But our reason for not putting it aside will be less that the author adopted it, after whatever degree of scrutiny and reflection, and more that it may be a close reading or commentary or translation by another before our time that was made in good faith. Is reading the original better than reading the original and the translation together? Perhaps reading the original is better, if the original was inspired and the translation is not. Perhaps it is not better to put aside the translation if the translation is inspired. We are led to the question of what the indicia are of inspiration and good faith in commentator or translator, to the problem of text and tradition, to the possibility of a changing text at the center.

III.4 ☞ *King's College Chapel*

King's College Chapel, Cambridge, built in the fifteenth and sixteenth centuries, gradually weathers away. Walk around to the hidden side of the building and pick out a stone from the rubbish bins filled by the masons who are almost continuously at work on the decaying fabric. You have in your hand an illustration of the difficulty of defining an entity physically, without reference to noncorporeal design and the good faith of restorers.

There is similar difficulty in giving any substance to the term "law" without reference to good faith.

You have also an illustration of the difficulty of distinguishing between action and inaction in a world that is active over time.

There is similar difficulty in law in distinguishing between act and omission.

The eventual replacement of all the chapel can be conceived. That it *is* "King's College Chapel" would then be taken by the observer on faith, a faith that reflected an assumption of good faith among the restorers, and in saying "restorers" in the plural it becomes evident that the chapel persists in its form only in records and the mind of more than one individual. That so much has to be taken on faith is one reason why the molecular original of a thing where it can be had is of such importance. One need not rely on another in one's access to it, except, of course, to believe that it *is* the molecular original.

But this is no less true of the fabric of a document; or, to take the next step, of the form that is repeated through copying; or to take the step after that, of the mind and heart, to which one seeks access—in the law as in art.

III.5   *Right, as a Word*

Legal thought seems to consist heavily of placing. The word "right," so dear to lawyers, reflects this basic activity of lawyers. All the senses of the word—adjectival (*correct*), noun (*a right*), verb (*to right*)—come together in the placing of something or someone.

Then when the rush of time is introduced, and with time the dissolution of all things and thoughts that are not constantly rebuilt, "placing" becomes an act of orienting rather than of locating.

III.6   *Neither Detail nor Whole*

Such attention to detail we show, to the perception, recovery, preservation of it. Restorers clean the nine statues on Michelangelo's Medici tombs using feathers, lancets, cotton, and nothing stronger than water and a few drops of turpentine. They take three years to do it. Joyce's editors, two generations after the publication of *Ulysses*, undertake to build up a new copy-text word by word, feeding in corrections, omissions, and changes, from manuscripts, subsequent manuscripts, corrected galley proofs, and other editions, producing an authorial text (that was never to be found embodied in a single document) differing from the first publication in some five thousand places. They devote a great part of their maturity to this task, of producing and reproducing authenticity of detail.

And such freedom we retain, to conclude that a detail is a flaw in a work. Daily we do both, whatever our profession—labor for the actuality of detail, dismiss and ignore details as flaws, in knowing any friend or listening to any person's talk.

Why such labor for details, such devotion of lives to their recovery, when the general outline of the whole is there, and when in the end we are not bound to respect the detail we recover, or to preserve it further?

Because detail may be critical to understanding: the change of a window changes a facade, the change of a word changes a statute or a poem. We say easily there is agreement in "principle" but not yet "in detail"; but all know that the principle will be revealed in the details, and that agreement is unreached until the details are, so to speak, discovered. (The language of discovery is in fact used: "Let's see what they really mean.") This is why the original is sought, the original rather than a reproduction or slavish imitation of it—the authentic rather than the imitative, the merely imitative, the slavishly imitative meant to express nothing new in the reproduction of it. An imitation, even a crude one, can spark the memory of a beautiful or meaningful form—a sculpture, a chair. But the sculpture or chair cannot be read for its beauty or meaning in or through a crude reproduction or imitation, nor perhaps in a "good" reproduction, the "good" having fewer omissions or interpolations of detail. The imitation or reproduction is read for itself, as part of the history of forgery if it seeks to pass itself off, or as an acknowledgment of influence and expression of admiration and joinder if there is no passing off, in which the modifications, the differences, the omissions, and the additions are expressive and not flaws to be read away.

A text full of chance omissions, chance interpolations, cannot be read for its meaning either. Nor a text full of what are equivalent to the effects of chance, omissions and interpolations effected for reasons that, to the spirit of the text, are contingent, reasons that are secret, reasons of one not *in* the spirit of the text but using it strategically. Detail is too important. If one has not seen the text before, no memory of it can be sparked by this equivalent of a crude imitation or reproduction of a sculpture or chair. There may be beauty in it still, an outline, a form, but, Keats notwithstanding, the beautiful and the meaningful may be different, certainly proximately, perhaps ultimately. The music of the spheres that says no more than that it is may be beautiful, but it will be empty of meaning. If it is read for its meaning, it leaves one with only what one already knew. It is a stimulus of one's own thought, like the eye lighting by chance on an object that sparks a thought. It is not an expansion of mind, a source, a source of meaning in a search for what to do and how to think about what to do begun with a genuine question, "What am I to do and how am I to think about what to do when I do not know what to do or how to think about it?"

But then the restorer, or the editor building a copy-text from the ground up, devoting years of life to the grinding daily labor of it: what drives this remaking of the embodied work? There would be no remaking of the text if something—shall we call it the text?—were not there touching and inspiring the worker. Of course the work could be a job and claim to income, better than alternative ways of spending one's workday hours. One may be caught up in a game, the game of detection. But the thirst for the original and the authentic, which must drive the imagination in the search, and justify the life devoted to it, would not be supplied by these; and the product, of the work, would not be touched by that which would make others pay attention to it.

Convention might be thought to provide the push. One might imagine textual work being done on a Supreme Court opinion because convention has placed Supreme Court opinions in the canon for reasons—of focus, common discourse—not associated with the texts themselves; but in fact Supreme Court opinions compete with each other for attention, and convention itself cannot keep them within the canon and within the focus of workers laboring on them asking the question "What am I to do and how am I to think about what to do?"

A pattern may be recognized in the text, an "idea" from the "history of ideas" that are said to have an evolutionary process of their own: this may be thought enough to spur on the work. But it may be only the appearance of an idea and not an escape from solipsism—the details will tell, which have not been discovered. Life and choices in the use of the text stretch on.

What does supply the drive, that does appear to be there in us, in others, to work and work on the particular texts and objects we and others work on?

The detail—omitted, added, modified—can change the whole. The detail has not been discovered or established. But if detail were all there was, expression and the expressed would be the same, and the difference between expression and the expressed is precisely what allows us to dismiss or ignore the detail we do find and establish, as a flaw. There is something other than the thing as it is, that is perceived—and more than perceived.

A garbled score of Mozart's would summon one or many of us to work and would have authority for us—lay claim on our attention—because Mozart had spoken elsewhere and otherwise. As the lawyer well knows, what is being said is generally determined by reference to texts in addition to the one being worked on, and the remark of a friend is never heard in isolation nor its meaning sought in itself. Inspiration speaks to faith and sustains it, until faith is abandoned. Work is rewarded, or it is not. True, what has inspired may be a mistake in transmission—the detail discovered can change the whole: what was heard was not being said, what inspired was stimulus only, not source. But mistakes may also be made by the person we are seeking to hear. That is for us to judge, and we are always actively making such judgments. We may lose faith in the detail, while maintaining faith that we hear a voice, maintaining faith in the whole that is now a product of our work and judgment. Back and forth we go, from detail to inspiration, and back to detail, reaching beyond what we already have (what merely is) and making it our own.

This is why one oneself is not lost in what is beyond one, why one is not the pawn of it when it has authority and one hears the author of it: because one is author of it also. Without faith, we know nothing beyond ourselves. We start with acknowledgment that our self of the here and now is not enough. The voices we hear and that we are convinced we hear, because we go forward, speak to faith. Lawyers call it "good faith."

III.7 ☞ *Rational Units of Reference*

Faith is not without reason. Irrational it sometimes is said to be, but that is because its units of reference, the objects of faith, are not so limited in time, space, or concept as those of mathematics or as those of thought made suitable for mathematical treatment. Reason in its largest sense, respect for evidence that includes all experience, is the very ground of faith.

III.8 ❧ *Difference without Separation*

The actor is different from the action, but is not separate from it. There is a mode of thought that makes actor and action the same, by eliminating the actor—dissolving the actor into what is, what happens. That is not legal thought. An always continuing difference of the actor and the action, despite the absence of any separation of the two, is what permits criticism of what is or what happens, as never enough, always a tragedy small or large; just as the difference between actor and action is itself consciousness of what is or what happens. The normative, the purposive, the moral, live and have their very being in this difference, and consciousness does also, these two together making the human.

III.9 ❧ *Character*

To defer truly to another's statement of "fact" or of "law" is to give weight to that other's statement, for the reason that it is that particular other who makes the statement, in coming to one's own conclusion and to one's own statement of "fact" or of "law" that one makes to oneself or others. Deference is inclusion of the identity of another in one's own decision making (true deference involves making a decision that is one's own and is not merely the appearance of being a decision that is one's own). Deference is thus most personal. That someone does or thinks something, not why someone does or thinks it, is reason, not complete reason, but reason, for concluding it should be done or thought. This is sometimes known as the influence of character, or paying attention to the character of another.

Such responsive deference is at the center of authority. It is a reflection of the connection between personification and authority. Respect, obedience indeed (the reciprocal of authority), is paying attention to the person of another as one goes about in the course of life making one's own decisions—those decisions of one's own that give one one's own character and authority.

What is *done* by another and what is *thought* by another may not be entirely interchangeable. That something is thought by a person for whom one has respect may be reason for entertaining the thought, trying the thought, tentatively thinking the thought, proposing the thought to oneself. But actually thinking a thought may be actually believing it—not actually to believe it may be not actually to think it. Whether one does come actually to believe it may depend on how it works out in one's thought; the fact that another believes it may possibly drop out in the course of one's thinking. Or, it may be, if one is unable to believe it and therefore actually to think it, doubt arises whether the other believes it and actually thinks it—the fact, that another thinks something, quivers. There is in addition the difficulty that what is thought, the "thing" that is thought to which we colloquially refer, blends into why it is thought. The expression of the thing thought, a particular text, is not understandable without reference to much beyond that text. To think the thing thought is in some sense to understand it. To objectify any particular text, which is one among many, which is transient and aging rapidly, is to move away from true attention to the text, and put oneself in a condition where one may find, to one's surprise, that one's true attention is focused elsewhere.

So, in deciding whether to *do* something, the situation may be different. One does; one does not simply tentatively do something. What another does, does not melt so into why the other does it.

But the break is not sharp between thinking and doing. One does, but one also undoes. One does again in new ways. One does in ways that attempt to preserve options for correction. What exactly is done by another is not wholly separable, as a descriptive matter, from an understanding why it is done. It passes, difficult to catch—it fades into something larger—it comes undone as one tries to draw a circle round it and capture it. And concomitantly, it is not as possible as it may seem to make all one's thinking one's own, to reflect on all one's thinking all at once, to change a part of one's thinking at will if other parts are connected to it. There is a doing involved in thinking too, a doing that is less a matter of the will perhaps, less a decision, but still decisive.

Therefore, doubt that one can actually defer to another's thought may extend to whether one can ever actually defer to another's action. But the reverse is also true, that the fact of deference with respect to whether to do something, and perhaps the necessity of such deference, extends also to thinking. Both questions, to defer or not to defer in deciding to act, and to defer or not to defer in deciding to think, are addressed hourly by ordinary practitioners in working with cases and opinions. The opinion in a case, if it is not an advisory opinion or a moot case, represents a decision by someone to do something. The opinion, an invitation to think something, is itself sometimes referred to as the decision. What is done is difficult if not impossible to state in the absence of an explanation and a specification of the case. Paying attention to, or instead essentially ignoring what is done, turns on the grip the writing exerts on the deciding mind asking itself what should be done now in a new case, and how one should think about what to do.

III.10 ❧ *The Rule of Law*

Traditional accounts of the Rule of Law mislead, and mislead particularly those in the scientific community who seek to reproduce legal thought, or explain it, or use it for explanation.

The Rule of Law is law speaking to everyone: no man or woman above the law, least of all the legal analyst. The postulation, in traditional accounts, of the prior existence of abstract "rules of law" that are applied to "the facts" is only a means of expression of this universal permeation by law, and the idea-in-action may be fleshed out in shorthand fashion less misleadingly today by saying simply (instead) that under the Rule of Law determinations of law emerge from working with texts that are common and public.

III.11 ❧ *The Peculiar Joining of Is and Ought*

Why men and women obey the law and whether there is obligation to obey the law can be folded into the question what the law is. Whenever we refer to law we refer to an ought—that is why we use the word *law* rather than "orders" or "another individual's will." We don't say, "It's another's will that you do this or that"; to invite something beyond a fight or treachery we say, "It's the law that you act in such and such a way." And there is always and will be always a question of what the law is as long as "law" does not collapse into "another individual's will."

III.12 ❧ *Law as Prediction*

What the law is, is what someone truly speaking for the law would order someone else to do or think in circumstances legally determined. But one's truly speaking for another, and one's not finally determining oneself the fact that one is truly speaking for another, are always linked. The linkage between speaking for the law and not finally determining oneself that one speaks for the law appears both in legal method and in institutional expression of method.

III.13 ❧ *The Author of a Legal Text*

That a lawyer or other writer of a legal text "does not speak for himself" does not leave a legal text without authorship, nor separate legal texts from the intent or meaning that comes with the identity of an author. And to stop searching for intent in legal texts and stop constructing it, to remove it at the start, is to leave the words dead, possibly uninteresting, certainly without capacity to raise thought of fidelity or obedience.

III.14 ❧ *The Authority of the Past*

Law is pronounced the dead hand of the past. Law is hangover, in almost all senses of hangover—architectural, something solid jutting out and shadowing; historical, an anachronism; even physiological: it is the vise grip of a morning after. Law is the old, all that weighs on us, what the young who are young in age or in mind delight in escaping or confounding or defying.

But the authority of law is not the clutch of the past. Law itself has a word for the dead hand of the past, *mortmain*, which is a pejorative. The fact is and should be obvious that we cannot be afraid of the past. The "dead hand of the past" is just that: dead, gone. The past cannot touch us. And if it were fear of the past that kept the past in our minds, the past would not have authority over us and we would not be paying any true attention to *it*. We would be paying attention rather to its consequences and how to predict, manipulate, and avoid them—as we do in science or medicine with the consequences of our physical past.

The past and its texts enter the experience of legal authority through legal method and its presuppositions, which are subtler than statements commonly made about law would suggest to the nonlawyer, or to the young introduced to law in the course of life. Experience of authority, in law as in other fields and aspects of life, is experience of true attention to something in itself, attention that has as its ultimate effect an embracing and perhaps a merging, such that thought and action that are associated with what is attended to can be said to come from within. There are all manner of words or phrases in law that point to attention, to embracing, and to the within as part of the phenomenon of authority—or respect—or true deference. Many such characterizing words or phrases invoke "faith," which is a notion in some academic trouble. "In good faith" is one of them, peppering statute, rule, opinion, doctrine, and discourse in corporate and securities, constitutional, civil rights, and criminal law. "Bad faith" (which is the opposite of "the bona fide") and "fidelity" and "faithfulness" cluster about the standard phrase. And the words "real," "actual," "genuine," "substance," "spirit" as legal terms have a similar function, referring as they do to the object of faith. Lawyers, legislators, and judges do not bracket them when using them. They are used rather unselfconsciously, and they are used pivotally, which should make law an object of amazement to the modern and postmodern mentality.

What cannot sustain true attention is not part of the experience of authority. Insofar as what cannot sustain true attention does have an effect on us from without, it can be characterized pejoratively as well as descriptively as the authoritarian, which of course we all also regularly experience. The question how the past enters authority is thus virtually the question why pay true attention to what is past, as such. Why, we may ask, pay attention in law?

The question is rarely asked, which is an oddness, though an oddness matched by the oddness of metastatements about law—metastatements by contrast to the fine structure of legal discourse—that seem in fact to cut against any association of law with authority and to speak only of convention. When for instance someone asks a lawyer not "What should I do or think?" but "Why should I do this or think this way as you have told me?" the lawyer's reply may well be, "Because it's the law. What is done is done because that is the way it has been done." There may be a quotation from O. W. Holmes, Jr., "Judges are trained in the past which the law embodies." Then there is a shrug.

Such metastatements about law and the past rest upon a perception of law and its method, and it is a misperception, albeit one often purveyed by lawyers themselves. This one proceeds from the ease with which law is reified in the metaphors we have to talk of it, rather as reference to the "ground" of a decision might suggest (if one did not stay alert) something that would stop the foot if stamped upon, instead of the glowing ineffable that it is.

There is no law to which anyone can direct you to see or to repeat or perhaps chant out loud, neither in general nor on some particular subject or question. There are instead only statements of law. And they are statements of law only if they are made in good faith, responsibly, after the exercise of legal method: if statements are not made responsibly, if they are made not believing in them, in bad faith (the pretense that they are statements of law being a useful move in the feint and thrust of conflict or game), or if they are made without engaging in legal method (like pronouncements about conclusions of experimental science by someone who has no understanding at all of experimental method), they are not statements of law at all.

But even if they are responsibly made, they remain only statements of law, not the law. Any of them can be challenged. That is lawyers' work, to challenge them constantly—part, at least, of lawyers' work, another part being making statements of law. Even a Supreme Court opinion on a matter is not the law. It is one more statement of law, and often one which some justices bringing the vote on it to a majority have signed all the while full of troubled reservations, and to which dissenting justices deny any lasting validity beyond settling the immediacies of the immediate case.

There is thus no set or network of rules to which any lawyer or any official or judge could lead you by the hand and point to as the law, and which you might find old, dusty, and of antique design but nonetheless ancestral or venerable or at least venerated by lawyers because of its age. If there is to be discerned a relatively stable pattern of behavior or widespread agreement, from which such a set of rules might be induced in the manner perceptions of scientific rules (also called law) are evoked, and if this pattern or agreement and the rules induced from it could be linked to the past as the way things have always been done, our practice and understanding seem clear that a pattern of behavior or widespread agreement is not, as such, the law. This has always been a stumbling block for legal positivism. The *Dred Scott* decision, that constitutionally a person with a dark skin was not a citizen, and the hundred years of practice following it, is our most prominent national example, but there are hundreds of ordinary examples, from the practice of bribery to the discharge of mercury waste into waterways. The claim of illegality, persuasively made, is always the claim that what is, even if it has always been done, has no authority.

What then is the connection between the past and law? The past enters law and the experience of authority in law wholly through legal method, not descriptively or definitionally, and certainly not of its own force. The past enters, very simply, because lawyers work with texts in making statements of law and the texts with which they work are from the past.

If you go on to ask, as you should, "But why do lawyers *pore* so over texts from the past?" the first reply must be that those are the only texts there are. All statements, and all statements of law, are immediately in the past. And if you go back one step and ask, "But why turn to texts in the first place?" a response to that deepest of questions (also rarely asked) might begin by recalling another question most actually do ask themselves at least once every hour, "How should I act in or begin thinking about this situation?" The very asking of that is to turn outside oneself and look beyond the way one does act and behave, or outside a self so imprisoned in the here and now. To answer oneself by saying "I do this" or "I think that" is no help. Neither is the present behavior of others, as such, any help. Thus the attempt to read others, who have asked the same question in other situations; thus texts; and thus the past.

The difference between texts in general, and texts from the deeper past with which lawyers work more perhaps today than professionals in other fields except theology, is a difference of degree. There is no line of substance that is crossed as one reaches back or down. But the relative antiquity of the texts with which lawyers work remains intriguing and even striking. Lawyers try to spruce them up—for instance, lawyers change the spelling and capitalization and italization of eighteenth- and early nineteenth-century Supreme Court opinions. Their age, in the modern world, is very slightly an embarrassment. But legal texts are there in the deeper past, and not closer to the present, for several large reasons. One has to do with the imperatives of common reading and organized discourse among many individuals. There are texts that are focal texts, and perhaps there must be focal texts to which other texts and present or almost present statements make reference as commentaries or interpretations.

Focal texts are to be found in most disciplines. If they are from the founding moment of a reading community, they move back as that community continues to live and develop. Those of the Confucian, the Hindu, the Judaic, the Buddhist, the Christian, the Islamic, the Enlightenment, and the Marxist traditions are grand examples. The Sherman Antitrust Act of 1890, now a century old, is an example from one of the smaller worlds of law. Insofar as texts are not associated with the founding moment and do not begin as but rather become organizing texts—and the hierarchical institutions of Western law are designed to permit and promote this—it takes time for them to move to a central position. Once they are there, much time must pass before they are replaced, not only because it takes time for others to move to a central position, but because the number of aspects of life to be addressed is large in relation to the span of individual human life. All aspects cannot be addressed at once, and no one aspect can be readdressed in a close and serious way without leaving statements on others to continue aging.

Once there, at the center, they are read and reread, not because they are old, but rather because they are central. There is, moreover, an inevitable inertia in their centrality. Once other statements are made referring to them and organized by them, they cannot very easily be let go without deracinating those other statements as well. And so they tend to remain, moving ever deeper into the past. One would like to think they invite and reward rereading.

Their presence at the center is some evidence that they do. But read and reread they are. In fact, close interrogation of texts, in and of itself, may work to hold them in place, even as it also presses to eliminate them as they fail under the pressure. Close reading, reading in every detail and in every way, is at the very center of what lawyers *qua* lawyers do, and other parts of lawyers' method and the institutional structure of law are designed to make close reading possible. Anything closely read and reread must be there some time, always aging, if only to permit rereading. The rereading of some texts, the Confucian, the Vedaic, the Torah, for example, may go on forever.

But the large fact remains that in law focal texts, no matter how old, are not fixed. No legal text is immune from challenge and substitution, not even statute or constitutional provision. If one does not understand a text despite all efforts of one's own and others, if in the end it does not fit, has no resonance, it then cannot hold its place. What in it lawyers are paying attention to is most certainly not the words, which in themselves are sounds like sounds of the sea, but what is being said. If what is being said has no meaning, attention must shift. And as real attention shifts from it the text loses its place in the creation of authority, however much apparent attention may still for a time be directed to it.

There is a second reason, or one that can be separately stated all-encompassing though it is, why the past is not progressively abandoned in law and left behind for historians. No one, again, simply mouths the words of legal texts. They are read for their meaning, translated, restated by one who, responsible for the effects of what he says and does, will give orders or contribute to orders as he believes himself to be ordered by what he hears. The search for authority is a search for a voice beyond the brute facts of the past unfolding into the present. The voice is not less real for having had to be constructed by active work, but real it must be, actually heard, before it can be made one's own voice. Our looking to past efforts to hear and state what is heard is driven by our thirst to have all evidence of mind available to us as we listen for mind. We and our contemporaries and our immediate predecessors are not likely to have heard all there is to be heard.

Of the operation of precedent in law there is nothing different to be said. In the very word, the pre-cedent, seems to lie the proposition that what comes before governs what comes after, precisely and only because it comes before. What has been done in the past, the notion of precedent suggests, determines what is done in the present. But precedents are texts. A precedent is what was said as well as what was done. What was done is guide in understanding what was said, including the characterization of the situation itself, but one hardly knows what was done without looking to what was said. What was said may or may not grip the attention. If it does not, attention moves to other texts, including other precedents.

To be sure, each decision, each opinion accompanying an order made in a case, is written as a statement of what the law is. There is no tentativeness, no language of mere possibility. The closer the statement is to the focal center the more confident is the customary style of writing. This may be the only fitting convention for statements that are made responsibly and that will have long consequences for individuals involved in the case. But as soon as the statement is made it moves into the past and takes its place among all statements made, including all statements made by the same utterer. All are written in the same confidently assertive manner and, for the lawyer, there are thousands, hundreds of thousands of just such statements. They must compete, at the least, for attention.

But even then, competing for attention, they do not wave and step forward and present themselves to the mind wholly by their own motion. They do not even present themselves as candidates for attention. No one of them will be picked up or even glanced at until a situation is characterized, until it emerges what a case is "about." And as to characterization, two situations are never utterly the same. A responsible act is required, a response to the whole, if part of the living world is to be broken off and given a name and character of its own. Such a responsible act, not itself governed by precedent, must be the beginning of any search for voices that seem to have spoken about such a part.

Reference to reliance is often associated with invocation of precedent. But because the past can enter the present only through legal method and legal method is not a form of copying, what are called reliance interests are not themselves grounds for doing things the way they have been done before. The notion of reliance upon the law assumes some previously fixed object that might or might not be changed. What is there to rely upon? Not some particular statement of law, however definitively and confidently it may be written. The only possible reliance is upon our thought. The fact that we as individuals do things the way we did them before, or that natural systems do so, does not mean that creations of mind have this quality or even capacity. Law is always reaching into the future, and why the hopes of some should dash the hopes of others no reference to reliance can answer.

Reliance is sister to notice, always deemed a basic ingredient of justice. But in the same way, the notice one has is of the evidence of all the law (it being not forgotten that at some high level evidence of law is in the breast as well as in the books). The modern business executive who has proceeded without regard to worker safety in his factory or environmental safety outside it, and who is prosecuted for common law homicide or for poisoning waterways under the Refuse Act of 1899 when employees die or deformed children are born, may want to say he had no notice. But he has really no claim of surprise. The texts are there, the common law, the Refuse Act enacted almost a century before. Legal texts generally, including even those of corporate and securities law itself—those speaking of fiduciary duty to corporations, corporate purpose, disclosure, shareholder access to the corporate proxy, corporate constituencies—contain too much tension and debate and too much challenge to any proposition that worker safety or public safety as such and in and for itself is irrelevant to business decisions.

Reliance interests are no doubt attended to. A judgment about the good faith of those who read the law differently from the decision maker in a case (who contributes a statement of law to past legal texts) will affect the remedies given in that case. But reliance interests cannot govern what the law is; there is no way, in view of the actualities of legal method, that law itself can be viewed as a wall or a web of protection for them.

So too with a vision of law as fairness, invoking the past through the claim that, independently of reliance, those in like situations must be treated alike (unless, it is said, intervention of an unchallengeable and arbitrary power from outside overrides the law that exists, a revolution or a legislative act). There is the same necessary action, responsible to the whole, of characterizing and naming the present situation before what was done in the past can be compared. And in any situation in which there is appeal to equality of treatment, there will be other interests claiming their own legitimacy, other hopes demanding protection. That the hopes of some were realized in the past has never been, in itself, sufficient reason for denying the legitimate hopes of others in the present.

III.15 ✤ *Poetry*

What makes words poetic? We must think we know. The terms "poetry," "prose," are with us and there is a reach to categorize with them, a tendency to do so of the sort we tend to think and call natural.

Sound and form contribute to the poetic but do not define it. Rhymes or lines shorter than the width of a page are not enough. Might poetry not be rooted in its layering—in its echoes (toward which rhyme points), its double meanings, its references back—which represents the truth of experience many-layered, everything unfolding, everything having many meanings at once; which represents the truth of experience better than any linear abstraction that separates experience into units and places units one after another? Is this not why poetry so often appears condensed, and why, more even than the frequency in it of rhyme and rhythm, poetry is associated with music?

Legal texts are similarly many-layered and full of multiple reference. Linear and abstract in form they may appear, but they are closer to poetry than to prose.

III.16 ✤ *The Units of Legal Language*

A pitfall, yawning to receive its victims, is the thought that legal language consists of arrangements of units of greater or less generality. So, units of less generality can be placed in those of greater generality, which can be placed in units of greater generality still. A pitfall one step beyond, spread for those who are inclined more toward the horizontal and the egalitarian than toward the vertical and the hierarchical, is the thought that legal language is a system of units mutually defined by their differences from one another. Both are pitfalls mathematical thinking has left as it has moved beyond its own territory and passed through law.

Legal language does appear to be open to either characterization. "Is this included in that?" is said. "Shall we apply that term to this?" Or, "Is this phrase not too general to give any guidance?" Words in a statute or in mnemonic formulas drawn from common law materials are indeed presented as technical terms each with a definition that could be substituted for it save for inconvenience, the terms of the definitions themselves definable in the same way until all linguistic space is filled and the system is closed.

But appearance, this appearance, is denied by the realities of legal practice. The units of language, the words, the phrases, the terms, the titles, cannot be even conceived as boxes into which particularities can be placed or as solid, impenetrable shapes with contours ultimately molded to one another. Every use of a term in law is a metaphorical use. Every term is an expression, an expression better or worse, more revealing or less revealing, more resonant or less resonant. There are no fixed units of discourse, to be related to one another in a hierarchy of generality and particularity, or horizontally as in a puzzle. This would be mathematics, not language, not legal language. If a term does not express, it is abandoned, by speaker, or by listener, or by both. If a term has different lights in a succession of statements, its lights are blended by looking to person and meaning as a whole, which as in all metaphor is the only referent.

III.17 ❧ *Supposing*

You are not supposed to be there, says authority. What is
in that word "supposed"? You are not supposed to be
there (in the middle of the road, if you are a pedestrian, or
at the end of a chain of reasoning, if you are an agency of
government and relied upon inadmissible grounds in your
reasoning) not because some big person outside told you
not to be there, as a child might hear the words, but because in the contemplation of order and the way things
are supposed to be *you* are not there, and your being there
is not what you would suppose either if you sat down to
work it out. That of course is a challenge, and the beginning of argument, about what you would suppose. In the
end the proposition is that *you* are not there rather than
that you are not *there*.

III.18 ❧ *Law and Mathematics*

Some of the general difficulty in thinking about legal
thinking can be traced to an assumption that mathematics is language, an assumption that has been with us a
very long time, perhaps from the Greeks.

As long as lawyers and judges went ahead and did law
themselves, their assumptions about the relation between language and mathematics had minor consequence, at least in Anglo-American jurisdictions. It did
affect Europe if Max Weber's characterization of the common law, in a passage doubting whether the common law

was a "true" or genuine "legal system," may be taken to paint by contrast a picture of the reality of life affected by the existence of Roman or civil codes: "[In the common law, concepts are] not 'general concepts' which would be formed by abstraction from concreteness or by logical interpretation of meaning or by generalization and subsumption; nor were these concepts apt to be used in syllogistically applicable norms. . . . [R]easoning is tied to the word, the word which is turned around and around, interpreted, and stretched."

But now, in the late twentieth century, both the contemplation of and the practice of not doing law oneself, but of having it done for one either through machine inquiry or by bureaucratic delegation in newly bureaucratized courts and law firms, have made the difficulties introduced by the mathematical assumption more acute and have brought it more to the foreground.

The question in the late twentieth century is not whether legal discourse fails to reach the ideal of rationality represented by mathematics. It is whether legal discourse will be eliminated by mathematics. An exposition of philosophical texts on the nature of language can begin with a "phrase" from mathematics, "sixty-eight plus fifty-seven," and assert that the problem to be addressed in the example applies to "all meaningful uses of language" (and then go on to present, as Wittgenstein's view, that the meaning of "sixty-eight plus fifty-seven" is quite indeterminate). But no a fortiori conclusion follows for the language of law from any inquiry into "sixty-eight plus fifty-seven." The reason why not takes something of the form *nihil ex nihilo*. A mathematical statement never was meaningful, because it is not about anything. It is empty, dead. "Two plus two equals four" may mimic a sentence in legal discourse, but the similarity is in form only. "Two men plus two women, or two Asians plus two

Europeans, equal four human beings" would be a legal statement, which is about something, but by the same token it would not be a mathematical statement. Sentences in law are "Bargain in good faith with a labor union" or "Do not be cruel to children," and in speaking of *faith, cruelty, children, labor,* we speak about our lives and what is alive for us.

It is sometimes said that when one uses a word, and is challenged (or challenges oneself as one uses it), one must justify its use by reference to a rule, and this—justification of action by reference to rules—is what makes mathematics like law. But if you say to me, in law, "What is the meaning of that word? Justify your use of it," and you say it as a move in a game (as you would in setting up an equation to define a relation in mathematics, and not as just one way of getting discussion going about what someone, or I, may mean), then it is best, for you and for me, to decline to play the game. It will get us nowhere. If you are asking what do *I* mean, and are using your focus on a particular word as a way of talking, that is useful.

Then I might respond with another statement, and you would respond with more questions, two would be talking to each other about what is important to them, and we would have an instance of human language. To concentrate otherwise on a word in itself, and to ask for *its* meaning or for justification of *its* use, is like concentrating on one legal text to the exclusion or others in the universe to which one looks in determining the law. In law, one justifies by reference to the whole, not to a rule; one does not ask, "Does this rule fit?"—for the rule is not given until analysis is finished—but rather, "What is the law?"

Underlying the failure of the analogy to mathematics, whether for law or for human language, and any analogy to a set of rules like those of a game, is the elimination of the person speaking and listening. There is no one who cares what is said, any more than a programmed computer cares about its use of terms. Mathematicians talking to one another about mathematics may be talking about something they care about, but the language of their talk is then not mathematics. And in the development of linguistics and artificial intelligence in the twentieth century, theorists' reification of words and their assumption that there need be no one who cares before one has even an instance of language pull them away from what we all—and they themselves—actually do in speaking to one another, which is not to define words and keep them constant, in systems, but to express, to speak in metaphors that stretch, transform, and appropriate the words, and to read the whole—words in sentences, sentences in paragraphs, paragraphs in statements, statements in lives. For while theorists would like to think and do say that something "is" or "is not" legally valid, "does" or "does not" impose a legal obligation, "is" or "is not" the law, as in mathematics A "is" or "is not" B, practicing lawyers know that these are all matters of degree, even that in expressing what they know in terms of degree they use the mathematical term "degree" only metaphorically.

III.19   ✿   *Real Cases*

Legal thought works with real cases. If the case is not real the reality of law is lost. Ortega y Gasset was willing to say, "When a concept is formed, reality leaves the room." Rootless, legal thought would lose its grip on the mind— the authority that attends authentic expression of the unexpressed disappears.

III.20 🐦 *Civil and Criminal*

If in some particular field one's judgment about what the law is turns out to differ from the judgment of officials with current responsibility for the field, one's material expectations may be defeated. Flows of money may be diverted from one's pocket to the pocket of another—though both expectations and present arrangements of money flows can anticipate and discount to a degree the possibility of such a difference of judgment.

This is the legal phenomenon of "civil liability." By contrast, criminal liability and punishment rest upon an inquiry into belief (though liability which is not "criminal liability" but which is based upon and justified by blame does shade into criminal liability). Regardless of the fact that there is a difference between one's judgment about what the law is and officials' judgment, prosecution and punishment do not proceed far if it appears one believes in one's judgment. In itself this does not make the criminal law what anyone responsibly, authentically believes it to be. Differing responsible judgments remain only evidences of the law. But if others do come to a conclusion that one authentically believes one's interpretation, their interpretations incompatible with it must be put in question for them and the authenticity of their own belief must once again be a matter for their own inquiry. And for purposes of blame and punishment, the fact that others can believe you believe says something, perhaps enough, about you (and them). This is the source of the great changes brought about by heroic dissent. What one is *punished* for, positively, may be only one's not following one's actual belief in the matter.

III.2 I ✤ *Levitation and Law*

A command to levitate either means something other than what at first glance it seems to mean, or it is not the law. If it is a "command to levitate" it is unenforced and unenforceable. It cannot be obeyed. It is ignored, laughed away. It is not serious, unmeant really, only a bit of play, a joke—perhaps a cruel joke and serious in its consequences, but a joke nonetheless.

A claim unenforced and unobeyed may not be the claim it seems to be, and read differently may turn out in fact to be enforced and obeyed. It is not, merely because unenforced and unobeyed, therefore not law. That would be "what is, is right" in negative form. There could be no thrust of hope, no eschatological thrust in law if that were so, if no eschatological thrust no authority, and no law. Law speaks to the spirit, which can fly. But there may be something like gravity in the world where the spirit moves, and a spiritual determinism, such that statements purporting to be law that demand the spiritually impossible are, in that perception, perceived to be not law, just as a demand is seen to be not law to the degree it demands the physically impossible. Levitation does occur. Gravity is transcended. But the spirit, when it takes flight, does not find itself with nothing around it, in the nothingness of infinity.

III.22 ☞ *Propitiation*

You drive over the posted speed limit and a trooper stops you. You say truthfully, "I am trying to get to my dying father." What does the trooper do, or the prosecutor? What does the judge do? What is the law of speed limits?

The trooper will help or the prosecutor will wave the case away. In the extraordinary event of prosecution, the judge may find you not guilty of the crime of speeding. The sign by the side of the road is not the only text.

If the trooper does cite and the prosecutor prosecutes and the judge convicts, but the judge then suspends sentence, could they all be propitiating a demon?

III.23 ☞ *The Sociology of Law*

"Everybody is doing it" is no defense to a charge that it is "against the law." What everybody does is only the beginning of a defense, evidence, that may lead to persuasion it is not against the law because the law is not what the accuser makes the law to be. What law stands against, at the outset of any analysis of what is against the law, is "what is, is right." "What is, is right" is temptation toward death within; "what is, is right" is tyranny itself. Thus the part words play in law, texts: words are protection against temptation, escape from tyranny. Law is not convention.

Words of law are not givens of the world either, right because they are. Movement away from the tyranny of "what is, is right" is not a lateral move to an equivalent tyranny in linguistic form. The literalist dreams of this (the literalist would not want to live it in reality), such rest where the dream can be dreamed away from the responsibility of determining what the law is. The very words themselves are not given. They are found. Even focal texts, that become concrete particulars of the lawyer's world for a time, carry no meaning a lawyer can reach up and break off like a bit of crystal. Constructing a statement of law to be acted upon, a lawyer constantly seeks a real meaning, drawn from all the evidence.

The evidence is not only other words. It includes action, what is done. A circle then, back to "what is, is right"? No. The evidence that is garnered is evidence of belief. Actions may be renounced, as words may be renounced; actions that are not renounced are affirmed in words or else buried under succeeding actions, forgotten and lost in the webs of cause. Words that are not renounced have their thrusts. Law's denial of "what is, is right" is not itself denied when a meaning that is real is sought in all the evidence.

The question what the law "is" is not so very different from the question what we "are." We seek ourselves in evidence of ourselves. Little other way is open to us. What we do is evidence of what we believe, despite what we say—or is evidence of the meaning of what we say. But even to begin the search, and necessary to the undertaking, we must presuppose that that is not all there is, that we are flawed, that what we do is flawed and what we say is flawed. Escape from a circle that would have us dying into what merely is, into the material or into history, is the ordinary, daily, constant experience of human existence. Escape from such a circle is nothing arcane or peculiar to law. Are we in essence who we say we are, or are we as we are? We are the joinder of both, and both what we say and what we do must be read.

Something of an image of law's sense of itself can be seen in lawyers' work in criminal law. An individual characterized in the course of the criminal trial is never merely what he said he was or says he is, hypocrite that he may be. Nor, however, is he merely what he does. What he does must be connected to him; the meaning of what he does is found not only in its consequences in the world but also in what he says. (Were legal consequences visited on him purely for the consequences of what he does, that would not be through the criminal law, or not for what lawyers call a "true crime": that would be "quasi-criminal," perhaps necessarily or "constitutionally" so; "strict" liability, the person as such not the focus and not much blamed.)

And where the defendant is not an individual but, as so often in the late twentieth century, a corporate organization that operates more by formal utterance than most individuals do, this mirror image in the small of lawyers' search for what the law is appears more sharply. The merely stated rules of an organization are never enough to exonerate the organization and separate it from what one of its employees or members does, by putting that employee's act "outside the scope of his employment" (as it is said). There is a most natural move, by judge and jury and legislator before them, to look to all that all those acting for a corporation do and do not do encouraging, or preventing, or accepting profit from the loss of the legally protected value, in the course of judging the place of the value in the corporation as a whole, which is the defendant, and the defendant corporation's connection to and blame for the loss of the value at the individual hand of its member. The stated corporate rules, the speech of office, the canon to which the defense keeps pointing, remain as evidence of corporate *mens rea* or lack thereof, but there is a sociology of the words, undertaken by second nature before deciding to blame or not to blame. Natural, because it is something of the reverse, rather like a mirror image, this inquiry for purposes of blame, of the search for the mind of the law for purposes of praise—the praise of attention, conformance and imitation, internalization.

There is sociology on either side, determining what is against the law, determining what the law is. Blame tracks the way of praise, though in a conclusion of condemnation faith is given up, in response to a perceived breach of faith, and in determining the law faith is not given up (and thus the "is" in the "what is, is right" that both blame and praise reject is not entirely the same "is"). The sociology which is the sociology of law reconciles rejection of "what is, is right" with a determination of what the law is that includes all the evidence—in the evidence itself there is escape, from action into words, and from words into real meaning that is embodied because present, but not limited by mark and space and time. The evidence with which the sociology of law works is evidence of actual belief, and because belief is belief and within, the great issue always remains with us, as we escape and escape again.

The great issue is the challenge posed by, and to, sociologists who would distance themselves from both blame and praise if they could, and who would stop—if stopping were not death, as they know it is. Put, again, of ourselves, rather than of law, the issue is the finality of the evidence. Are we free of what we actually believe as that is revealed to us by all we say and do? Do we actually believe that that may yet not be what we *actually* believe: can faith be kept that what we actually believe is worth believing, is right? One can only ask. But any of us can wonder whether the same "irrepressible self-consciousness" that "distinctly answered, 'No'" to John Stuart Mill's enormous question he put to himself (would it be "a great joy and happiness" to him if all his "objects in life were realized"?) may be speaking to each of us about the finality of the evidence of ourselves.

III.24 ❧ *Positivism and Literalism*

In "the great grain elevator scandal" one company was fined five hundred thousand dollars for false export statements because it deliberately set its scales at one-twentieth of one percent greater than true. But as was pointed out by the defense, regulations required scales to be accurate only within a tolerance of one-tenth of one percent. What was the company doing other than profit maximizing within the bounds set, which some argue (those who also can conceive law as bounds) corporation law requires? Yet the company was condemned. Here the corporate officials involved were not likely misled by positivism preaching the possibility of literalism. But positivists preaching the possibility of literalism do mislead some when they make statements about law.

III.25 ☙ *The Shadow of Heresy*

Office, which lawyers have, brings with it the problem of discipline. Shadowing discipline is the question whether there is some notion of heresy in legal thinking, as there has historically been in theology. Lawyers do not find the question a very agreeable one. Everything in them longs to say no. Modern discussions of heresy seem a holdover from the infancy of Western European thinking—atavistic, the rites of a cult, a very large cult but a cult nonetheless. The mainstream of twentieth-century thought, indeed the mainstream of thought since the Enlightenment, appears to have no place for any notion of heresy. If an accusation of heresy were leveled at an earnest speaker at the American Law Institute or a section meeting of the American Bar Association, there would be shudders, laughter, thoughts of freedom.

But there is still a notion of error in law, within which the sporting talk of arguments and winning or losing arguments is set. A lawyer or judge can be viewed as making statements of law which are simply wrong. Moreover, if they are not only wrong but willfully wrong, the response is not merely to ignore them or filter them out of meaningful discussion, but rather to do something about them. If a professor at a law school taught that the Fourteenth Amendment applied only to descendants of slaves or the Bill of Rights did not apply to the states, went to original sources to prove his thesis, and dismissed the institutional elaboration of the Fourteenth Amendment in the constitutional opinions that are the usual texts for study of the amendment in courses in constitutional law, he might well not be allowed to continue to teach his course by his faculty. At the least it would be made difficult for him. In any ensuing debate over academic freedom references would be made to the agitation, uncertainty, and confusion that would result from his willful and deliberate promulgation of error, and the judgment made on him would be cast in terms of competence. If his faculty did allow him to continue teaching, central accrediting agencies from the American Bar Association or the American Association of Law Schools would begin to take note.

So too with practicing lawyers. They teach the law to those who come to them for advice. Action might be taken against a lawyer today, for example, who was retained by a corporation and who insisted to management that her only fiduciary duty as corporate lawyer ran to management, and that her duty did not run to the corporation and all associated with it. She would be teaching the management false doctrine. If a practicing lawyer gave advice on the Fourteenth Amendment of the kind just described, the disciplinary committees of the bar would intervene. A litigating lawyer arguing to a court that abandonment of the gold standard is unconstitutional may be fined or imprisoned for contempt and disbarred. Court and disciplinary committee would take action not just because the lawyer's clients would lose as a result of her positions, any more than a heretical priest is disciplined just because those whom he advises and influences might lose in another world. Everyone is thought to be affected, in somewhat the same way as everyone may be thought affected by a crime.

Is all this, if truth be told, *heresy* still with us alive and well in the twentieth century? Given the similarity of basic method in theology and law and the mutual resemblance of their institutional practices, it would be surprising if the notion of heresy were not in some way to be found in legal thinking. After all, the two white bands that judges and lawyers wear at their throats in Canada and

Great Britain are the same two white bands that Presbyterian ministers wear: they represent the two tablets Moses brought back from his encounter on the mountain.

The reason for the question, do modern lawyers have a notion of heresy and act upon the notion, is that there ultimately must be exploration into whether a notion of heresy attends every approach to authority, or whether a notion of heresy is instead merely a reflection of authoritarianism that can eventually be shaken off and left behind.

If authority, office, and heresy are intertwined, lawyers will at least have theologians to look to, however uncomfortable the looking may be. In the churches heresy is disciplined initially by exclusion from office, teaching or pastoral, and then by exclusion from the community of communicants. The community may be a local one of Mennonites or the worldwide one of Roman Catholicism. In those churches where every individual is a minister, which seem to have eliminated central institutions and thus departed from hierarchy and journeyed farthest toward freedom and equality, exclusion from office is the same as exclusion from the community. A conclusion of heresy is softened in the churches by the fact that one can set up another church. Hans Küng or Karl Barth, Roman Catholic or Protestant, may have his authorization to speak for the church and teach in the church withdrawn, but there are divinity schools that would receive Karl Barth and Hans Küng.

Not so in the law. Attendance at the ceremonies of the law is mandatory, and expressions of disrespect for the institutions of the law may be disciplined by gagging and shackling. Disbarment is total disbarment, conviction and imprisonment complete excommunication—though the consequence of a determination of error in law may be softened by a withholding of criminal condemnation in the presence of sincere belief.

But the difference is easily overdrawn. The theologian, like the lawyer, is seeking integration, and it is not simply that his old friends will not speak to him or listen to him, and he therefore must make new friends, that makes exclusion so terrible. The premises of his work pull him back toward the community that has excluded him. An austere truth known to him alone is not a satisfaction to him, whatever the stories of saintly heroism and lonely certainty circulated about those individuals, once reviled, whose thinking has since become one with a community's. Other individuals are part of his truth and sources of it. Action, practice, consequence in the world are inseparable from his statements and his thinking. Heresy, discipline, the means of discipline—the theologian is never far away when lawyers begin examining themselves.

III.26 ❧ Ontology and Methodology

If there is to be law it must be the product of legal method. You cannot ask, "Is there law to be observed here?" or "What is the law here?" without asking what has been done with the materials from which a statement of law has been drawn. What has been done? How has it been done?—you do not know whether there is law to be attended to or what the law is without inquiring into method. And to criticize the execution of method by which a statement of law is reached, or, stepping back, to raise a question about the possibility of fulfilling a presupposition of method, is to question the "is" in "law is" or "is the law," the presence of the law referred to in the statements "There is law to be concerned about here" or "This is what the law is."

III.27 ❧ *The Pertinence of Courtesy*

In discussion of anything human, and in all legal discourse, belief never lies very low and is easily stumbled over. A philosopher may write or say that one human being—I, you—cannot know that another is like him or her at all. If the reply were to be that such a statement shows how cold and unhappy the philosopher must be, if the reaction were merely one of pity, he would be indignant. Such a reply would be deemed ad hominem, unscholarly, most impolite.

Why would a suggestion that the philosopher needs help, or a different life with less philosophy in it, be treated as impolite? Because the philosopher assumes he will be treated by those to whom he speaks as a person like them, listened to, not observed as a case. And thus he assumes he will not be believed in what he proposes, at least to this degree—where he himself is concerned—and thus he reveals that he does not himself believe all that he says.

III.28 ❧ *Individuality*

Legal analysis is charged with a weary relativism, the passivity and the indifference to hope and cry that mark the absence of belief. Such a stance, so aristocratic (it is said), is possible only for the comfortably off; thus law, itself deeply radical, becomes a target of the anguished radical.

The defense of law points to individuality and law's protection of it, and *individuality* and *relativism* are then wrapped together, one entailing the other in the actual operation of the world.

But *individuality* does not need relativism to sustain it, and a threat to relativism is not a threat to individuality. Like Keats, who knew what a heart completely disinterested would be but knew of only two such hearts in history, lawyers, juries, legislators, legal analysts know what goodness is. The perennial difficulty is in realizing it. Kindness, help, generosity, interest in the other: questioning whether we can ever know what it is to do good is usually a way of avoiding the tragedy of the difficulty in realizing the good. So persistent is the difficulty of it, so apparently structural, that the difficulty of realizing the good has become part of legal thought and is transmitted when law is taught.

The difficulty is within oneself and it is within the other, the neighbor in the prophetic traditions. Within the other, good received can be a smothering, an invading, an overwhelming, an extinction of the growth of responsibility or the capacity to do good in turn. Within oneself (once one is beyond a contention with the inertia of complacency and the centripetal force of selfishness), the difficulty is like that which is within the other, consumption by goodness, giving the self away; and it is reflected, in the other, in the growth of neediness that consumes. The difficulty always is that there must be a fount to slake a thirst and streams kept flowing to that fount.

There is then a near inevitable holding back and thus a separateness. This is where individuality is found in a moral world, and this holding back is part of what, without denying knowledge of good, law protects in recognizing and protecting the individual.

III.29 ❧ *Contentment with Appearances*

The very act of close reading presumes or indicates that the meaning of another person makes a difference. One who reads hastily or sloppily may be taken to indicate that it is his own thought in which he is interested and that what he is reading is a more or less random stimulation of his thought: for purposes of random stimulation appearances may be quite as good as actualities.

Of course one who is truly interested in another's thought may be truly interested because he wants to know what he himself believes. It is his own mind in which he is ultimately interested. But if he reads hastily and sloppily and does not read closely and carefully when he has time to do so, he does not care what the other actually thinks. What the other actually thinks does not make a difference to him. Perhaps then he does not care what he himself actually believes. His experience of random thought is enough. He reveals to himself that appearances for him are as good as actualities.

III.30 ✌ *The Imitative and the Explained*

There is a connection between what is lost in a move to imitation or fakery—the authentic, in the sense of the real—and what is lost in a move to explanation: the reality to which the equations that move thinking into the mathematical form of thought, and limit thought to process, are false either in the units they equate (which pretend to be what they are not) or in their "equal" signs (which pass off one thing for another).

III.31 ✌ *Starting Points*

Is there any cut in a process other than an aesthetic or spiritual cut? Why do we divide some "finished" part off between the end of the process of "its" emergence and the beginning of the process of "its" dissolution—except that it is beautiful or has meaning and we frame and hold it?

How is the wolf separated from the process (or that slower process we call a system) which is the mountain where the wolf moves back and forth—except by our perception of its spirit or its beauty, that we frame and, in framing, separate from the mountain?

III.32   *The Evidence of Negation*

"There are no unicorns" is not a statement in which a person may be denying what he appears to be saying, as in the statement "There is no God." A unicorn turns out to be a horse with a horn added. But "God": what is this that does not exist? If an answer comes back in the form of a definitional sentence, it invites the response "That is not God." The beginning of an answer in the form of sentences would be *The Brothers Karamazov*, but the answer would not stop with the last sentence in the book. The discussion of what God is would be discussion of experience, not of a concept or of the definition of a word. And as discussion proceeded, if the person asserting "There is no God" did seem to the listener to know what he was denying the existence of, that person so speaking would more and more be evidence to the listener of the existence of God and to be asserting the existence of God in his denial of it.

There are many other instances of this form of assertion. An organism that has nothing to do with reason or purpose could not write, "Organisms, including man, have no reasons for acting, no purpose in acting." No-purpose invokes purpose, which cannot be broken down like a unicorn, unless the listener concludes that the speaker is not talking of what the listener understands as purpose; and the speaker will not stop at illusion of purpose: without purpose there will be no illusion of purpose unless his listener concludes that he is not speaking of illusion. "I should be the last to hold the individual responsible for conditions whose creature he himself is," says Marx, and in so saying asserts individual responsibility, which he and his reader must know to entertain a denial of it. The sociobiologist speaks of altruism as disguised selfishness, authenticity as successful deception. But altruism is no unicorn. Deception is deception only against the possibility of truth. If truth never is, neither is there deception. Masquerading it points to experience of it.

III.33 ❧ *The Relative Reality of Creation by Faith*

A person who believes she is determined, and who does not indulge in the illusion that she is not, would not go on. *She* would not go on. Which then is the illusion and which the reality? If we create by faith, what we create is the meaningful world. The fact we create it and must create it to live does not entail that it is not real or really meaningful. It is all we know. There is no comparison to be made of the relative reality of a meaningful world we create and the reality of a world we do not create. The world we know is the world where we live, the world where we live is the world that allows us to live, the world that allows us to live is the world we create.

III.34 ✍ *A Question of Method*

Death is a special kind of fact. There is a form of thought entered into when we conclude or infer from the fact of death that there must be hope to push us on to start what we cannot complete, and hope to hold us back and accept, generally, doing without that which we turn out not to have; and this form of thought continues when we conclude that this hope implies, most reasonably, that we see ourselves in those we love and leave behind—both those individuals, and those goods we strive to realize and with which we are identified. Death is a very special fact. What form of thought is it that reasons from it? Empirical, partly? Logical? A bit. Perceptual, really—humming a new tune and saying to another, "Is this right? Does this strike you as beautiful?"

III.35 ✍ *Aesthetics*

The golden section was discovered independently by Inca and Greek? If so, the notion that fashion, handed down, determines aesthetic perception—that beauty is in the eye of the beholder and that the eye of the beholder is the product of his cultural history—is challenged.

   The challenge of the golden section is uninteresting if the human neurological and endocrine system is so patterned that the golden section evokes a given response. But to speculate that that may be the situation is to leave out the beautiful. How easy it is, how accustomed we are to think of matters behind the screen of scientific method, leaving out their spirit: to say the golden section just *is* beautiful is to evoke something mechanical, even static. The line of emphasis should be drawn under the *beautiful*, not the *is*. Then we might remember we can never capture and can hardly say what we mean by beautiful, any more than we can say what we mean when we exclaim that for a moment in a sunny woods we felt safe, young, and free. What we are doing is pointing.

III.36 ❧ *The Status of Lawyers' Presuppositions*

Compare the lawyer's situation to the scientist's. Use an extreme example of the scientist's situation for the clarity that contrast can bring.

Evolutionary biologists have moved to the study of things human as Darwin never did, particularly as they have shifted their unit of reference from the individual or species to the genetic material that families share. Their speculations are interesting, but far more interesting is the transformation, by some biologists, of a predictive tool into a creed. The predictive tool is a supposition that the process of natural selection acts in such a way as to preserve only genetic material that maximizes its own survival. The creed, the positive assertion, is that "we are nepotists and nothing else."

Using his supposition or predictive tool, his pretending, the biologist asks what we would expect to find in our experience. He looks around and finds this or that, and is not discouraged. Some things as he finds them would have turned out as he predicted if his supposition were part of the structure of the world. And then the shift occurs: every human phenomenon, law, morality, thinking, learning, speaking, has, it is asserted, an evolutionary mission. All our traits and tendencies are the product of evolution and the purpose of all our traits and tendencies is to maximize reproductive success. The shift is over huge dimensions—the assertion is of the same order as the statement "Man was born to suffer" (though the evidence of suffering is far more consistent and universal than the confirming bits that biologists find as they pick over human experience).

Much has been written in ridicule of the Articles of what may be seen as the New Biologist's creed. Much of the ridicule goes too far, utterly denying that in our thinking, choosing, and creation we must deal with inherited structures not of man's making. Even though biologists seem not to understand what law or moral reasoning is, their warnings are useful. But there is, after all allowance, something ridiculous in the New Biologist's posture. The biologist of the positive assertion simply excludes from the evidence his own experience of love, of meaning, of purpose, of language, of death, of beauty. Indeed, he excludes the evidence of his own use of the everyday words "I" or "we."

And much of the biologist's difficulty is the difficulty every scientist has, which lies in the difference between being inside and outside an experience. For the new biologist all things are behavior, what is *done*, and this insistence on remaining outside drains of meaning what is important to us and makes it virtually unrecognizable. A greeting is a wave of the hand, nothing more; love is the phenomenon of flesh on flesh, nothing more; a smile is a pulling back of the skin covering the teeth; dignity is measured by the relative angles of backbones.

Scientists know that none of this is true to their experience of greetings, love, smiles, and dignity, and they demonstrate in their lives that they do not believe it. Nonetheless, here is the spectacle of analysts transforming into positive assertions presuppositions that are methodologically central to their work. Do lawyers do the same?

In presupposing mind and creating persons are lawyers deceiving themselves, or at the least engaging in the same kind of slippage from the hypothetical and the pretend to the credited and the real? Admittedly there is some of this. The strong question is whether this is what lawyers really do across the board, so that in their creation of persons they have no more claim to credence than do some scientists in their elimination of persons.

There is a difference whatever the final judgment on lawyers' assertions may be. Lawyers presuppose mind, to be sure, as they go about their business, but they are not doing so for the purpose of "seeing what would happen if" or of predicting. The presupposition of mind is a useful presupposition, has a use, in securing willing obedience and the joint pursuit of shared purposes as they are expressed through law, which is derived by legal method. But this usefulness—if the term useful can be used without moving into a detached and manipulative stance—is not realized without belief. It is the positive assertion of the existence of mind and caring person that makes the presupposition useful in law; whereas in science it is not the assertion that is useful but the hypothetical proposition, which is set up and sought to be disproven and which is refined and changed as the facts are surveyed. Indeed, in science the transformation of hypothetical into positive assertion gets in the way of modifying or discarding the predictive device. In law the assertion or the belief is prior to the methodological presupposition, though certainly lawyers (and people generally) work to maintain the possibility of belief. And hearing and understanding, willing obedience, mind and meaning, are part of the experience of the lawyer and the nonlawyer, part of the evidence, not merely propositions derived from the evidence. The evidence (again, if experience of these things is to be treated as *evidence*, to make the two cases at all comparable) is not of a kind which a scientist would admit, for the scientist is always detached and outside that with which he or she works.

Belief in mind and assertion of personality are thus not precisely equivalent to their opposites in their derivation and claim to credence. It is the very attempt of law to be true to all human experience, to be universal in its reasoning and that from which it reasons, which saves law from the unreal, playing, gaming quality of all those discussions of human affairs from which the speakers themselves seem to be missing. Of the scientific mentality, it is often said the distinctive characteristic is the desire to control. The very value of or in prediction lies in the sense of control and command that the capacity to predict provides. One who knows what another will do can manipulate. Prediction is not for the purpose of understanding; understanding is exactly equivalent to successful prediction. Prediction, manipulation, and control are no doubt also part of a lawyer's life. They are not, however, distinctive characteristics of law and being a lawyer. In law the prediction is of what one would oneself think or do as a result of thought. One is inside, not outside. The manipulation and purposeful change in which a lawyer does engage when making statements of law are of and in the structure of thought which he or she shares with others, and from which he or she, like all others, stands somewhat apart.

Again, scientists live in two worlds, one where they smile and love and grieve, the other where they manipulate and calculate. If it is of significance that lawyers seem a particularly manipulative crowd, it is also of significance that distinguished scientists sometimes abandon the limitations generally associated with the disciplines in which they have built their reputations, and concern themselves particularly with those parts of human experience they could not allow themselves to touch before. The dilemma at the end of Darwin's *Autobiography*, his wishing he had dosed himself daily with literature, the work of Penfield or Schrödinger or Polanyi seeking to bridge mind and matter without denying either, are in fact an introduction to what the ordinary lawyer must labor to do every day.

III.37 ✍ *A Challenge of Postmodernism to Legal Method*

Michel Foucault is said by a contemporary to have been active in sadomasochist practice. Suppose this to be true.

Foucault's thought about the subjective and the self is read as dissolving the self into power. Playing on two of the senses of the word *subject* represented in "subjective" and "subjection"—"subject for" and "subject to"—he is taken to propose that the very sense of self is sense of power or sense of being defined in the exercise of power by another or by a system. Sense of self appears in and is equivalent to the exercise of power over another—as a flash appears in the course of lightning and is equivalent to lightning itself, neither the cause nor really the effect of it. But formless as the subjective and the self must be, if power has no end or purpose beyond itself, the subjective must, like the flash, dissipate. And if concrete existence can be experienced again only as an aspect of power, there may then be a reversal and a shift from active subjecting to being subjected, to being formed from without.

But the form thus given from without is hollow. It is not one's own. The sense of the subjective that arises with the imposition of another is also only a flash, and the dominated may seek again to dominate. It does not matter which human being is in which position; each would act the same in either, and the same human being may be in one or the other position in different contexts, notably so in a hierarchy where each is submissive from above and dominant from below. Both situations can be imagined played out within a single human being. The invariable is that the subjectivity that so appears, that merely is, as the flash of lightning merely is, is meaningless and is not maintained. Alternation, repetition, or progressive tightening of the bonding or the ordering proceeds along until death, presenting to the analyst the truth of the process which is the limit of human experience. Self-consciousness is awareness of power and awareness that this is all there is.

Similar visions of a cyclically destructive and self-destructing human subjectivity based loosely upon sociology or psychiatry have been presented—the psychology of the Crowd and the Survivor, or perception of a perpetual child within alternating between childlike aggression reaching for total domination and consumption of the world, and childlike dependence and total submission. Foucault is not alone. It would be odd if Foucault were alone, for such visions might be expected as outgrowth or response to the axiom of science that all is process, there is nothing more than process. But for many, Foucault's texts are central texts, the texts assigned and taught. They are discussed as perceptions of the truth of the human condition rather than as the cries of a tormented man. What is to be done with the possibility that Foucault, hating himself and repeatedly seeking to erase self (and gain some other) in action, sought also to erase self in thought?

To explain Foucault's work, to reduce what he says or writes to a symptom or a reflection of personal tragedy, is to accede in one's method of working with texts to the very erasure of voice he seems to propose—a stance at war with the presupposition that must underlie reading him at all. Is all ultimately misleading in its reach for the universal (except insofar as it demonstrates that there is nothing but what is), all ultimately infected by and reflecting (in truth, in fact, behind appearances) the personal failures of the individual life of the writer of what is proposed to be read?

The implication of the very notion of failure suggests otherwise. Some texts are inauthentic and are put aside. But if any texts remain to be read and reread as authentic attempts to struggle to express what is perceived, they must be read together—the whole evidence of meaning. Foucault's practices—if biographically true—do not make him blind so that his urging what he says he sees is like a blind man describing a sunset. His experience of himself may permit him to see things as others do not or things that are clouded by denial, in a way perhaps not wholly unlike a parent's love of her child may enable her to see truths about the child that others have not seen. The question—a question posed by method—must remain: not what do Foucault's texts say, but what does Foucault say in texts that keep one reading.

III.38 ❧ *Form and Substance and Mens Rea*

Legal discourse turns to "form" and "substance" to express what is to be condemned. Whether a decision maker is criminal or not depends, it would seem from reading explanations of condemnation (or approval), upon whether there is substance to the form of what he has done.

If you pursue the terms "form" and "substance," as the counselor must implicitly do if she is to give counsel, you come to see patterns of other words associated with form and with substance—constellations of words that appear around "form" and "substance." When, for example, does the structuring of a transaction move from tax avoidance, which is allowed and expected, to tax evasion, which is condemned? When the transaction is "artificial," it is said, and there is then raised up the alternative to "artificial," which is "real"; or when the structuring of the transaction is playing a "game" with the law or with those—administrators, prosecutors, judges—responsible for giving force to the law (a responsibility counselors undertake also on admission to the bar), and there is then placed against game playing its alternative, which is being "serious"; or when the transaction is "sham," which raises up "sham"'s alternative, what is "actual"; or when the structuring is an "abuse" of form, raising up the alternative to "abuse," which is "caring" or "concern." The presence of one points to the others and to its alternative, and rarely is the alternative not to be found voiced in some explicit way, if only in a "really." The discourse is not definitional. Word opens to word, term is added to term.

So artificiality, playing, misleading appearance, uncaring abuse, are arranged against reality, seriousness, actuality, and concern. And on the one side is the attribution of criminality, and on the other side is the deference given to responsible action, nonintervention—enforcement, indeed, of an individual's decisions in the various ways individuals' decisions are enforced through law.

Look at the constellations of words on either side. *When* is there present the unabusive caring or the "serious"? *What* is the "actuality" and the "reality" with which these are associated? It is the person, the caring mind, which a system, the objectified working of rules, can only mimic and pretend to be. Or, on the other side, what is the "appearance" *of*? What does not engage always in game playing? What is "mere" about the merely formal? Criminality is the absence of the person—*mens rea*, that which makes action criminal, is largely omission, absence: as responsibility is presence.

As the circles of words widen, associated with condemnation (and thwarting through law) on the one hand, or approval (and enablement through law) on the other, the constant that links them will be found to be the person, the active presence of responsible and caring mind. A decision maker may ask a counselor not, "What ought I to do, or how ought I to go about thinking what I should do?" but instead for an "exposure index" cast in probabilistic terms that can be fed into other calculations, and that would include, in addition to the counselor's relative confidence in her reading of legal texts, a factor for the probability of being detected, to be multiplied by the probability of being prosecuted, and then by the probability of being seriously disadvantaged by a sanction. There is resistance to the request, condemnation of counselors who accede to it. But what is wrong with it? The answer found is often that it introduces a "cold" stance toward the law, the gambler's stance.

So the treatment in law of a gambling upon one's own criminality appears (outside law) to be circular. If one places a bet that one will not be found to be a criminal, one may discover that whether one is found to be a criminal depends upon one's *mens rea*, and the *mens rea* that leads to one's condemnation is one's betting, one's gaming. Cost-benefit calculations, placing beside lives or suffering, translated into dollar figures, the market-supplied costs of alternative courses of action, for instance in the design of a consumer product or of a manufacturing process, are viewed as very possibly inflammatory if presented to juries considering punitive damage awards. They are associated with raising the level of condemnation. They are viewed as at least evidence for the prosecution, in a charge of reckless homicide when a death occurs, proof of the relevant *mens rea* that is described as "disregard" of the value of human life. Pursue the language of the explanations why this should be, and you arrive also at the term "cold." What is condemned is not mistakes in calculation, nor reasoning itself. What is condemned is an absence, one's abandoning oneself, who is represented by the alternative raised by "cold," which is "warmth." In law's insistence on staying with the internal—on not leaving the internal to move outside—there is reflection of the widely understood artificiality of the self-conscious, in contrast to the genuineness of the "unself-conscious." "Self-consciousness"—in this instance a pejorative and not what is celebrated as the culmination of evolution—puts one outside oneself, detached, unintegrated, ultimately manipulative of oneself through the crude and frozen categorizations and loss of sensitivity that accompany all manipulation of the nonmaterial. What is missing is living concern, the animated imagination, that can achieve what no lifeless working of rules and blind manipulation of forces can achieve. What is missing—so that only the form of it, the misleading appearance of it, only the shell remains—is the person that law, the legal mind, and legal discourse presuppose, create, and demand.

III.39 ❧ *Praise and Blame*

There is no complete detachment of the "responsibility" that is associated with a judging mind—the word "responsible" being used in its central sense—from the "responsibility" attributed when legal remedies or sanctions are invoked. As praise is not accorded without perception of central responsibility, and the paying of close attention to a person or a statement may be the most basic form of praise—*reading* may be praise—so also is there at least a resistance to blaming without perception of such responsibility.

The two are certainly not parallel. Consequences may be visited upon someone and blame implied thereby, to a degree that would not satisfy the instinct to praise. The attribution of statements, actions, and outcomes with attendant use of the term "responsible" does not follow precisely the same pattern of thought in praise and in blame. But just as praise can be pushed only so far, blame can be pushed only so far, and when blame does go too far there is movement to a different form of analysis and a departure from the world of obligation—or a move to redefine the person being blamed or to redefine what the person is to be blamed for.

III.40 ❧ *Law's Kindred Subject Matters*

Everyone knows, and shows it in a thousand ways, that a puppy's charm is lost somewhere on the way to causal or mathematical explanation of it, and that what is explained in the end is not charm. The same is true of the selflessness of the selfless, altruism that surprises, a lover's love, a penitent's penitence, a forgiver's forgiveness. Each escapes along the way. The explanation offered may be very interesting, but it is an explanation of something else.

III.41 ❧ *Punishment*

We are up against a strange circle in the moral life. It appears also in law. To explain all is to forgive all, but at the cost of losing respect for and even interest in that which has been so fully explained. What seemed the greatest gift, of pure forgiveness, turns full circle to be total withdrawal. What starts as strenuous effort to avoid inflicting pain ends with greater pain. But the circle is strange, only because the human is strange in a world in which the reflective mind is occupied with the tenets of science. Against explaining all is the mystery of the person, never explained; understood rather than explained, but never fully understood; never put behind, finished and filed. Against the gift of forgiveness is the self-assertion of repentance, the claim, made back, to respect as a full person. And associated with repentance—mystery reestablishing mystery—is a place for punishment in the human world (the thought of it is hard), the mystery of pain consuming pain and leaving the person fresh.

III.42 ☞ *Weber*

Max Weber puts legislation at the center of law. But legislation is a problem in law, not central to law. Weber separates fact and value. But in law fact and value are always linked in action. Weber individualizes the person. But in law the person is someone always to be identified. Weber treats value as a mere product of an act of will, a pure creation. But this is at war with the evidence of lawyers' discourse and action. Weber makes legal analysis the application of rules. But legal analysis is the reading of texts. Weber emphasizes that his view of law is from the outside. But law cannot be seen except from the inside. Weber assumes that what the law is on some matter is evident. But what the law is on a matter is always a question. Weber speaks of concept, logic, deduction, transparent clarity. But in law all is metaphorical and moving. Weber portrays law as a closed system. But law is open: systematic, but not, in the end, a system. Weber proposes that lawyers can be entirely self-conscious. But lawyers do not have rootless minds. Weber is drawn toward disenchantment. Lawyers work toward enchantment.

III.43   ✍   *The World of Intellectual*
History: An Exercise in the
Identification of the Nonlegal

Work in law is not scholarship, at least in the newer sense of "scholarship," which is intellectual history. Law is scholarship in its older sense, a working to achieve a correct text. Every lawyer writing a statement of law in good faith is seeking to write a correct text, better than any other. But law has not moved to become intellectual history, because lawyers cannot confine the meaning of words in legal texts to the time and place of their utterance.

Lawyers listen for the live meaning of the whole of what they read. Intellectual history necessarily involves objectification of ideas and the separation of the reader—the scholar—from them. Intellectual history is part of a larger move which is the literalization of language itself. Words and forms of words acquire fixed meanings at a time and in a place, about which the scholar can be quite definite, which can be traced genetically, and which crumble and transform themselves into other fixed meanings at other times and places, about which the scholar can also be quite definite. The scholar is unaffected by the words and the meanings of words thus fixed. The things he identifies, combines, and traces do not draw him into their spirit. He is, looking backward, always superior to them, seeing them for what they are. Belief, in the objectified "ideas" with which the scholar works, is not a category relevant to the work. It is a psychological state, about which one liberated from it may be curious; but were one to slip into such a state of belief oneself, it would interfere with scholarly work.

To the lawyer, by contrast, all language is metaphorical. Ideas are not confined to words and forms of words, and words that a lawyer perceives to express an idea do not have a definite meaning confined to their time and place. For the lawyer is not separate from the ideas, and in law neither ideas nor language have been or can be reified. What is expressed is live and present—in the present. It is beyond language, not reducible to the linguistic, not identical with it or a reflection of it. What live that is being expressed is of course new: all things of the present, things not dead, are new as each minute is a new minute. And of course the lawyer looks through and beyond as the intellectual historian cannot. Something that has authority for you draws you into the spirit of it.

The failure of the historian as such is in not fully reifying. The failure of the lawyer as such is in beginning to reify and thus, in her statements to the world, to deceive and manipulate. An example of the contrast can be seen in the biblical scholarship known as "form criticism," devoted to establishing the social and political contexts of the utterance and preservation of biblical texts. Some among form critics read the earliest New Testament texts, the letters of Paul, as political and organizational documents never intended by their author as more, though kept by their recipients and read regularly out loud. The object of writing the letters was simply the survival of organizations of mutual support waiting for the end of the world soon to come. Some among form critics, perhaps seeing their own twentieth-century world as a world only of systems contending, are comfortable seeing the theological statements and appeals in the Pauline letters as post-hoc justifications, persuasive devices, pragmatically spoken in the hope that they may work to achieve the immediate then-contemporary organizational object, and selected by Paul from the range of possible theological statements of the time and molded in their specific form by the political and organizational object. That the recipient churches kept the letters and read them regularly (as Melanesians in a Cargo Cult might keep a packing case or an airplane) was only an irony, a matter ultimately for quiet amusement among those now who can look back and see the letters for what they really were.

Paul, in this scholarly view, becomes much like the modern litigating lawyer, uttering words he does not himself believe—or disbelieve: he is detached from his words. His words are thus no access to anything in him or beyond of which he and his words may be an expression. Or Paul is seen as the modern executive whose words are also detached and no access to anything beyond, who characteristically signs or speaks statements written by others, not saying what he means because the words he speaks are not his, while those who select the words for him to say do not mean what might be said because the statement to be made is not to be their statement.

This, of course, is a strong charge in a theological context—that a belief stated was only the manipulative appearance of belief—unless it is thought that it is no charge at all but a statement of the obvious about all such appeals at all times and places. Insofar as evidence or argument for the proposition, this strong charge, is thought necessary and is adduced by the scholar, it is in the form of a demonstration of theological contradictions in the letters. That the statements made by Paul are contradictory is the conclusion of analysis of them using the tools and assumptions of intellectual history. There are strains of ideas that are historically identified by their terms, the linguistic form they take and to which they can be reduced. They can be seen genetically combined in Paul's speech. Their combination there produces nothing new. The historian knows already what they are, and sees them occupying the transient mind of an individual for a while and passing on. An individual, like Paul, may attach himself to one or another of them in the psychological state called belief by the analyst who is outside and free of belief. But if there is an apparent attachment to two strains of thought that do contradict, the proof is sufficient that the individual does not believe either of them, but is instead pragmatic in his use of them (and successful to the degree he conceals his indifference to belief from his listeners). The scholar's certainty that there is contradiction is the product of the scholar's larger commitment to literalism in language. The meanings of words and associations of words are in the end plain, genetically fixed, most certainly not in mind beyond.

The lawyer, on the other hand—ironically, in view of the scholar's universalization of the picture of the litigating lawyer, archetypical persuader with an ulterior motive—cannot approach texts in this way. The very nature of the language with which the lawyer works is different. It is expressive, not fixed. The lawyer would not be so certain that statements which seem opposed to one another are opposed. Approaching texts in good faith, the lawyer does not know in advance what can be said and does not have independent measures by which to determine contradiction. The lawyer may determine that a part of a text, or the whole of a particular text, is inauthentic, and will drop the part out or will put the text aside and cease working with it. But the lawyer is listening to the whole of what has been uttered in texts to which her own statement as a lawyer, if it is thought a means of access, may be added. The history of words and patterns of words is interesting to the lawyer, a tool in the work of listening, but the lawyer, not separate from what she hears, does not assume that the person whose words she reads is detached from those words. Quite the reverse: the lawyer, unlike the scholar or the historian, approaches the words with a faith to be tested in her work with them, for her object is the evocation and justification of a similar faith toward her own words on the part of those to whom she is going to speak.

III.44 & *The Self and Ultimate Foundation in Legal Thought*

The ultimate faith of Buddhism—or hope, or perception—that there is no self and that the reality, the truth, the only knowledge is that there is no "foundation," may be very close to the ultimate faith, hope, or perception in legal thought.

Perceiving that there is no self and no foundation becomes, apparently paradoxically, itself foundational and source of the strongest sense of self. The paradox is only one more illustration of the difficulty of using a language of words that are largely materialist metaphors. Parallel with, on the one side, faith that there is no self and no foundation, are, on the other side, the person of Buddha, the texts and work with the texts through which perception of the authoritative is achieved, and the community that is knit together through texts and the effort to model individual selves on the person perceived who in turn has perceived—that modeling, which is conforming, which is obedience, but which is conforming only to the meaningful as the meaningful is heard and perceived.

Authority in Buddhism, or of the Buddha, is actually what maintains the self against death or loss of all in the meaningless and endless processes of the world. Yet the Buddha's authority is in his actual, incarnate perception that "there is no self." Emphasis should be put under the *is* in the expression "there is no self." "There is no self" is an acknowledgment of ultimate freedom. The self does not merely exist, is not *is*, is not graspable and reducible to something other than itself and most especially not dissolvable into the processes of the world that merely are. The self is not in time and space. Similarly "there is no foundation," because nothing can be found into which the self can be transformed, no foundation in the scientific sense of the word, an ultimate ground of all being that simply is. There is no foundation because whatever is proposed as foundational cannot claim authorship of the self.

Modern (or postmodern) historicism, with its ancient roots in stoicism and courage despite despair, dissolves the self into process—linguistic, cultural, social, economic, political—denies the self, and denies the possibility of authority, because, it is said, there is no foundation. Law and Buddhism affirm the self and make possible the self, a sense of identity, of community, of that degree of certainty that can lead to responsible action and responsible self-restraint, because, it is said, there is no foundation. But by "there is no foundation" lawyers and theologians mean that the processes of the world are not all there is, a proposition the historicists, children of science, could not begin to accept, at least during the day in their professional lives.

SECTION IV

Present Meaning

On the Personal in

Legal Thought

IV.1   🙟   *The Merely Extant*

Your own voice and the voice of another (yourself and that which you are not or are not yet) are not substances that continue despite your cessation of work and belief. The substance of life is nothing like the substance of an element that goes on regardless, in passive experience of itself and its surround. The substance of life—the self that speaks, the self that hears, and the self that is heard—arises with, is the product of, is inseparable from work and belief. It does not exist apart from the active source of it, and the puzzles that might torment the mind if it were such a passive extant (waking up surprised, to further passive experience on the other side, and meeting eternity and infinity) are not its puzzles. If there is belief, and work that belief makes possible, there is life.

Therefore there is creation, continuous creation. The person, the self, is not an already-created, a given. Nor (though it may have its own necessities) is the person's own self tied to the fate of the already-created and the given. Nothing that merely is can encompass life. A person is, in actuality, and in every detail (though a detail may be a flaw), but a person is not merely extant, is never passively so, would not exist in actuality if that existence were mere existence.

IV.2 ❧ *Inconsistency and Objectivity*

Legal thought seeks the authentic text, the exact words, the embodiment of a statement in all its detail. But legal thought goes on to restate anew, judge flaws, put away, add, to achieve a more exact form of the always unwritten text behind each original so closely read. The lawyer listens to detail, speaks generally, is listened to in detail. In legal thought the detail is necessary to reach beyond detail.

In legal thought the meaning of the word or words is not separate from the meaning of the speaker. The quality of language in law is metaphorical, not literal. The details of a statement—the particular word, the phrase at the beginning, the phrase at the end, exactness in which is sought in seeking to know the original—are read together, and the meaning of the detail emerges from the meaning of the whole.

Yet the lawyer judges what is read. There is a judgment of the good faith of the speaker, that the speaker is in what is said, that the speaker believes what he or she says. The judgment may be of the whole, or of any detail, that though it is original (as emanating from the speakers's hand or tongue) it is still not authentic. There is a judgment of flaw, that despite good faith the speaker is not in and does not believe a detail of what is said, a word, a phrase, a thrust.

For the listener, language heard is evidence. The question is what the evidence is of. A detail may be put aside as inconsistent and inauthentic: details and parts are inevitably put aside, dropped, ignored, in any listening to any course of talk or in reading any text. The evidence is fragmentary, the fragments put together are chosen by the listener. There may be a revelation of belief in a buried word that makes much else, even the bulk of what is said taken quantitatively, inconsistent with what is meant and in-authentic. Or the buried word may be glossed over—a *gloss* being an explanation, an explaining away—and put aside as inconsistent. The judgment is made, daily, hourly, in all talk and reading.

Unbelieved, judged to be unbelieved, a word or phrase withers as if its root had been cut. But a speaker's explicit declaration of unbelief is judged much as a speaker's avowal of belief: a statement that she does not believe in something, or that something does not exist, raises for the listener the question what it is that does not exist for the speaker or that she does not believe—whether it be a color, or kindness, or God—and demands that the listener determine, in order to understand the statement, whether the speaker knows what it is she is denying or whether what she is denying is something else and not what it ini-tially seems to be, and then whether, if she does know and does mean it, it may therefore actually exist for her and she does believe in it.

But that this is so, that there are judgments of inconsis-tency (and of meaning, in order to make judgments of inconsistency), and that there are conclusions of authen-ticity or inauthenticity based upon judgments of inconsis-tency, suggests a standard of inconsistency beyond the person being listened to, and a meaning being given to words a person uses other than the meaning of that per-son. And there is thus suggested a literalism in legal thought and language despite its devotion to the meta-phorical, and an objectification in law despite law's de-pendence upon the personal.

In part the difference between the literal and the non-literal is a difference in approach or in cast of mind encountered within oneself as much as among one's acquaintance. It is the difference between an assumption that one knows and an assumption that the other knows, between (at the extreme) arrogance and humility, between allegiance to the past of one's experience and openness to the new, between unwillingness to do the work of understanding (though perhaps because of a lack of faith) and willingness to attend and to work (which is the beginning of the granting of authority).

But the "literal" would seem to remain in either approach, though faith and authority are touched in one and not the other. The resolution between the metaphoricity of legal language on the one hand—the inseparability of its meaning from the person who speaks it—and the very possibility of flaw in a person's statement, on the other, lies in the joinder that produces this daily difference in practice between the easy, literalist inconsistency and a hard inconsistency, the inconsistency that (as in law) is hard to come to and to admit. The possibility of flaw is the very possibility of the personal. Nothing a machine does is error for it. What it does is what it does, no less, no more. No less: nothing it does *it* didn't really do, or was not itself when it did it; no more: nothing it does means anything more than that that was done by it.

The listener is constructing meaning from words beginning with the uses he and others whom he understands have put the words to, but open to idiosyncrasy (idiosyncrasy that could not be given a statistical location, but is instead perceived as a difference against a background of prior experience with persons). The listener does not declare inconsistency lightly, but only after effort is exhausted to understand words in a new way, and inconsistency is never declared as a result of placing words against a standard of received relationship between units that have a previously given quality. The declaration of inconsistency is a declaration of a lack of understanding.

But a declaration of inconsistency is also the entry of the listener into the constructing of the person heard. The meanings of the words used are necessarily the listener's meanings also, affected though they be by his encounter with this other. The standard of inconsistency that is the reference of understanding or expression of it is necessarily the listener's standard of inconsistency, thus beyond the person heard. But then too not beyond, for the person heard is the person heard by the listener, constructed by him, and therefore, in the only way in which it could be that *person's* standard, it *is* her standard. But because the listener is listening and not just speaking, listening only to one whom he actually believes to be another—another in actuality and not in imagination—so that he is not listening only to himself speaking nor hearing only what he himself speaks and what he hears is new (and thus makes him new as he hears and understands it, absorbs it into himself and makes it his own), that standard which is that person's standard, in the only way it could be that *person's* standard, is not merely the listener's standard imposed on or inserted into the person, as it would be if the person were the pure creation of the listener alone and from his (old) self alone—a fiction. The standard is the standard of them both; and the person who is heard is a listener also, understanding herself in part by understanding the other's understanding of what she herself has said (since she too knows of flaw, and that what in particular she says she too can hear as not herself speaking), and herself constructing the person who speaks back that understanding of her, herself discarding some details in his statement, accepting others, approaching words used back in a new way, acting on an equal faith that the person speaking back is not an echo or mirror reflection nor pure creation, fiction, but exists in actuality. She must construct the person who speaks back, acting on equal faith, in order to understand that understanding of her. She does so by a standard of consistency that must necessarily be hers, but is not hers as it was before she spoke and listened to another speaking back.

The standard is hers, in the only way it can be hers, but not only hers; the standard is another's, in the only way it could be another's, but not only another's. It is a standard for them each in actuality, existing not apart from them for even an instant of time but in them as they are related to time and as they are in actuality, each of them a creature of faith (the faith of each of them and of both) in the actuality of themselves and of the other. The standard of consistency is—insofar as it is actual, and not a fictional plaything unbelieved by anyone—never a standard of any others than these, any others who are not heard with equal faith or spoken to in equal faith, or who do not speak or hear with a faith that is perceived enough to make these undertake the work of understanding them. The standard does not exist "in society" beyond these and regardless of speaking and hearing, regardless of faith and regardless of person, any more than the actual meanings of words exist anywhere other than in the meaning of persons who are actual, the creatures of listening and speaking with faith.

IV.3 &ᵣ *Syntax*

The distinction made between syntactical nonsense and objective (or definitive) syntactical sense is sometimes shored up by an effort to demonstrate the possibility of syntactical sense despite *semantic* nonsense.

But there is no semantic nonsense if a speaker means what he says, means to say what he says and means sense by it. Words need not necessarily mean some particular thing or be equivalent to some particular thing. They do have associations rich and deep, echoing and reverberating until too faint to hear in any conscious way. But they cannot be confined. The statistical frequency of their use in a context says something of ease and difficulty, nothing of meaning. There is no legislative authority in a majority of the users of a language.

Something of the same may be true of syntax. Nonsense in it may be claimable only with reference to the speaker. No one can legislate that things are singular or plural, present or past, aspects of something or unconnected with it, active or inert. The very categories of syntax are abstractions from experience and often puzzling to us as we try to fit experience to them. A speaker may make a mistake in not saying what he means to say or would say if given another opportunity. But a listener or reader granting him respect will not assume immediately that he has made such a mistake. And a speaker with respect for his readers will no more use a word of action generally used in connection with a unity when he has in mind a multiplicity or a manyness, than he will use "desert" to refer to "sea." But if he does, he may be indicating something about his experience of a manyness— that it is in some sense a unity, an entity of thought, a unit of reference and in reference—just as he may be indicating something about the experience associated with "sea" by referring to it as a "desert." Obscurity eventually defeats understanding, but no more than a clarity false to one's meaning. Whether and when reading breaks down depends upon the reader's will to persist, upon the intensity of the reading that is evoked by an encounter with the text and the continuing experience of the effort to understand.

IV.4   *The Language of Responsibility*

Delegation of thought and writing in legal institutions threatens responsibility and, with responsibility, the authority that is built on it and the deference that responds to it. But how can this be said, if in law responsibility is imposed, located, allocated in the design and modification of a system, and judged according to its practical operation and consequence? It can be said because responsibility is not entirely a matter of lawyers' choice.

Even in the extreme case of complete delegation, of which the Queen of England, adviser rather than advisee, may be taken as an example, an official may continue to sign statements with her own name and announce decisions in her own voice. We might be tempted to think she remains responsible, simply as a matter of definition. But in this we would not be true to law's usage. There is a difficulty, to be sure, but law's use of the term "responsible" handles the difficulty by moving through appearances to the actuality of persons.

In law, when we insist that someone *did* do or say something and *is* responsible, we generally mean she should take the consequences of her acts and statements. She is civilly responsible, and should be a source of compensation. She is criminally responsible, and should be deterred or punished. She is politically responsible, and may be replaced. But if what is at stake is the very *making of the decision* with respect to allocation of civil liability or the very *statement of the considerations to be taken into account* to avoid condemnation, then we are not interested in money payments, deterrence, or punishment. We do not say the speaker or actor *is* responsible. We say she should be responsible, or we want her to be, because we want the *decision* or *statement* to be a responsible one. (And if it continues to be the case that no one is responsible, political replacement is of no avail.) The decision or statement must be responsibly made before we can truly take account of it—before it itself can have much in the way of consequences in the world.

In this context the legal term "responsible" is used somewhat (though not entirely) differently from the way it is used in the phrases "civil responsibility," "criminal responsibility," or "political responsibility," for we are in some sense prior to the structures of discussion by which we determine responsibility of these latter kinds. It is thus possible to say that a person not responsible for a decision *did not make it,* and that what she appeared to do *she* did not do (as in the case of the Queen). Human action and responsibility are still conjoined, but the mind's movement is from responsibility to speech or action, rather than from speech or action to responsibility. Connections with law's expression of insanity are evident.

IV.5 ✌ *Meaninglessness*

"Colorless green ideas sleep furiously," says Noam Chomsky, to demonstrate that a meaningless sentence can be syntactically correct and therefore that there is an irreducible difference between syntax and semantics. But is the sentence meaningless? Found in a poem, "Colorless green ideas sleep furiously" might be thought a rather nice line. We have known that ideas can be green since Marvell's

> The mind, that Ocean where each kind
> Does straight its own resemblance find;
> Yet it creates, transcending these,
> Far other worlds, and other seas;
> Annihilating all that's made
> To a green thought in a green shade.

We know ideas sleep. There can be furious sleep, dream-tossed sleep. A furious man can sleep. When he sleeps he sleeps furiously—and who knows what sleep really is?

And when is a green leaf colorless? When life is colorless; when that color green is there, perceptible, but does not reach you, as that which is furious often can't reach you, as often nothing can when you are furious.

The reason one would not interpret the sentence in these ways, and the only reason, is that Chomsky, the speaker of it, did not mean anything by it when he said it—did not mean what he said. The sentence is meaningless as all machine-produced sentences, sentences produced by rule and rote, are meaningless. Meaninglessness comes not from the words and their juxtapositions, but from Chomsky; and the meaning of the line must also come from the speaker. Is syntax inherently meaningless?

Only if it has nothing to do with human language, for which there are no rules laid down. To speak and be heard, to understand and be understood: pattern emerges from these, and from the long lives of those who speak.

IV.6 ❧ *Dissolution to Process*

Nietzsche notes we say "lightning flashes" but lightning is not a subject that acts in a verb. Lightning *is* the flash. Therefore conventional description is false to experience. His corollary is that the presence of the word "I" as a subject in language may also be false to experience and there may be no "I."

Certainly the corollary does not hold: The question is what we mean, subject and verb notwithstanding. But what we say is also evidence of what the experience is.

There may be no personification of lightning at all in making *it* the subject of a verb, as there is personification when the human subject is constructed out of evidence over time and on faith. What, in fact, do we believe of lightning? The assertion confidently made is that lightning *is* the flash, that there is nothing separate from the flash that might flash: that this is the truth, or at least the truth of experience. But we could find some way to designate in ordinary usage that lightning *is* the flash and does not "flash," if that is what we want to say. The fact we do not do so is some little bit of evidence of what our actual experience of lightning is as we live our years in the world. Perhaps we do imply that *lightning* does not flash when we say lightning flashes even if we do not imply the equivalent when uttering "you" or "I": that remains to be seen.

IV.7 ❧ *The Possibility of Progress*

Law cannot accommodate to the view of man that lies behind cognitive science. Relativism is content to equate what is new with what is true but then History steps in to observe that the new may be only reversion. The vision of man in cognitive science does seem a step back, a return to an earlier vision of demonic power—man as possessed by forces from without. John Macquarrie: "A more advanced theology . . . protests against the idea, as one that is destructive of human responsibility, that men's actions and their history are determined and then given effect by superhuman powers, whether good or bad, that can 'possess' men or 'instigate' their actions." And Macquarrie goes on to say, implying the connection between the responsible and the real that is made in law and that appears explicitly in the language of legal discourse, "This seems to make everything we do unreal."

IV.8 ❧ *Stating the Epiphenomenal*

"Mind," says the epiphenomenalist, "is nothing but the glitter on the water."

But this is no effort to capture any real sense of mind. This is instead an expression of some sadness, in an image of smallness and insignificance, of little lights dancing on the deep and of transience, no light coming again ever to the same place.

But then there is that word "glitter." The epiphenomenalist knows full well how the word is used. If the word could speak, it would speak of jewels, Christmas trees, the lights at parties, winking lights, smiling lights. In that one word is a radiance at war with sadness. It is evidence, not to be ignored in analysis, never actually ignored in judgment, of the true sense of the experience of mind the speaker has.

IV.9   *Presuppositions*

You ask someone, "Where are you going?" The answer you receive is, "I don't know because I don't know how to get there."

What do you do with such an answer? You may think the person did not understand your question, or is drunk, or is strangely ignorant of the difference between ends and means. You will make a decision, to dismiss this and start again, or simply turn away. Or you may do something else. You may take what he has said quite seriously and puzzle out its possible meaning. Perhaps there is no difference between means and ends, though you had always thought there was. Perhaps for any of us what we had thought to be destination, existing whether or not we reach it or could reach it, is in fact not conceivable unless we have some sense that it is reachable.

But you would not be pushed by this answer to engage in such speculation unless you allow that there was something behind the words you heard. It is that something that makes you pause when you do pause before dismissing the word-sounds you are constantly hearing as the product of ignorance or drunkenness; pause, reflect, and listen.

IV.10 🐦 *Materialism*

The advantage of materialism is dialectical. It pulls away from abstraction of the spirit and back to our actual situation, albeit through another abstraction, now of the body. The assertion of the materialist, that the Cartesian mind-body or psychosomatic distinction will not do because there is no mind or psyche, is of less importance than the assertion in the same breath that the two are one; for the word and use of the word—mind, psyche, spirit—imply in the most determined speaker an understanding of a spiritual aspect, the same understanding he evinces in his loves or she in hers.

IV.11 🐦 *Mind and Person*

There is in the English Protestant Book of Common Prayer a prayer for "those who are ill in body, mind, or spirit." Who are those *those who*? The reference is not tautological. *Those* in the phrase are as separate from illness of mind as from an illness of body. They are not equivalent to the illness of their minds; they are not their minds. Perhaps they are not equivalent even to their spirits. They are they, lost or hidden, mute or trapped. The presupposition of usage, reflected in our action toward these *those* (though it may not be reflected in the theory to which we presently shift when we conceptualize the world in a conscious way), is that they are not gone, nothing, without existence.

Consider the stroke victim; people outside not understanding what the afflicted tongue says; people outside coming in to the inside all garbled. Note the *I* or *me* who struggles against her own brain in therapy, and to whose hope, courage, and will therapists make their appeal. Note who is dissatisfied with loss of words and confusion of memory.

IV.12   Conscious Mind

Mind is not exhausted in consciousness, with whatever is beyond consciousness then being not mind. Consciousness, if it had such an edge, could be pinned down. It would be *there*, and mind with it. What was in consciousness would be *in* it, and we would know what there was in it, and know where those things started and stopped, so we could tell whether they were in it or not in it. But consciousness has no edge. It cannot be pinned down, nor can what is in consciousness—any more than the self that is in consciousness of self. We do not know where the presences of which we are conscious begin and end. They are not things. We do not fully grasp them.

Mind is not suited to any such nice definitional equation. Mind is not known before it is searched for. Pulled by intimation of it, driven by faith in it, we are always groping for evidence of mind, reading words including our own that may emerge into it and from it, looking at forms the hand and eye have made, listening to sounds: we even look at the lines traced by mountain ranges, and into the eyes of animals.

IV.13 ❧ *The Fully Human*

Mathematical physicists search out a place for mind in their cosmology. Some seek genuinely to achieve a real existence for it there. But they do not or cannot take the step lawyers must take, to find a place in thought for the real existence of caring mind. Lawyers might be inclined to say that a step from matter to mind is not a step to mind at all if there is no caring to it, only an expansion of cold system that cannot be acknowledged as mind.

Mathematical physicists do use faith and the negative in their work with mind, as do lawyers in their work with caring mind. The reductio ad absurdum of contradiction, which presupposes a faith in the consistency of the world, is presented in physics as proof that what cannot not exist must exist. Absurdity threatens faith, absurdity follows loss of faith, faith denies absurdity, in both physics and law. The difference between lawyers and physicists, that takes lawyers to caring mind, is the difference between a logic of mathematics, where the entity is discrete, as a number is discrete, and the logic of life, where neither "this is not that" nor "this is equal wholly to that" are essential to reason.

IV.14 ❧ *Personification*

What does a person *really* want?

What does a *person* want?

"I want to die," a person says.

"No," comes the frequent response. "*You* don't. You are not being yourself."

This *you* is not an immediate phenomenon heard materially here and now. This *you* is an existence over time, with a past and a potential, whose voice you listen for continuously while making judgment after judgment whether to respect or to discount the words you hear one after another.

IV.15 ❧ *Truth and Person*

How can you respond to someone who takes the physiochemical stance? "Man is nothing but a physiochemical system." "Mind is a set of physical and chemical reactions." Can there be only silence and brute obstinacy in the face of such assertions? They may be aggressively spoken by someone schooled to repeat them from an early age. Child of modernity that you are too, must you acquiesce if you can think of nothing really to say, stand defeated if you want to continue to count yourself reasonable even though agreement be against your deepest inclination?

The physiochemical stance is a credo, and can be received as any other credo. Look at all the speaker says and does in his life. If there is inconsistency with it, point out the inconsistency; if what is said is something written by someone beyond call, do not let what is said in this one instance overly bother you. You are not overly bothered by single statements in other contexts, made face to face or in writing.

But you may think there is still the question whether what is being urged is true, regardless of whether the speaker of it acts and talks inconsistently. Could you not ask yourself the same question, "*Is* man nothing but a physiochemical system, man's mind a set of physical and chemical reactions?" so that you are the speaker of the question and it is your question?

Of course you could. In answering such a question put to yourself, you would decide whether an affirmative answer took into account all your experience, of yourself, of music, of death, of love, all your experience to the furthest reaches of it. If an affirmative answer did not fit your experience, you could not make such an answer to yourself and believe in it.

But the person not yourself who is making the assertion to you is still there. If you are face to face and if, returning from putting the question to yourself, you find you cannot persuade the other who is saying this to you to give it up, the fact he is making this statement to you surely must put you in some doubt about your own conclusion.

But is the speaker saying this to you—or saying something else?

You are the one who must determine that, and you would determine what the speaker was saying by looking at the whole of what the speaker says, interpreting what the speaker says as a whole. Could not you understand what the speaker says in the part and grapple with it? But that would be cutting the author off from the text. That would put you in the position you find yourself when you try to read a sentence composed by a computer or a word traced out in shells and stones by waves on a beach. You could not read it except as itself a system, grammatical or otherwise, which tells you that it is and nothing more, only that it is. Pulling out the part is severing the spoken from the speaker, leaving the spoken, the sounds, the shapes, without authority, without that claim to your close attention and struggle to understand that authentic human speech makes upon you.

Is this the abandonment of objectivity? It is if by objectivity one is to mean staying outside. To stay outside what both you and the speaker are inside is to avoid grappling with the phenomenon itself. There is no abandonment of objectivity, rather the reverse—a move toward full objectivity—if by the objective one means the empirical.

Is this reducing truth to persons and to how you respond to a particular person? It is. "Love," says the speaker, "is a physiochemical reaction." Do not rush to respond. Act as you do, often quite unconsciously, when those around you are speaking of smaller things. Look at what the speaker does, if you can, and watch the speaker use *love* in other contexts, before you draw a conclusion about what is being said to you.

IV.16 ☙ *Euthanasia*

An Alzheimer's patient taking her own life—those around her understanding, if not approving—is a picture of an ordinary view of the person. The ordinary view of the person is abandoned only in the hermetic world of scientific discourse. *She*, who is now and was, will be gone when the ganglia of her still-persisting brain are twisted and shriveled. Most, perhaps all, understand that, including the scientist in the evening. The scientist at work during the day cannot allow it. There is no she. The brain of today is not qualitatively distinguishable from that future brain, not better or worse. There is no qualitative, no better or worse. The Alzheimer's brain, indeed, may be viewed as more highly adapted to exploiting the environment and securing others to take care of it, under current social and economic conditions. There is only a system and process now, and a system and process then, and change from one to the other, but no loss.

That she is gone is an ordinary view believed and expressed in understanding the action of taking one's own life. It is ordinary in the sense in which ordinary is used in "ordinary man," man not in a role, such as, for instance, the role of a natural scientist. Against it is the view that we do not know and cannot be confident she is gone when her ganglia are twisted and shriveled. This is another ordinary view, believed and expressed in opposing her taking her own life and in maintaining her body's functions when her ganglia are twisted and shriveled. But the scientist during the day cannot allow this either.

IV.17 ☙ *Bird Song and Personification*

To know the songs of birds is to name the birds. Here is the thrush, the hermit thrush; there is the cardinal, there the warbler. Naming enriches the world, populates it with more than the sounds that were there all along in the ear. Why? There is a consequence to naming, that anyone can experience. Why such a consequence?

Is there, in the consequence, to be discerned an assumption that the bird is speaking? Certainly there is a progression. There is less in the world if you know the source of the sounds only as "birds," less still if you know the source only as "animals"—if one can imagine oneself in such a relatively nameless state. The progression the other way is from knowing the songs as those of the thrush or the warbler to knowing the individual bird. The analogy, with us, is the progression from knowing sounds, to knowing them as human sounds, to knowing the language. The so-called postmodern would like to stop at that point; but there is a step we take, impossible at the moment with the hermit thrush, which is to know the individual, who is no more lost into *the language* than the hermit thrush is lost in "bird" or *the language* is lost into sound.

But in moving to and naming the individual, there is an assumption, motivating and revealed, that there is someone speaking.

And this may be motivating and revealed in learning the songs of birds, even though the further step that can be taken with man cannot, or not yet, be taken with birds. An experience of heightened interest, of enrichment, comes with learning the names of flowers, even rocks, but it has a different cast: one does not feel less alone for it, as one does feel less alone knowing bird songs even without knowing whatever individual variations of song there may be. The repeated forms in song may be truths— though there would be no truth in them if they were only forms. Man is not much moved to name the sounds of the waves rolling forever on the shingle, even less to conceive of capturing and naming the sound of an individual wave.

The postmodern does not want to take the step that can be taken with man, because for all his postmodernism he is still a scientist of the fundamentalist kind. How opposite, an interest in naming and in bringing out particularity, and the modern scientific interest in eliminating particularity, that driving interest in modern science, that near delight in saying there are only forces, simple equations and a few constants that when fed in produce and therefore are what we see and hear.

Part of the difference between art and science lies in this opposition. Art begins with the imitation of natural forms, and informs them with the meaning they would have if they were the product of a designing hand: art assumes such meaning in moving to imitate them, and as a consequence, a consequence made possible by that assumption, gives them meaning. This is what we know as *creation* —

—Just as in personification generally, in law or elsewhere, even listening to the songs of birds. But, in law or elsewhere, one must believe in the person or meaning assumed, before person or meaning can be created. Only if there is belief can there be creation. It seems an oddness, but is the fact of the world that gives us the world.

IV.18 ⟡ *The Personal in Scientific Discourse*

It is a little pitiful, the naming of scientific rules, reactions, and effects after the individual human beings who perceived them. A Willgerodt reaction, a Mach number, a Heisenberg principle, Planck constants, Bernoulli effects, de Broglie waves, Ward identities, Brownian motion—this naming is a small protest against the axiomatic impersonality of the world to which the named devoted themselves, a quiet denial of it, a side glance to a world of nature that like the world of art may be as much created as discovered: a hope that the named, and the namers, are not truly lost in the world conceived by them.

IV.19 ⟡ *Authentic Belief*

Belief is not a "state" like a configuration of a system— "Ah, I see that system has gone into a state of belief." It is not a property of a system, a feature of a thing. Belief is not separate from what is believed, nor is what is believed separate from what you—or he or she—believe, or separate from you. You become what you believe, are identified with it. That what of the world, which is believed, is concrete, it exists as you exist, it is an extant; but since you are not merely extant, belief or what is believed always brings a beyond with it into which the words of its expression shine little beams of light.

IV.20 ✒ *The Individuality of Justice*

Mass justice is not justice. Justice is individual justice, and mass justice is justified as some justice, or as more justice than no justice at all—all are still left seeking a way toward the defining goal, which is not quantified or an aspect of majority rule or utilitarian. A device adopted for mass justice is a temporary expedient, to be discarded if some way is found. The fact that more cases may be decided correctly through mass procedures (determined by some sampling method and some judgment of outcome, which is itself most difficult since every case is unique and the values are living) has never absolutely outweighed the injustice of the individual case. This is the overriding difficulty of statements of law given out in the form of "rules," always leaving out relevant considerations, and why such texts produce such tension when made central texts and, after a fashion, decay of their own accord.

IV.21 ✒ *Judicial Decision and the Unconscious*

What is unconsciously motivated is not for that reason inaccessible, secret, arbitrary, with *us* being little balls tossed about by dark forces below that are not us and alien to us. Nor, in law, is the power of a judge, who is one of us and like us, therefore a blind impact upon us from the unknown. *We* blend into the semiconscious, the subconscious, and the unconscious.

The whole person acts and speaks. In talk and action and in writing one obtains evidence of what one thinks, oneself, as a whole, evidence that one then interprets, and not against some independently accessible conscious intent but as one would interpret any authentically meant writing. Words and means of expression come to mind. Then one sees them.

So with the legal decision maker. She decides, or concludes she has decided. There is a motion of her mind. *What* does she decide? Happily she must justify her decision. She writes and looks, and the whole may surprise the part and summon her in a different direction. When she publishes, she reads what she writes in company. Where is her power, the power she has in and of herself as judge? Her power beyond the case is in her text. And if there is an appeal in the case, to judge the judge's text, her power even over the case itself is limited, to the degree she has genuinely sought what she truly thinks—which seeking is itself a limit on her power as she comes to the decision that is reviewed.

IV.22 ☙ *Determinism*

We have particular desires that give us our substance. We seek meaning.

About these, the wanting, and the plantlike tropism to meaning, we can do nothing. They seem to exist within us unwilled. We are determined to that degree.

We do have an ultimate freedom. We can refuse, choose meaninglessness. But we know then what we have done, and cannot say we actually want the result. There seems cruelty in this, a setup, a ratchet to unhappiness, the provision of only a negative door out away from command.

But the truth is that meaning is not just light from outside to which we open our petals, any more than particular objects of our desire are hard givens in our substance. We construct meaning, so that it is as much our own as it is a merging with something beyond us that is not us and acts through us: just as objects of our desire, which can be affected by our choices and change over time, are creatures of what we do or choose not to do.

IV.23 ❧ *Escaping the Given*

A live sense of history helps one escape one's own patterns of thought—psychoanalysis and history have much the same purpose and effect. But to conclude that one is oneself constructed by history, the product of history, would make inquiry into antecedent of no conceivable interest. If there is inquiry into antecedent, the one inquiring is outside history, structured, limited, but outside, measuring the product of history against unarticulated hope. One is not only what one is.

(Of course much that one does not like about one's structure one cannot escape and must pass on to others in the flow of history. Over and over one does not know how to separate what one does like from its involvement with what one does not like, or one does not have time. Still one is not only what one is.)

IV.24 ❧ *Destaging*

We assume roles—we play a part—but, then, we move really to assume the role so that it is no longer so much played. The part ceases being part of a play, and becomes a part of us who have many parts combined into a whole.

But though we live the part more, and play it less, genuineness is never and perhaps never can be absolute, any more than we can live entirely in the present or wholly in the concrete. When we take a role on stage we throw ourselves into the character. Yet we are not the character. Traces of this remain in ordinary life. We always remain somewhat detached, outside, beyond.

IV.25 ❧ *Identity and Identification*

Past and future are perhaps understandable in a mechanistically ordered view of the world, perhaps not understandable when one introduces a choosing agent into a view of the world.

What would be the difference between you in the future and any of the great number of yous, which could be set side by side, each emerging from a different path followed from a different decision you could take now? From the vantage point of one of *them*, *you* in the future are but a might-have-been, one of a great range of might-be's fanning out from the possible decisions at an earlier point of decision. And so too with that earlier point, which is the present now, back and back, the numbers increasing and increasing, to the you that might not have been born if your mother's head had not turned with just that smile. It seems that we, who see in the present, are the ones that are; but then, this present, where *we* are, always stretches over time, some time. How much time? There is no one to ask. How are what is, and what might have been, to be distinguished? Only by the choice and act of our own that takes place, and our choice to identify with the one and not the other.

IV.26 & *The Biological Analogy*

Working with intellectual structures that are results either of no choice or of choices made that we dislike may be a bit like working with genetic predispositions. If we know of such intellectual structures, we may be able to do something about them in the long run, either individually within a single lifetime, or as an organized society affecting its future nature by present decisions.

And so legal work with law's structures may be like any other work within a given inheritance. But though there is this semblance, inferences can be drawn from biology for law only with great caution. Biological thinking suffers markedly from the unreality, the quality of play and game, the pretend, of all those descriptions of human affairs from which human beings and particularly the speakers themselves are missing.

Darwinian theory supposes that the sole measure of success in life is reproductive success. Nothing that does not translate itself into reproductive success is of any significance, because it will not last. The "because" in the formula is a nonsequitur. Making beautiful music is of significance even though the music itself does not last a moment after the end of the performance (though beauty may evoke beauty in the mind and then an expression of beauty, that might pass for reproduction). But in this context the use of terms such as "success" and "significance" is wholly tautological. Success and significance are simply defined as survival, and the fact, for instance, that man can conceive the world better off without man would have no bearing on this definition.

Sociobiological theory supposes, further, that all man is or does must be traceable to man's genetic material. The student is then invited to note that there would be nothing man is or does that would not contribute to reproductive success. Otherwise the behavior, characteristic, tendency, capacity—call it what you will—would have been selected out in evolution and would not be there (assuming, it must be remembered, that there is nothing in man except what can be traced to man's genetic material).

This would seem to have consequences for any concern for equal treatment of individuals. Must that concern for equal treatment not be illusion and self-deception? The individual is the product of her genes. Her genes are interested solely in maximizing their number in the next generation. Therefore the individual looking out for her genes will look out for her close kin, children, nieces, nephews, uncles, aunts, first cousins, and so on, who share genes with her. The genes within an individual are quite indifferent whether it is they themselves who survive or their identical copies in other individuals. Therefore the individual will act accordingly—less concerned than might be supposed for her individual interests, most concerned with the interests of her close kin. Equality of individuals before the law appears to be much more than difficult to realize. It may be unnatural.

But it must be remembered that these conclusions and others like them are not conclusions about the world or about reality of the sort lawyers, judges, and juries are called upon to make. They are conclusions that follow from definitional rules. Some scientists do seem to believe in these definitions (except perhaps when they deal with their friends, lovers, and co-workers). But it is best to think of them simply as parts of a closed system of thinking, like logic or arithmetic, which is not open as legal thinking is to the whole of man's experience. The statement that an individual is interested only in her genes is a flat assertion. To say that genes are interested only in their reproductive success, and therefore an individual will be also, is a nonsequitur. An individual may have her own concerns, and not be interested at all in the fate of her genes. The statement that an individual is interested only in her genes is possible only if a definition is introduced, that an individual human being is nothing more than the product of her genes. In support of its truth there is no evidence of any direct kind. What happens is that the sociobiologist says, "If it were true that the individual were the product only of her genes and that the individual looked out for her genes' interest in survival, we could predict that individuals would engage in nepotism, that is, favoritism toward their closer kin. And we do see evidence of nepotism in human society." But this is small proof of the assertion made. The proof put forth in discussions of assertions of this kind is usually of laughable thinness, threadbare beside proof offered to the child for the hypothesis that the earth is round. Put side by side the evidence for an assertion that an individual is nothing but the product of reproductively interested genes and the evidence for an assertion that there is, let us say, divine intervention at each human birth, and the assertion of divinity would win hands down.

There is the additional difficulty that the evidence that tends to prove what the sociobiologist proposes to believe—in general, or in particular—tends at the same time to show that nothing can be done about any of it. As long as man remains the product of its genes, resistance is futile (if indeed resisting oneself is a notion that can be entertained). What one is trying to do will be doomed not to last. There is always a strong flavor of "what is, is right" in any scientific observation. In response to this sociobiologists often introduce a new mechanism, man's capacity to learn, to explain why the state of affairs that would be predicted is so often avoided where the actors are human individuals rather than the lower animals.

A developed mechanism, for learning, answers no question of interest to lawyers or others in the world. Untouched are the questions "Learn to do what?" "Learn to seek what?" "Learn to avoid what?" which may be implicit in the very use of "learn," even in biologists' use here when speaking as biologists (just as there lies in the cold medical use of "deficits," when speaking of schizophrenia as a chemical situation, the condition of "no deficit" that is normative rather than normal and has implicit in it an opening out to the question "What to do?" with a mechanism that at last is without deficit). Nonetheless biologists have been pleased with the evidence they have found in the course of seeking to prove the truth of their definitions where animals are concerned, and it is more than possible that there are tendencies in the human species that we may have to reckon with continuously in our practical thinking, rather as we have to reckon with and deal with the phenomenon of anger. There is a great deal in us that reflects our biological heritage, and few would deny that we should be alert to how much there is so that we will be better able to nurture what we find within us that we trace to another source, to our humanity or our divinity, or, more simply, so that we may move toward the freedom of reality.

IV.27 ❧ *Legal Trusteeship*

An individual is the way he is. I am the way I am. You are the way you are. Capacities we may once have thought limitless have become limited, and allowances are made, though any of us is free to deny any limit and continue to struggle. But closer to us than our capacities are our urges and desires. They too, welling up in us, seem given to us and not made by us.

An individual's experience is experience of being in a situation. If his situation is different from what is celebrated as the ideal, he really may have no choice in the matter. Though he is or can be made conscious of the way he is, and of his desires as "desires," and is able to conceive an alternative to the way he is (he himself not being the same as the way he is, or absolutely identical even with his desires), he may be unable to move his capacities or desires toward an alternative. It is too late to change—his very desires will not change if they truly are givens of his world. If he nonetheless celebrates the ideal, he must live it vicariously, and few do not, in the end, live ideals vicariously.

But suppose an individual does not celebrate the ideal. Will there then be a shameful affront and denial of his dignity if what is called ideal continues to be celebrated and called ideal and, especially, celebrated in law? Does an absence of individual choice, on any matter, once that absence is finally acknowledged by others (with whatever reluctance), make him equivalent to a person with a particular color of skin, and distinguish the ideal he does not celebrate from other ideals individuals do not live?

Short of fatalism or the entrusting of all to chance, whatever is not genetic must be a subject of choices by trustees of the future (and now the genetic itself presses to enter the arena of choice). Trustees may be unable to choose for contemporaries around them, who cannot change, or even for themselves, who also cannot change. But until a capacity or some substance of desire is shown to be hereditary, the absence of choice on the part of individuals with respect to themselves does not entail (morally or logically) that there should be no choices made on behalf of individuals to come or that there should be no ideal maintained to guide such choices. If an individual's situation in life is determined—beyond heredity—by factors now identified as sociocultural, psychodynamic, situational, or biological, then inevitably choices must be made in molding the nature of family life, the culture, and the situations that in turn will guide and mold the individuals developing in them, regardless of whether the individual may have little or no choice when his or her development is over. That as an individual one can emerge far from ideal need not be viewed as tragic only and cause only for sorrow. This is also the comedy of life, in which all play a part; and good humor and good grace, which an individual may also find he has despite himself, are what have been relied upon to get through it.

A trustee is as beyond his own desire as he is evidently able to push toward capacities beyond his own. The tolerance and more than tolerance—the empathy of the similarly situated—that has always marked a civilized present lives within the sustaining of ideals for the future. For a trustee as trustee, there must be a decision beyond desire, whether to reproduce desire. Whatever his own situation as an individual, he is not, as long as he decides and acts as trustee, mechanically or genetically reproducing desire. Fate may reproduce desire into the future willy-nilly, chance may affect it, including the chance built into the legally modulated processes of elections and voting. But the spirit that reads and is read in legal method works against fate and chance, however slowly and partially. Thus if trustees clash, or think they clash, over whether to reproduce a desire—as that desire is thought to be—it is no reason to withdraw from action, desist, that a challenger has no choice as to a desire. Equally it would be no reason to continue, persist in decision and action for the future, that one oneself has no choice: if one exists, if there is a choice whether to persist, it is oneself persisting and not forces of which one is the object. There are mechanisms for settling clashes over time by surrendering something to chance—hierarchies of appeal, multimember bodies, legislation. A trustee losing in these mechanisms or thinking there has been loss can continue to think things will come right over time, not least because of the working of legal method on the texts that emerge. The legal trustee dissents, but reads.

Not merely children's beauty and charm it is that makes a child-centered society the happiest that can be conceived.

IV.28 ❧ *Fidelity to a Text*

There are Asian literary and philosophic traditions in which scholar-practitioners seem to feel less obligated than would their occidental counterparts to maintain the details of a text. In seeking the meaning of the text they seem to feel freer to change the text while passing it on.

This might be taken, by observers in the West, as production over time of a negotiated text or a text with multiple authorship. But such a description would not comport with the scholar-practitioner's own view of what he was doing. Like a Western lawyer writing, such a scholar-practitioner is not, in his own view, speaking for himself.

IV.29 ☞ *Speaking and Speaking Through*

If a speaker speaks through me, I am not a text to be read. I am not a text to be read, because I am not a creature different in kind from the speaker speaking through me. What I *say* is a text to be read, but *I* am not a text.

IV.30 ☞ *Bureaucracy and Lying*

It makes little sense for me to ask your opinion unless I suppose that you believe in the opinion you offer me, which is the same as to say that it is *your* opinion. And when you offer me an opinion, you know what I must have supposed in asking for it.

It is not yours, though, if it is someone else's. It is not yours if it is a mere mouthed formula. And it is not yours if it is inaccessible both to you and to me because it is an amalgam of interpolations and changes by other minds—when, if either of us is puzzled by it, reading it closely and flipping back and forth among the words and sentences will do no good.

IV.31 ❧ *Orientation*

Socrates is still for many the beginning of any discussion of authority. In the *Crito*, Socrates wants to know whether to obey an order given him to drink hemlock.

So the laws appear before him as persons. Plato invokes a personified law to express why Socrates would obey, why Socrates might feel within him an obligation not to find his way around the order. In the *Apology*, Socrates' attitude toward the assembly that was the Greek jury, from the internal machinations of which a verdict would pop, is very different. The jury cannot come as person to him. It is system only.

The end of the discussion of authority will not much differ from its beginning.

IV.32 ❧ *The Evidence of Legislation*

Lawyers are caught by legislation and their reading of it. Either they must believe what they do with legislation is often foolish and deceptive; or they do believe and confess a belief in an informing spirit in the legislated words that is beyond individual legislators. As in all large matters, there is mixture, the usual combination, of doubt and belief, made easier to live with, as usual, by strong doses of self-deception.

IV.33   ❧ *The Normative and the Positive*

What makes a difference to us is meaningful. It has a reality for us, wholly separate from all to which we are indifferent. Conversely, what is real for us is meaningful, and to it we are not indifferent.

So the first and last thing we know, the ultimate object of knowledge and belief, is a person, not a principle. To a person, who is not merely a reflection of ourselves, we are not ultimately indifferent. This is what we know, what is real, what has meaning.

If the object of knowledge were a principle it would be a reflection of ourselves and, like the image in a mirror, not in itself real to us. Inevitably we would ask the question (or overhear it being asked), "What difference would it make to us, really, if this principle (or any principle) were not true, did not exist?" The answer would return, "No difference, really"; and if the existence or not of some thing ultimately makes no difference to us, it is ultimately not real to us. It comes to reside with all that is hypothetical—it is idle, without force for us, as idle speculation is idle. We do not *know* it really, because ultimately indifferent to it, passing the time by occupying ourselves in our pursuit of it, we have not been sustained on the path to knowledge. We do not try as hard as we could try if we were sustained, because we cannot try so without being sustained. The last reach, for knowledge, is not in us.

IV.34 ❧ *Evolutionary Contingency*

A friend sees experience in the faces of Rembrandt's portraits of the old. But in the faces of the crowd looking at the Rembrandts on the wall he says he does not see such experience, authentic experience—such substance.

If Rembrandt has seen and conveyed and not created only, if the lines of the elderly faces are lines of his subjects' faces and not only lines of one or another face of Rembrandt's own, those lines in which my friend sees authentic experience are not simply the remains of their history, like scars that mark past accidents. They have been molded into meaningful form as if life had been an artist working on the givens of nature. Those lines of flesh, the nose, the eyes, the mouth, the delicate forms and shadows around them: seeing meaning in them is at war with any thought of pure contingency in their origin.

Imagine what it would be, truly to keep in mind that we all and all of each of us are purely the product of chance, our faces, eyes, noses, the chin, the hand, the nape of the neck—to see always endlessly stretching away alternative after alternative, five eyes, stumps. As one cannot love a system, one cannot find expressive what is only the product of chance, what, in the perceiving of it, one overlays and replaces instantaneously and continuously with transparencies of jellyfish mouths, gills, whatever might have been or might yet be. The very attempt to see the eyes and mouth of a human face as a jellyfish's or worm's raises a problem, for perception, as serious for seeing the human eyes and mouth as for seeing the human experience they convey.

If my friend, or I, or you, do see meaning and acknowledge it as such, that is as much a datum or part of experience as the data which underlie the vision that all has proceeded from origins over time and that all which has proceeded from origins is a product of chance. And evolutionary contingency actually adds nothing to the contingency already surrounding the individual. That the human race or the form of the human face is not the foreordained product of evolution, but chance, is lost in the sea of chance in which we live. That the human being, viewed abstractly as an organization (of components) of a high order, cannot be the object of evolution because increasing combinatorial complexity (from a lower-order organization of components to a higher) is not to be predicted from the laws of nature acting over time, is equally an observation hardly worth notice. It is a matter of chance, a contingency, that any of us is here at all. The day we were conceived, the location of our birth, our individual makeup, our talents, tendency to quick anger, ease, are all a matter of chance. Each moment we live is a gift. The train rushing by might have been switched mistakenly and hit our train. Any time we drive a car our attention is seduced constantly away from the road; we need only have glanced away once in wrong circumstances and we would not be. A live sense of evolutionary contingency adds nothing to this, so large is it already. In fact those who have focused on the luck involved in life, in economics, for instance, have not known what to do with the perception. Stripping away from us all that is a matter of luck, including our talents and vices and perhaps our virtues as well, has led only to the urging that we should love one another more, for we are all the same. Otherwise there is silence in the face of what is: this happened; that did not; and that is all.

IV.35 ❧ *The Materials of Individual Life*

THE PATHETIC FALLACY AND THE
PROBLEM OF LANGUAGE

One's own existence is bound up with one's creation of it. One is never alone in the venture—one takes as well as gives—and the extent of the creating, as a question to be talked about, ultimately touches upon the question of meaning or absence of meaning in natural forms. This is raised explicitly for the young student not in the first instance by science. The student may be in the very midst of discovering nature and responding to its moods and beauties, and science feeds on such repeated fresh discovery. The question is raised rather by instruction in the Pathetic Fallacy: that nature does not weep, that rain is rain not tears, that the nobility in the cloud forms of a beautiful sky is projected on them not taken from them.

The question of meaning in natural forms then leads to and raises a question, if it has not been raised before, about the "objectivity" of language, to the forms of which the student is also being introduced. This question about language grows as the student matures in its use, and ultimately touches back upon that first question of the extent to which one is creating by oneself—and what it is to be an individual.

These are of course human questions that can be sensed by the schooled and unschooled alike. They are associated questions and not the same question: an answer to one of them, meaning in natural forms, "objectivity" in language, even perhaps the extent of creating in the end, need not fall in with the answer to another. But their association magnifies the importance to law and beyond law of a response to any of them. The question of meaning in natural forms is hardly special to law. It is carried forward generally at some level into adulthood, and eventually asked of what catches the eye and what is seen at some point, for example on a long walk in the country. Closest to the immediate concerns of the lawyer, and the question to which lawyers can speak most directly from their experience as lawyers, is that which comes with experience of the forms of language.

In law and it would seem in the use of human language generally, one is not outside and in control of one's language, the individual words one uses, or the phrases, or the whole of which words and phrases are details—one does not have it in hand so that language is in this sense a "subjective" affair. Nor is language a given, again outside oneself, which one fits oneself to, well or badly, always with a risk of demonstrable error in working with it—so that language is in this sense an "objective" affair.

Rather, one treats with one's language, almost as with another living being, a living but inarticulate being. To be sure, the word you speak aloud is access to you; it does not speak aloud except to say that it is, a sound, a shape. But before you speak aloud you speak to yourself, and after you speak aloud you read what you have spoken, not only from another's point of view but as yourself. When you face words that you yourself speak, there is no question of a meaning asserted by another calling it the literal, nor of the likely response of another: you know well that only you can say what you mean, and your response is not some likely response, it is your response. It remains constantly true that the life words have that are not dead words is your own life. Still, you listen to the way words work, even as you try to make them work. The way they work when they do work, their music, seems part of the access they offer, and seems to beckon also when they do not work and music is not achieved, the usual case when trying to speak or write—the even occasional reach, the maintaining of the effort for a time, is some evidence in itself. Certainly everyone knows the experience of waiting for a word. And one tries to open oneself to a word's resonances just as one does when one consults one's own mind, settling oneself to listen rather than speak, trying not to drown out its remarks. Sometimes one experiences a sense of a word's inescapable rightness, which remains even if one chooses not to use it after stepping outside and looking back at it and predicting how it is likely to be read.

The question of the *objectivity* of language then, still and perhaps always with us as a question, is whether word or phrase or language itself can in fact tell us something, of substance and not just of itself as a means, something more than the history of the word's or language's own making, and what the conventions were that happened to obtain at the beginnings of our various overlapping generations, and what of these conventions chance allowed us to absorb individually—something more than any of this, something akin to what flows from understanding another's new use of words, something said to us by words as if musically in their resonance and rightness in expression (since words cannot use words to express themselves) when we treat with them within and propose to give them new life.

IV.36 ﺏ *Mathematics and Consciousness*

To consciousness add self-consciousness, which con-
founds all objectifying, systematizing, historicizing, all
the science of what simply is. To self-consciousness add
meaning and with it caring, the dynamic of purpose and
desire. Then, from self-consciousness and meaning comes
the person, which combinatorial thinking cannot handle,
nor the units of calculation represent.

But if combinatorial thinking is thought, if calculation
is thought, and if the two exhaust what thought is so that
thought is combinatorial thinking and calculation, then
the person must be denied if thought is to proceed. So law
stands in the way of science; law, and person and sense of
self, are mutually sustaining and interpenetrating. So law
stands in the way of self-destruction, and the person
stands in the way of destruction, for the loss of self and the
loss of law proceed together, but grasping the one stops
departure of the other.

IV.37 ❦ *The Subversiveness of Law in the Twentieth Century*

Extreme forms of dialectical materialism, that gripped the minds of many earlier in this century in Europe and still have force today beyond Europe, maintain that subjective consciousness is the product of economic arrangements and is of no independent significance. The inner life is epiphenomenal, a reflection of economic arrangements whether the glass is accurate or distorts. The inner life changes in predictable ways with the predictable development of economic arrangements. Thus neither condemnation of an individual nor restraint from condemnation turned any more upon perception of the individual's intent or state of mind. What was criminal before was not; what was innocent before could be treated as criminal.

In any period or place where dialectical materialism has had force, law has stood in symbolic and practical opposition to it, subversive, for reasons never really understood or satisfactorily articulated. They become more understandable thrown now into relief by law's equal opposition to the core of what goes by the name postmodernism in literary and philosophic studies. For postmodernism too, the inner is illusion and history is all there is and history is unaffected by self because the self is a contingency of objectivities. The difference from dialectical materialism is the absence of a belief in known laws and predictable outcomes. But that is immaterial. There is no interfering in history in either case. The important feature in each is the leaching away of the person, into history. This legal thought does not do.

IV.38 ☞ *Law as Artifact*

On a pedestal in the Detroit Institute of Arts sat a plain, smooth, closed wooden box. There was no door, lid, or opening. There was no way to get into it. You were about to pass on when you noticed faint sounds coming from inside it. The sounds were sawing, hammering, planing, brushing, the clink of tools. What was inside was accessible after all, but what that turned out to be was a record of its making played over and over.

Self-referential artifacts speak to the emptiness of that which is only a record of its making. But there is an oddly greater emptiness—more than a matter of degree—in a written statement that proves to be the same. The difference is that on the pedestal there is a box, nicely made, before the viewer, whereas the statement (it may also be on a pedestal), which is nothing but a record of its making, may in itself, in its words and punctuation, warrant attention only for the statistical normality of its grammar and spelling.

IV.39 ☞ *Minds and Kinds of Minds*

Any writing to be read that is not mindless is written to reader as friend whose mind is a mind and not a kind of mind. Even writing to persuade the reader, or to persuade oneself, that mind is only a kind of mind is written ultimately to the friend whose mind is a mind and not a kind of mind.

Thus whatever your persuasion on the matter of mind, I can speak to you of the larger meaning of law for the modern mind or the Western mind, themselves kinds of mind. And whatever your persuasion, you can continue with me because yours is a mind and not yet a kind of mind. You may have wanted immediately to point to mundaneness, the ancient enemy of larger meaning, and the mundaneness of doing law. What you would point to is the everydayness of law. Transcendence of time and of process and of the merely extant remains necessary to law in its everydayness, part of it. You may maintain, as a reason to the contrary, that law then must present a direct challenge to the dominant and increasingly dominant form of thought in modern life. Law does, when that form of thought presses to occupy all the mind and the minds of all. But so does my speaking to you, and your reading me, present a challenge to the dominant form of thought in modern life, or what is called dominant because it presses to occupy all the mind.

Could some fall into what Blake envisioned two centuries ago as Newton's Sleep? We would not know them if they did, nor they us. Our movements would mean nothing to them, theirs would make no claim on us. Legal thought, which is everyday thought, works to keep each of us from this, to keep our minds from becoming kinds of minds rather than minds, our hearts from becoming emotions rather than hearts. Legal thought is the daily exercise that not only allows us to sleep in peace, but keeps us from Newton's Sleep.

SECTION ❧ V

The Pull of the Real

On the Active in

Legal Thought

V.1 ❧ Choice and Undeniability

Authority is real. The person facing authority does not choose to grant authority—authority is not a matter of choice. One can deny it. One can deny anything. But one does not deny authority without striking at one's own integrity, one's identity, one's own reality, one's self. Or should it be said that one can seem to deny it but, deep within, one does not or at least there is then awareness enough one is at war with oneself and one's actions and statements are not one's own.

The reality of authority is like physical reality, which one also does not deny except at great cost or by a seeming, a self-delusion to which one is a knowing party. But not wholly like: there is a passivity in acknowledgment of physical reality—less passivity perhaps than there may be thought to be, for psychology suggests much activity at semiconscious or unconscious levels before the simplest perception: but there is at least a sense of passivity in physical experience, which happens *to* me though I may struggle to evade it. In the experience of authority there is no such passivity. There is a moment of stillness, at the point of recognition, but the authoritative that one recognizes takes work to find. Activity precedes recognition— listening, discarding, listening again. And ample incentives to the work though there be, the work is always hard. The student of Torah, whose wanting to know the law must be so strong, if he is actually to know it, that his wanting can only be described as love of it; the priest making himself ready for a visitation; the Buddhist breaking through—all are working toward that which they must acknowledge.

They do choose to work, but in the end they do not choose to hear what they hear.

V.2 ❧ *Flaws*

A flaw is but a fading out of faith on the part of one who declares "flaw." Aspect, detail, line, trait that is not understood is not immediately thought a flaw. There are degrees of modesty in readers but few are so immodest that they need undertake no work at all to draw out meaning and to understand. The moment work begins, faith enters. What drives the work would not be a static statement to self, "I do not understand," but a statement pointing forward, "I do not yet understand." This line, this note, this proportion, this action that appears wrong, awkward, contrary, inadequate—this rhyme that does not rhyme, this sudden cruelty—I do not ignore, forgive, or condemn, not yet. Nor of course do I dismiss the whole on account of it and move my attention more profitably elsewhere. I attend, I work, here, on this.

Spending time and continuing work is a testing of this faith that the object of attention can be understood and that the difficulty is not in it but in one's perception. Then comes the point when one works no longer and spends no more time. Then faith is given up, and as it is given up, the appellation "flaw" emerges into the mind to be attached to the object from which attention passes, and to be left behind to mark the giving up of faith.

This is never done in science. There is no flaw in Nature, which is to say, faith that the difficulty is not in Nature but in one's own perception is never given up in science. There is no flaw in God. One does not judge Nature, one does not judge God—

Or perhaps one does. The scientist alone among us, or in us, entertains no thought of flaw in Nature, no thought of taking the action that follows a declaration of flaw, which is resisting, ignoring, or dismissing. The scientist alone will not fight Nature or move attention beyond Nature. Others of us, or other parts of us, will fight Nature, ignore some aspect of it, even in the extreme dismiss the whole of it as fatally flawed—as dead to that which, because outside it, can look beyond its bounds. And so perhaps also will we act with God, at least the God of the theologians, and so perhaps with any person: where flaw is in question, it is not clear there is a deep difference between the details of Nature, of artifact, or of character and action.

Only the all-encompassing that encompasses oneself within the all is immune to judgment and immune to loss of faith—does not depend for its very presence upon faith. This may be what love is, the all-encompassing beyond faith, the only all-encompassing, in which condemnation and abandonment have no place.

What of law? Law lies somewhere between Nature or the God of the theologians, at one end, and an artifact or individual, at the other. Law's authority suggests that (if it has authority) one does not judge it, one only seeks to understand it: law's authority suggests that one does not cease in faith when working to understand it. Like Nature or God, unlike a poem or an individual, one cannot easily do without it, condemn it, push it away and go on to something or someone else, take that ultimate action that can follow a declaration of flaw.

But law does come embodied in artifacts. A detail, line, aspect of one of these artifacts can be declared a flaw. The faith sustaining work to understand the detail can fade, the detail can be ignored, indeed condemned. Even the entire artifact of which it is a part can be put aside; other embodiments of law can step forward to take its place, and it is in fact the distinguishing feature of the Rule of Law that this does happen and work then continues.

Though law then, because work continues, looks again close to Nature, as if the spread continuum of faith and flaw were a circle, Nature actually is of another order. For whether faith, in the law that is sought in and through flawed constructions of it, continues, or falters, whether faith is or is not maintained, the fact remains that that which is not understood will not be obeyed. Until that which is not understood is understood there can be only the pretense of obedience. Whether flaw is declared, or not, the consequence for human action beyond the work to understand will be the same. And oddly, if there *is* obedience that is sensed as true, as a person can be sensed as true and not mere facade, there is evidence one understands more than one knows one understands. Understanding Nature, on the other hand, does not entail obedience, and failure to understand does not lead to pretense. Nature gives no orders.

v.3   ⚓ *Obedience to Law as Activity*

The Koran has been aging for a millennium and a half; the Torah, the Old Testament, for two and a half millennia; the New Testament for two. The very language of theological texts ages and they need translation. Translation always raises a question of faithfulness and accuracy. If texts are very old, there is a question of textual accuracy—faithfulness to the original, not of the translation but of the text itself—which is the origin of "scholarship."

If there is a question of textual accuracy, the text has to be constructed. Judgments have to be made about the words the text is to be cast in. Such construction is a reading of the textual materials, a reading that is then given written form and called the text. And just as this scholarly construction of a text to be read, the deciding what the text is, is itself a reading, so translation, which is also deciding what words the text is to be cast in, is also a reading.

And since a translation does not deny that it is a new statement, keeping translation in mind makes it easier to hold in mind, against the grain of intuition, that reading itself is a new statement, a statement of the meaning of the text for the reader. When a reading is written out, it is sometimes called a commentary, a commentary being a form of translation (as the Translators' Introduction to the *New English Bible* of 1970 is at pains to point out) and a translation being a form of commentary, both, reading or commentary and translation, not being different in kind from construction or reconstruction of the text, choosing what language or parts to include and what to omit. These near equivalences are standard understandings in theological work.

Construction, commentary, reading, the basic terms of theological work, are terms just as familiar to the lawyer. Constitutions age and their language gets old. The Treaty of Rome has begun to age. Though the accuracy of legal texts is not as often open to question, they need translation and restatement quite as much. Statutes get old. Some, like the Sherman Antitrust Act, are half as old as the United States Constitution itself. Judicial opinions certainly age. If one goes to the rare book room and looks at *Calder v. Bull* in 3 U.S. Reports or *Marbury v. Madison* in 5 U.S. Reports as they actually are—or were—one is surprised by the strangeness of their punctuation and capitalization, the italics that appear everywhere in them, their spelling and those fuffy *s*'s of eighteenth-century writing. The great cases of administrative law, that still-new subject, appeared when the grandparents of today's beginning lawyers were young. Any statement of law, any of the materials of law with which lawyers work, must age. Theology and law therefore present parallel methodological problems, and these parallel problems are similar to those presented by art. They all raise the central question: what really is the reason for concern with the original?

Historical work on the social, political, economic, and linguistic context of the making of a legal or theological text proceeds as if it had a purpose other than mere knowledge of *how* things once were. There would not be even an attempt to read and reread, translate and retranslate the ancient Hebrew, and how ancient it is, unless it were thought the ancient Hebrew—the language and those who wrote in the language—were understandable and, since understandable, were evidence to us of what we are and can think. In the case of constitution or aging statute or aging judicial opinion no less than in the case of Bible or Koran, arguments are made that current readings are not *faithful*. Protection of small business to achieve the Jeffersonian ideal was originally part of the Sherman Act's purposes, though the economist thinks it destroys symmetry or coherence; or it was not there originally, and has crept in over time. The Framers of the Constitution or the People voting for it did not really approve of capital punishment—or they did; were truly opposed to—or were not opposed to—the infusion of religious value into the constant reconstitution of the voting polity. Something, in law as in theology, turns on the outcome of arguments such as these about the original. And the answer to the question "Why should anything turn on the outcome of such arguments?" is much the same as the answer that would be given in the nonlegal and nontheological activity where the original is also significant, in art. If the text is going to continue to have authority for us, which is to say, if we are going to continue to read it, we can be content with nothing less than all mind. The reading of the legal text is for the purpose of producing an authoritative statement, translation, restatement. That is why it is "cited" and why citation and quotation appear so explicitly in legal (and theological) works. Without an attempt at faithfulness to the original, we read only ourselves or only ourselves and our immediate predecessors, which tells us too little about ourselves. We are adrift, we have an object too much like a stone or stick of wood, an *objet trouvé*, and not a work of art to which we can respond.

But note that interpretive equivalences can be reversed. Just as translation is a form of reading, restatement, and commentary, so reading is a form of translation, restatement for ourselves, of what we understand and what has meaning for us: certainly mere mouthing the words of a text does no good, for they are mere sounds like the sounds of the wind. And just as construction, out of underlying materials, of a text to be read—the original scholarly endeavor—is ultimately a reading of the evidence, so reading is a construction of a text to be read. Rereading, or reading anew, which is done in each legal argument and each case and each time a lawyer turns to the texts, involves seeing words or phrases that were not seen before (and, therefore, were in a sense not there before), emphasizing words or phrases or sentences or structures that were not emphasized before (and, therefore, were not in a sense there before), moving aspects of the object in or out of attention. The question in law is always what one emphasizes, concentrates upon. Any written text is open to this, and all music. A reading one year is rarely the same as a reading another year.

There is thus no way we can escape participation in and responsibility for the creation of the meaning that we take from this activity we call reading. Turning attention back

to the original does not allow us to escape it. When we get
back to the original we must still read it. But—and this
the reversal of interpretive equivalences also helps us to
remember—we are not alone in our reading. We are not
alone as individuals, nor alone as a contemporary community of readers (however that might be conceived when in
successive instants it stretches seamlessly from those just
about to die to those just being taught how to read). For
any text that is read and reread, there are intervening readings between its first appearance and our encounter with
it. These, the tradition, may ignore a thrust of a text and,
in a sense, drop that thrust from a text. Though our rereading may seek to reinsert it, as if the text were being
retranslated or reconstituted for the purpose of translation, the intervening readings do not vanish and are not
merely evidence of others' limitations. The intervening
readings may themselves be evidence of what the original
mind saw, or thought, or sought to express. Playing eighteenth-century music in the twentieth century, we do not
abandon the nineteenth-century pianoforte when we re-
discover the fortepiano, for we know that composers may
dream upon their instruments and may have heard a
pianoforte sounding, and we know we are not uniquely
wise, looking for the first time with unblinkered eyes.
What is that original mind if not a mind something like
our own, and what are it and our own but pointers to a
larger mind. If we are seeking truly to read, and not just
pretending to read, we give up neither our thirst for the
original nor our attention to the way the original has
come to be read over time.

When we note finally that there must also be a determination what texts are to be read and perceive that commu-
nities over time do make such determinations, we find
ourselves even more fully involved. As reading, or translation, or reconstruction of texts moves words and pieces of

texts in and out of that to which we attend and respond, so texts and works are moved in and out of that necessarily limited group of them to which we look, and look to as if it were a larger text to make sense of as a whole—the canon, which we find in art and literature as well as in theology and law. In reading we not only drop things out to make sense of what we read—flaws, imperfections, details to be paid less attention to or no attention to; we drop out whole objects. We do this in art and in literature. It is done in theology. Lawyers constantly do it with judicial opinions and with statutes, which fall in and out of use. We do not force ourselves to continue looking at a thing. We can put the thing aside, move it to the storeroom, relegate it to history, cease gazing at it.

But free to do that much, we are also free to do less. We need not eliminate the work entirely. We can eliminate details, even parts. And in eliminating the detail or the part we can think that the original maker would have done so too, if only he could have lived so long and had a chance to read his work again. This we do in reading any text, indeed in knowing any friend and listening to any person's talk. At each point in the course of hearing as well as speaking, reading as well as writing, looking as well as making, there is an assertion of responsibility, which itself is an assertion of *being*. It is most active. It does make a difference whether you, as listener *or* speaker, are there, in the same way it makes a difference that you are there if you are a mother to a child, in the same way it does not make a difference if you are thing, slave, wholly exploited, passively used, one for whom a substitute could always be found. That corrosion of being, the thought that one might as well not be there, which afflicts the pure observer outside it all, that fading of a sense of one's own existence, is not to be found in any actual speaking, or hearing, or writing, or reading, or the making of an expressive thing, or the looking at an expressive thing. There is no passivity or being merely used in any of these. Quite the reverse.

v.4 ☙ *The Sanctification of Convention*

There is oneself, who must decide, and find ways not only of doing things but of thinking about ways of doing things; and there is the world, and the world's ways. Doing things in imitation of the world's ways, doing things in the ways the law sets out (not "commands" or "prescribes" but sets out), may once have been accepted, by those long ago who like us had to decide, because they were meaningful ways, *the* meaningful ways, meaningful because they were expressions of the Creator. Obedience then was imitation. Only the meaningful was to be imitated, but it was not the known purpose of the world's ways that produced or justified obedience in the form of imitation, but rather that they did have whatever purpose the Creator had, shrouded though that might be.

But the world's ways are no longer the ways of the Creator. And the world's ways are not *there*, set. There are patterns, but obedience does not consist of imitation of them, for they are not meaningful. They are merely patterns, changing with the times. The transcendent may still speak. But the transcendent, if it speaks, speaks through a great variety of flawed and conflicting texts that continue to be heaped up as time goes on. What is said must be constructed—there *is* nothing that can be merely repeated, imitated—and construction proceeds by unshrouding purpose.

V.5 ✤ *Authority and the Invariant Text*

In religious thought the authoritative may be the sacred, the sacred may be the unquestionable, the unquestionable may be the central text which does not change—the Torah in Judaism, the Koran in Islam, the Vedas in Hinduism, Scripture in Christianity.

In law, the text changes. Statements of law are added and read in light of prior statements. Texts move in and out of the focal center.

If you ask of a believer in a religious tradition, "What is authoritative?" you might be taken by the hand and led to look at the invariant text. But there is no law which anyone can take you by the hand and point to. There are only statements of law. Of course law has its bits of relatively long-lasting constitutional text; there are in fact four versions of the Parables, seven versions of the Koran, different versions of the Sutras spread across cultures; within all the great canonical works there is much room for shifts of attention: this difference between a religion's text and law's moving and amended text is not sharp. But a difference seems to be there. In the experience of authority is this a difference of importance?

In pointing to the marks on the pages or scrolls of the manuscripts of sacred texts, no one is saying that *they* are authoritative—are the law. Always the authoritative is in what is said in them. Lawyers are as attentive as priests to the details of a recorded statement of law. They are not casual about the change of a word. The absence in law of an invariant text that is unquestioned may mean only this, that in law there is no mark that marks being inside belief or outside it.

The religious believer is identified by belief in, acceptance and adoption of, the unquestioned, and the unquestioned is the invariant text. In perceiving human experience of authority in religion, one can, perhaps must, take the stance of an outsider vis-à-vis the authority that is experienced if one does not oneself embrace the invariant text. In the absence of an invariant text, one need not, perhaps cannot, take the stance of an outsider vis-à-vis the authority that is experienced. If ritual acceptance of the invariant text is the beginning of religious authority, in law there is the engaging in the method of law itself, stepping into the practice of law, adding to the statements of law that are closely read, and then *acting* and thus investing oneself in one's conclusion. One's engagement and one's taking action that is not inconsequential reveal to oneself and others—as at the furthest reaches of revelatory action martyrs do—one's own implication in the presuppositions that attend the use of such method.

v.6 ❧ Fictions

Sociology assumes law and cannot replace it. Like economics and political science, sociology and even anthropology are laden with legal terms that have no meaning except as writer and reader shift to the understandings involved in the exercise of legal method. Lawyers must nonetheless be concerned with the sociology and anthropology of law, with the law-in-action as it is called raising somewhat the misleading suggestion that there is law that is not in action or that action is not to be read in reading law.

Any lawyer must pause before saying "this is the law" if he knows that he or another lawyer quoting his words would be uniformly ignored or that his words would be viewed as a flaw in the whole of what he said. In Catholicism and Islam, formulations of words that were termed "rules" against the charging of interest on money were quoted for centuries. But income flowed back from the lending of money, in one way or another. Was there a "rule against interest"? In American state corporation codes, sections can generally be found requiring in mergers of corporations that a vote be taken among affected shareholders and the appraised value of shares be offered in cash to those who lose the vote. But mergers are routinely achieved in one way or another, involving several steps or the temporary creation of "shell" or "phantom" corporations, without allowing votes or appraisal. Sometimes state legislators address those ways, with further words. Sometimes legislators remain silent. Was there a requirement of shareholder voting on mergers?

Something indeed may be expressed by a formulation that appears to be without effect in the world, some pole of thought, some force, and maintenance of the formulation in discourse may be a self-imposed difficulty that has its purpose as weight training for strength has its purpose. The strings of words lawyers craft and call "rules" are always pointings to objects, values, hopes—they are lawyers' special grunts. But their quality is never quite understood by social scientists turning to law, who pick them up and take them from law's own place, as they think, out into the field. No more do physical scientists understand, when they adopt the word "law" in speaking of Nature's "laws."

But like animal guides in fairy tales, sociologists can lead lawyers back from the hypothetical and the unreal to the living actualities of law; from some isolated part, to the whole from which lawyers, as lawyers, create statements of law. Though the law seized upon by sociologists may be fictional, there is a sociology of law nonetheless.

v.7 ❧ *Channeling*

The conjunction is interesting:

One popular paradigm of law is law as a system of channels in the form of clear rules, whose object is to prevent conflict and coordinate activity, quite like the channeling of energy by a machine. These rules (of the social engineer) speak for themselves or do not need to speak at all (so objective are they); an individual within the machine they form considers himself obliged to obey and does obey depending upon whether or not he approves the general object and justice of the system as a whole.

Side by side with this view is the equally popular view of working-to-rule—that is, acting upon the apparent meaning of rules, each of which by itself seems clear—as a standard form of disobedience designed to frustrate the system.

Lawyers who see law merely as a channeling system are in a particular difficulty. Their system, its parts fitting this way and that and hanging together in their contemplation, is a system of law. They must have constructed that system after much reading of law. But the reading they did was done on presuppositions inconsistent with a vision of law as merely a channeling system.

v.8 ॐ *Looking at Law*

How impoverished is a picture of law that puts at the center one individual giving *orders* to another. How impoverished is a picture of law that suggests even a disembodied voice giving *orders* to an individual. Consider the businessman. Few individuals are issuing *orders* to him as he goes about his business. He is making decisions, one decision after another. Around him representing the law are Securities Law, Corporate Law, Occupational Health and Safety Law, Tax Law, Environmental Law, the Law of Contract, the Law of Trespass, the Law of Homicide, the Law of Antitrust, the Law of Banking, the Law of Historic Preservation, the Law of Food and Drug, the Law of Immigration, the Law of Property. In his decision making, which goes on and on and on, he takes them into account or does not take them into account. They speak to him or they do not speak to him, they can be heard or they cannot be heard. When they speak and are heard they say "pay attention," but they give no orders, to haul a rope, to march.

v.9 ॐ *The History of Statutes*

Statutes and regulations are only candidates for attention, not just in competition for enforcement resources, but in the very analysis of situations. This is to be observed historically, from without. It is also experienced by lawyers, from within.

v.10 ❧ *Rightness*

Getting something right is less a theory of writing than a datum to be theorized about. Calling the experience of it "getting it right" is just trying to get it right. Lines and pieces of language sometimes come; where whole pieces of language do not come, individual words do. They just come. Why, we do not yet know. Once pieces of language or words come to mind, we semiconsciously judge whether they are right for that which is not yet expressed. We discard some and open the mind again—the first word that comes to mind is not at all the last—or we put them in combinations new or different. We stop, except for the exigencies of time—the competition within us for time— only when we experience the sense they are right or right as can be. Each time we stop with that sense we each change the use of the word ever so slightly.

This getting something right is not meaningless imitation. It is seeking to realize meaning. And it is not presumptuous. It is rather looking to something outside oneself, if the self may be temporarily so limited to make a statement about where, on a range between humility and presumption, lies the effort to get something right in the course of what is called creation.

But, you say, this experience is only of my separate and limited world, my context. Experience that I seek to express, the world of my mind, is different from yours.

Would I seek true contact with my own mind if in doing so I were not seeking contact with something greater? Of what interest or concern would it be to me if I were not? Would I seek contact with something greater, through giving form to and grasping what is in my own mind, if that something greater were only another particular? The experience of getting it right puts in doubt all separation of minds and ultimate particularity of experience, even if it does not demonstrate the opposite. And then there is action to take or not to take. We respect others by paying attention to them; but if others' getting it right is not at all our getting it right and what they seek to stay in responsible contact with is not what we seek contact with, we would not respect them. We would always use them for our ends when we did not ignore them, break them up when we could if we needed food or fuel. The reason we do not is not just fear, and not just that they have short noses, two eyes, and hair not all over the body.

There is action to take or not to take. We can intervene to feed, to protect, to rescue sometimes when we can—inaction is the form worn by true belief that mind is separate from mind and that experience is uniquely particular. Action and self-restraint as we practice them demonstrate belief in the opposite of separation and particularity, even if they do not demonstrate the truth of what they reveal is believed. If we allow ourselves even to think much mischief has been done by claiming a godly, a "right," perspective, we have used the word of an active person, *mischief*, who is making claims on self and others.

The lawyer is always trying to get it right: the lawyer is always facing action or withholding action.

V.II ✌ *The Aesthetic Analog*

Beauty can hit, as if physically; in music, over and over, in waves: felt once, its rising again can make the body physically flinch and steady. How can beauty be thought mere convention? What discounting, what ignoring of experience there is in the very thinking of beauty as convention, what turning from the actuality to be made sense of: what distancing, fear.

If Bach does not transport the Maori, but the Maori do acknowledge—and better than we—the beauty of what breaks upon them, it is no more difficult to say that there is beauty, but beauty appears in different forms, than to say that there is man, but man appears in different forms. If we say there is no beauty—or that beauty is mere convention, which is to say the same, that there is nothing but the form, the convention—because there is difference in the forms in which beauty is said to be experienced, then we raise a question whether there is man in the differing forms that come before us. (The classifications of science are of no pertinence. There is no *man* for science; respect, and communion, do not flow from its definitions.) To shy from one conclusion is to shy from the other. Is there not the distinction that we cannot feel the beauty ourselves the Maori feels, we only hear report of it, see its effects? But the report is of an experience we recognize, the effects are effects we recognize from its presence.

To be sure, Bach does not write new. He writes in a convention, a genre that has a history. He builds on it, shapes what he is born into. But to note that is to note no more than that Bach did not write by himself what he wrote. No one hit by the beauty in Bach's music can easily suppose that it is the work of Bach alone. Involving more of humankind, through awareness of the history of the form, does not change the substance of the immediate perception that the work is not the work of Bach alone.

V.I2 🐦 *Disenchantment*

In the complicated enchantment of the theater imitation of the actual has its own mimetic authenticities. Tarzan: boy or man-boy sits watching a movie Tarzan swinging through the woods uttering a victory cry and admires that cry. He wonders half-secretly whether that might be his cry too. It is deflating to discover Tarzan's yell is no human expression but a sound track mix of dog's bark, camel's bleat, hyena's yowl, and some snatches of Johnny Weissmuller. Or a dubbed film: the filmgoer knows the dialogue is written to fit the movements of the mouths of the actors (rather as a ghostwriter will write to fit the mouth of a purported author). It is not the same theatrical experience as the foreign film with subtitles. So, a glimpse of the sound man in the stage wings pressing toilet plungers against his chest is a real loss—the side curtains must be kept closed to the ticket holder sitting in the dark listening to galloping horses bringing rescue to a maiden.

In the modern experience of music, the rock fan basking at last in the presence of her favorite band feels less close to them when she realizes that in their performance before her they are simply mouthing the words and pretending to play their instruments, the sound coming from a tape played over a speaker system. The opera lover swooning to a beautifully executed duet between two sopranos broadcast on the radio, who listens to the rising interplay of the voices and thinks the perfect unity of two souls might be a real possibility, is jolted when the announcer tells him he has just heard Elly Ameling singing with herself in a splendid demonstration of electronic technology. His thoughts do not fit.

Disenchantment is occasionally depicted in itself and in a way that makes possible a laugh about the loss. At the beginning of *Monty Python and the Holy Grail* the galloping and clomping of horses' hooves are heard in the forest. Then a knight appears trotting along on foot as if he were on a horse, and behind him appears his squire laden down with backpacks and pots and pans, clip-clopping together two coconuts to give the effect of a horse. But there is a difference between ordinary experience and the experience of law or the various other disciplines of inquiry. The laugh is less possible. We might be better off thrilling to the rescue of the maiden, admiring the victory cry of the noble savage, basking in the presence of the rock band, swooning to the duet, if the price is merely being deceived. That may be a matter of choice. But if that is a matter of choice, to pay that price for the return gained, the disciplines of inquiry, including law, do not have quite the same choice, for their methods are designed to unmask the unauthentic. They probe and they probe. That is what they do. That is the business of the practitioner of the discipline. If their material dissolves in their hands, they are not better off except insofar as the act of close reading was a pleasurable exercise in itself.

And there is not actually that much difference between the disciplines of inquiry and ordinary experience. Music and the theater come to an end and we go out into the dark. We keep only whatever of the actual and the authentic was captured there. Thrilling, admiring, basking are not just passive states. They push the person on to act in various ways, to take one turn rather than another in his or her life. One who admires will emulate, and if he tries a Tarzan's yell that is in fact made up of hyenas, dogs, and camels, he will find, like the legal analyst, that his material is not much use to him.

V.13 ✍ *Close Reading and Delegated Writing*

Put yourself in the position of a teacher reading a seminar paper. You are puzzling out what is being said, reflecting on what is being perhaps intimated about what is being perhaps glimpsed by the student that may be new and beyond your own thinking. Then you discover the paper was not written by the student but by a commercial term paper factory. The invoice left in the middle of the paper falls out as you turn the page.

You do not thereafter continue to work at reading it, and the reason is not simply that it is no longer the work of your student and a pile of papers sits waiting to be read. The paper is a different kind of text. Those who wrote it did not care or cannot be presumed to care about what they are saying; you presume now that they only appeared to care. What appeared to be an intimation may just as easily have been said quite by chance; the warrant for puzzling over it is gone. What was going through your mind as you read came from you, and so, not wishing to confine yourself to your own mind, you turn elsewhere.

v.14 ✎ *The Equality of Difficulties*

Of course it is hard to believe what you say. And it is hard to say it yourself and not parrot someone else's or an assistant's words. It is hard, whether you are practicing lawyer or judge, to keep up with your work without ghostwriters or mimicking. It is always hard not to be mechanical and mindless.

But is it also hard to say things you don't believe, and it is hard to listen to things said by others who don't believe what they say.

v.15 ✎ *The Foundation of Obligation*

This is the foundation of obligation, that in the end there is no foundation. The paradox in such a foundation lies only in the difficulty of using a language, our language, that consists largely of materialist metaphors. Paradox fades as the difficulty is seen only as a difficulty, albeit one that may be struggled with to the end of life. Even the word "be"—the "is" in our most triumphant sentences of discovery that marks movement of the mind from doubt, or from consciousness of illusion and unreality, to truth and a sense of the real—partakes of that difficulty, the difficulty seen in the word "ground," which, when used to speak of the reasons pushing and pulling a decision, might suggest something that would stub the toe. The person within—the self—and the person one hears and perceives are not absorbed into whatever might be proposed as foundational: there is no foundation in the sense presupposed by science or even history. The statement of the Buddhist faith or hope or perception that "there is no self" might be made also in law, as that which gives us law. The emphasis of the statement "there is no self" should be upon the *is*. The self *is* not, the perception being acknowledgment of freedom, and of oneself never captured or transformed into material or processes that merely are.

Of meaning, which fuels any sense of obligation, the same can be said. One certainty, one of the few, is that meaning is nothing that is, merely is. The satisfaction there is in a reach for meaning, the satisfaction of the moment, is the clarity of intimation. The presence of meaning points forward, the not yet known revealing itself now as knowable, "not yet" making all the difference between meaning—present meaning—and the unknown or the unknowable. When Moses asks the name of God and hears "I am that I am, tell them I am sent you," the Hebrew "is" and "am" contains a becoming, pointing forward to what can be. But even in this pointing forward, the becoming, the unfolding, there is the metaphor of flower, spring, the processes of the natural world. A metaphor from the child, who can be seen now to contain her future, in whose eyes is the whole of her life, would be better—but it would be too circular, too self-referential to be of much more help. Time itself, with its flow and its differences from point to point, is itself a metaphor, and the Hebrew "is" or "am," in reaching for Time to express the meaning of "meaning," does not seize meaning itself. What is known is never captured—"My soul into the boughs does glide; / There, like a bird, it sits and sings . . . "

v.16 ✍ *Return to the Aesthetic*

Law's thrust to action, its force and call in the mind, may possibly put it beyond the aesthetic, but the world of law is not wholly separate from the world of the poem or the picture.

Poisoned by what he heard during the great mid-century American confrontation over a statement made speaking for law that no one is to be separated off by skin color, Robert Hayden returned to a Monet,

> . . . again to see
> the serene great picture that I love.
>
> Here space and time exist in light
> the eye like the eye of faith believes.
> The seen, the known
> dissolve in iridescence, become
> illusive flesh of light
> that was not, was, forever is.
>
> O light beheld as through refracting tears.
> Here is the aura of that world
> each of us has lost.
> Here is the shadow of its joy.

The world "each of us has lost" was not wholly lost for Hayden, while he could say, assuming that he would be heard and understood, the words "each of us." Shadows and auras, that the eye like the eye of faith believed, were enough to continue.

Full Circle

On the Force of

Legal Thought

VI.1   Rules and Deconstruction

The notion of a rule, insofar as law is associated with rules, is part of what would link law to the tyranny of nature over us, link law to gravity when we would leap, to blindness when we would see, to addiction and decay— law's essence residing in the imperative as such, its givenness.

But there is no such thing as a rule that exists or even has force in the mind. "Rule"—sounding at once of authority, predictability, consistency, governance—and all that is put forth in discourse in the language of rules and changes of rules and exceptions to rules and violations of rules, will be seen by a lawyer to be but a way and only one way of seeking to convey what goes on in the legal mind in coming to responsible decisions. To speak rather of questions presented, and of taking various considerations or factors into account, giving relative weight to them, excluding some from consideration, is another way of seeking to convey and discuss what is going on: the discourse, the metaphor, is not itself what is going on.

There is always an enormous difficulty, an enormous struggle in law particularly, to recall and keep in mind that language is evidence of meaning, not meaning itself. The struggle comes from the thirst to know, for closure, that can always be slaked for the moment by illusion, but at a cost and often a terrible cost. The difficulty, the struggle, is the difficulty of listening, and it is a person one listens to—only a person, whom one approaches in good faith, which includes faith that there is a person to be heard. Axiomatic elimination of the person, at least from conscious presence in the reasoning mind, is a way of cutting short the struggle, stopping the work of listening. It is precisely the elimination of the person that permits one to think of rules not as linguistic evidence but as having a real existence of their own. So it is possible to take Hindu legal texts prohibiting killing to eat, for example, and then be amused at Hindus "getting around" the rule by eating fish who die "on their own" when removed from water. But what was "the rule" in Hindu law? What was "killing"? What place did "water" play in the mind? Both the general text against something called killing to eat, and the particular texts setting out the treatment of fish, are evidence. There can be no "getting around" a rule until there is a rule to get around, but that rule must first be constructed, and on the basis of all the evidence.

So there is always the temptation in law to approach a statute as if its words had meanings in themselves and by themselves—the authoritarianism sometimes shown by those devoted to maintaining the supremacy of democratic politics and legislative authority. And so, equally, the temptation on the other side to declare that a text, statutory or otherwise, is incoherent and without any meaning at all. Deconstruction, this last has been called in the late twentieth century—not hasty in its approach to the text, or cutting out evidence, or swallowing words without savoring them (as in taking a text and saying it has a plain meaning), but most meticulous, a child of the close reading that marks legal method. But the object in view—or the consequence—of that most meticulous reading is the demonstration of contradictions and therefore incoherence. Again, only elimination of the person— the elimination that is the presupposition of literalism— makes this possible. Without an assumption that words or patterns of words have meanings of their own, it cannot confidently be said that one thing contradicts another. It is ultimately open to a listener to conclude and to say that one cannot understand, or that one cannot believe that a person speaking believes what he says. But to say a text itself is incoherent, and to stop there, is to demonstrate the common reification of language that follows the axiomatic elimination of the person. There is no listening, really.

Lawyers are subject to all these varying consequences of stopping listening, to the authoritarian construction of texts and the equally authoritarian deconstruction of texts, all that follows the axiomatic elimination of the person. Lawyers are so subject if only because they live in close proximity to others of the highly articulate who play with in their daily work and profess a denial of spirit. But over the long run lawyers do not succumb. They pull themselves away from the common temptation. Something that has authority pulls you into the spirit of it. Without spirit there can be no authority. Without authority there is no law.

VI.2 ✍ *A Source of Positivism*

Nietzsche was no lawyer.

Law's authority, he proclaims, is in its pure imperative, its *non* sense. A book of law does not refer to reasons, "for if it did so, it would lose its tone of command—the 'Thou shalt' which enforces obedience; and this is the heart of the matter. . . . The authority of the law is established on the twofold principle: God gave it, our ancestors lived it."

No lawyer can point to an *it*.

VI.3 ✒ *Authority and Responsibility*

A legal scholar confronted with a passage in his treatise identical to an article written by one of his colleagues defended himself by claiming that whatever he might be blamed for he could not possibly be blamed for plagiarism. He had used student research assistants to write the treatise. It was one of them who was guilty, not he.

What then of the credit he received for the treatise? A means of exploring the place of authenticity in legal thinking is exploration of the connections between the possibility of blame and the possibility of praise; the connections between the possibility of blame or praise, and the possibility of reading for meaning; and, since paying attention is a form of praise, the connections between the possibility of authority and the possibility of praise or blame, that is, the connections between authority and responsibility.

VI.4 ✒ *The Evidence of the Child*

The connection between authenticity and authority begins in the child on the lookout for the phony in the towering adult. In lawyers the disconcerting child homing in on the phony is still alive. Lawyers' thirst for the actual is no mere consequence of professional training. Nor are children taught to read closely the adults towering over them. They simply do it, managing to do it even at the stage of life when whimsy and fantasy are entered into most willingly.

VI.5 ☞ *Speaker and Spoken*

Imagine the blush of foolishness if you found yourself mulling over a long letter of warm goodwill punched out from the sender's just-purchased program of letters for every occasion. The *Executive's Business Letter Book* promises "no more stomach-churning decisions on 'how to say it,'" and a quit to "wasting hours searching for the perfect words." The program contains "Building Employee Morale" letters ("Show your staff you care about them and hold them in high esteem!"), "Enhancing Shareholder Relations" letters ("Loyal stockholders are made, not born! Build a warm relationship with them"), "Building Customer Loyalty" letters ("It's ten times easier to hold on to an old customer than to find a new one. These letters will do the trick. Use them!"), "Building Personal and Community Goodwill" letters ("Your competitors often fail to use these kinds of letters because they're so hard to compose. Use them, and you'll tower over everyone, especially in the profit department!").

The blush of foolishness that comes with awareness no one is speaking is the same as that which comes with awareness that a speaker is speaking to no one but is handling, herding. No one speaking and speaking to no one are two sides of the same. The sensation is then followed by an incapacity to continue attending, paying attention, mulling, reading with care. Authority is not a matter of the will. Authority is not a matter of convention and habituation. There are in fact imperatives when authority appears, though they are imperatives of prerequisite and condition. All things can be different than they are? Not in matters of the spirit any more than in the physical world.

VI.6 & *Fear as Part of Legal Order*

Some observe that, human nature being what it is, we must be driven by fear and discipline as much as we are driven by desire and hope, and any arrangement for human life must provide a considerable place for fear and discipline.

In fact one of the attractions of an economic system designed according to what are called laissez-faire principles is that individuals' fear of the consequences of not striving may encourage productive activity; and early utilitarian psychology, emerging with certain Protestant views of damnation, placed avoidance of pain on a level with the securing of pleasure as a true source of human action.

That early psychology has contributed to the wide reception today of an axiom of thought, that all desires can be and are numerically ranked by individuals. It has contributed also to the accompanying assumption, on which the axiom is built, that when we realize in action one rather than another desire we really choose between them.

But in what way can it be said we *want* that which avoids pain? How can it be thought that discipline and fear would work to make us embrace or seek that which we would not otherwise desire? The torturer says, "I will make you beg me to beat you." Often (we are told) the time comes when the tortured does beg to be beaten, because he would rather be beaten than continue to suffer the other pain the torturer has devised for him. We can imagine him, or ourselves, saying, "All right. I give in. Beat me." But the torturer, if he is serious, might reply, "You are only deciding to *say*, 'Beat me.' You don't want it. I am going to make you really want it, really beg and plead for it"; and then he settles down to go on with his torture until he is satisfied that there is an actual desire being voiced.

Would he ever stop his torture? Can the victim say and actually feel that he wants that which his torturer is waiting for him to desire? Will his pleadings ever have the ring of truth to one who is listening to them closely? Can there be authenticity in his statements, real desire, identification of himself with that desire? We can think not, despite all we think we know about masochism. The torturer would know the absence of authenticity, real desire, identification of the person with the voiced desire, and the torture would go on until there is given up the very notion of a man's finally expressing in his choices in action the wants that animate and identify him. If it were otherwise, a man would be a humming system, a choosing machine and a thing only, which is perhaps indeed what authoritarian domination seeks to prove, if only to relieve itself of responsibility for what it does. But man remains rebel man. The negative is not the other side of the positive. There is only the positive.

VI.7 🐟 *Subjective and Objective*

In talk about law much is made of the subjective and the objective, the "merely" subjective, the "hard" objective. Oddly, the subjective is what has to be accepted, the objective is what can be argued over and is argued over. And the fundamental thrust in law toward free acceptance and law's characteristic attitude toward the authoritarian is revealed in a tendency to dismiss and ignore (once a dichotomy between subjective and objective has been so conceived) that which must be accepted and to concentrate on that which can be argued about.

But is there anything subjective that must thus be accepted by another? "I like that smell." Purely subjective? No need for reasons? But who is the "I"? A claim could be put that you deceive yourself. "I felt this." Did you? What is the *this*? There is a convincing that must go on and on.

VI.8 🏂 *Analytic Unities*

For the lawyer, the question of obligation to obey the law is a question of what one's attitude is or can be as one proceeds toward a statement of law. It is not a question whether there is or is not something attached to the something called the law, which can be described as obligation, prima facie or absolute. The content of the law, the obligation to obey it, and the specification of what obedience consists of emerge not one after another in the mind—or in legal analysis—but together.

VI.9 ✵ *Pattern, Systems, and Processes*

To know that a thing is a pattern, and not an open adventure, is to ensure withdrawal from it. To *see* it *as* a pattern *is* to withdraw from it. Building; consolidation; enjoyment—that is the sequence. We say, "Now is the time for enjoyment, since building and consolidation have passed." And one can enjoy. But one closes one's eyes a bit as in a trance, or as in a dance of patterned movement. The pleasure is not the same pleasure adventure brings. Adventure makes us one with our experience.

Dancing (to a pattern) is wonderful. To see oneself dancing and dancing again, and then dancing again, is not so wonderful. *That* pattern separates you from what you do. We would not in the end really want to predict all or control all. Aliveness and reality, aloneness and vanishing, are in the balance when the "all" is approached.

VI.IO ✵ *The Cosmology of Mindlessness*

No one thinking about law should be in any doubt about the importance of the impact of the spread of mathematical thought in disciplines beyond law and in society generally. If legal authority—or the possibility of it—is a desire, this is the principal threat to it. If, on the other hand, the persistence of legal authority should be considered an obstacle to social improvement, the spread of mathematical thought is the principal source of hope. Even if one were to succeed in remaining only an observer, this is the thread of development upon which one's attention should be concentrated.

Mathematical thought is translation of reality into process or system, with axiomatic exclusion of substance that might transcend any process or system. Materialism may be implicit in it, but its spread to linguistics, literary criticism, social theory, to the psychology of mind and even to theology makes "scientific thought" too narrow a term for it. As it grows to be characteristic of the contemporary mentality, academic and lay, engagement in legal thought must appear more and more unorthodox. Then the question is presented, to us in the present, whether legal thought in historical view is merely an anachronism or is the opposite, a seed of change in modern thought generally (though that question may be a question that only denial of an all-encompassing historical view makes it possible to ask). Legal thought itself cannot change in accommodation or emulation without abandoning its purpose. Its purpose is to search for authority. Simply as a matter of legal method, a search for authority presupposes the personal, in the individual and beyond individuals, and the personal disappears in process and system.

Legal authority presupposes the personal: can a universal claim be ventured, that authority as such implies the personal?

The question pushes not just beyond the legal to what Western usage terms the nonlegal but beyond the West and involves inquiry now chiefly centered in anthropology. But such a question is unavoidable, for any position and any tradition that denies translation of all to process has in it a thrust toward human universals; and the contrary thrust, toward acceptance of human differences unbridgeable in any present, may be rooted ultimately in a vision of reality exhausting itself in process. A fully self-

aware monotheism must address a similar question, perhaps the same question.

Science itself makes a claim to universality across time
and culture, but that claim of science repeats the underlying proposition of mathematical thought. It is rather the
response of science to the history of science, and to proposals to dissolve its fundamental understandings into
merely historical phenomena, or epiphenomena, that speaks
to the question of human authority. And whatever that
response may be, of natural scientists speaking for natural
science, there is doubtfully ever among natural scientists
actual belief in a cosmology of mindlessness. The thought
of mathematicians, at its deepest, may in fact not be the
mathematical thought that has spread so widely.

But to pursue this, one must pursue the pertinence, to
the seriousness with which a statement is to be treated, of
the speaker's belief in the statement; or, in interpretive
terms, undertake to expand the text to be interpreted to
the whole of what a speaker says over time and in all contexts—one must carry legal interpretive practice into
nonlegal realms.

VI.II ☞ *Clever Machines*

"Like the weather, vending machines are something we
all have in common. Who has not lost a quarter in one or,
dying of thirst, 'paid' to watch a cupless machine drink a
soda? On the other hand many are those who have received a cascade of coins from a haywire machine.

"Back when cigarettes sold for 35 cents, New Yorker
Ken Rubin brushed memorably one day with a machine

adjacent to a rest room on the New York Thruway. He routinely deposited his money, pushed a button, and received his pack of cigarettes. But when he turned to go, his shoulder brushed the machine and another pack came out. H'm, he thought, and then almost by reflex, tapped the machine again. Another pack. Short on pockets, Rubin undid a couple of buttons on his shirt and stuffed in packs of cigarettes as fast as the machine coughed them up.

"As he retells that story in the living room of his New York City brownstone, Rubin, a manufacturer's representative for a plastics company, smiles broadly. . . .

"The real advent of coin-operated vending machines arrived with the 1880s. America had shaken off the effects of the Civil War, U.S. industry was beginning to prosper, and people had spare coins in their pockets. A clever vending machine, New Jersey-inventor Clement Clawson noted, could easily separate the average American from those coins: 'Americans are improvident and never stop to think that 20 nickels make a dollar,' he said."

VI.12   *Railing At*

Obeying a process is as foolish as its opposite, getting angry at a machine, kicking it. No feeling is appropriate when facing a process or a machine save the one feeling of coolness—which is absence of warmth, of life, of being inside. No emotion is appropriate in one's relation with a process or a machine, nothing of that from which motion comes. You do of course get angry at nature. You rail against it as Lear railed against the storm. But you are either mad then, or personifying nature in your very act of getting angry at it.

VI.13 ✊ *Internalities*

The line and difference between what is within us and what is outside us marks authority. The very center of authority is in that the person to whom we listen and respond in good faith is not outside us but brought within us. That which we of the genuinely puzzled question "What should I do?"—we of the here and now—have a part in creating, is part of us. This is source of our response in good faith, of our true willingness in what we call obedience (to the degree we are truly willing to do what we do in our response and in our listening)—that all this which is beyond our hereness and nowness is within, as much within as our hereness and nowness is within.

VI.14 ✊ *Pathological Internalization*

A person adjusting to and internalizing the mere outcomes of processes—rules emerging from administrative or legislative machinery, for instance—seems the very picture of a person adjusting to neurotic, senseless parents. Perhaps you say the image is not apt. Neurotic and senseless parents, you may say, are deemed such only by contrast with parents who are not neurotic and senseless; adjusting to them is pathological only because it separates the victim from others who are liberated or not so afflicted. Here, in law, everyone (theoretically) might adjust if they adjust together. All are in the same boat. There is no separation. You may go further, and say that if in fact all rules are mere outcomes of processes the situation would be as if there were no contrast between healthy and neurotic parents, and the image fails on that ground too.

But if there is any connection at all between public and parental authority, what is known of experience of parents may throw some light on what often seems an almost innate resistance, on the part of the articulate and the inarticulate both, to entertaining even the idea of internalizing legal rules.

VI.15 ☞ *The Identification of Legislation*

The doctrinal expression of American law reflects a degree of skepticism about the political process one would not expect to find there. Throughout there is (at the least) a critical stance toward the proposition that the outcome of the political process is connected to the will of the people by reason of the fact alone that it is the outcome of the process. No such proposition stands as an axiom in legal thinking, and no such proposition can be taken as the beginning of positive law.

In some judicial decisions indeed there is a suggestion that limits should be placed on the amount of legislating that occurs, not so that the legislation that does occur will be more closely connected to the political process and the people, but so that there simply will be less of it. What is legislation? An aspect of the creative—an aspect of the essential in ongoing human affairs, which is perceived in perception of a person? As well, and what is not the same, legislation is that statement of law which can come into being without deliberation, without debate, without reason, and with no need (or perhaps hope) of justification. Legislation is the arbitrary which we allow—but also limit. To make the point in its strongest form, it could be said legislation is lawless behavior, except that by a paradoxical trick we make legislative statements materials which we use in determining what the law is.

These views or inclinations appear in a rather less veiled way than usual in the Supreme Court opinion written in 1983 to justify invalidation on constitutional grounds of the "legislative veto" provisions of statutes setting up administrative decision makers, provisions that allow two houses of Congress without the concurrence of the president, or one house, or even a single committee of a house, to overrule an administrative decision announced either in the form of a "general rule" (administrative rule making) or in the disposition of a "particular case" (administrative adjudication).

The case in which the opinion was handed down, *Immigration and Naturalization Service v. Chadha*, involved the attorney general's suspension, in a procedure set up by the immigration statute itself, of the scheduled deportation of an alien if he or she met certain humanitarian criteria set out in the statute. The attorney general was to report his suspensions of deportation to Congress. Within a stated period of time one house could by resolution veto particular suspensions.

The Supreme Court held that such a resolution was "legislation" that did not meet the requirements of bicameralism (or passage by two houses) and presentment to the president for signature or veto. But why was such a resolution "legislation"? Only if it was legislation did it have to be presented to the president and pass two houses before it could have legal effect. Not every act of a house of Congress has to meet the bicameral and presentment requirements before it has legal effect.

Any easy answer to the question "What is legislation?" is question begging: one could indeed say in a simpleminded and positive way that there can be no such thing as the unconstitutional delegation by Congress of legislative powers to another decision maker (in violation of the separation of powers), because if another than the legislature exercises the power it would not be "legislation." Or, if "legislation" is what Congress does, then a one-house veto is not legislation, because Congress as a whole does not do it; it is exercise of a delegated power that Congress as a whole, with the concurrence of the president, has authorized.

And no explicit statement is made or easy answer given by the Court in *Chadha* as it goes about defining legislation. As so often, one must read the majority opinion for implication and suggestion.

At its beginning the opinion refers to the fact that the bill denying Chadha suspension of deportation was not printed before the vote, the fact that there was no debate or recorded vote, and the fact that there was evidence, in previous cases of veto of suspension, that some members of the Congress had thought their resolution was carrying out the attorney general's decision rather than reversing it. A footnote is dropped at the end of the opinion disclaiming any intention of suggesting that valid legislative acts must be preceded by debate and deliberation, or that a legislative body need articulate its reasons for acting, or that members must know what they are doing. The Court leaves open the question why it makes these initial references.

Then, in closing, the opinion makes another reference, and an appeal. It refers to the bicameralism and presentment clauses (and the other procedural requirements for valid legislation) as having been chosen by Founders "who had lived under a form of government that permitted arbitrary governmental acts to go unchecked." The appeal at the end is to freedom, which is to be preserved by insisting that "the exercise of power [be] subject to the carefully crafted restraints spelled out." These closing comments pick up the reading, set out in the middle of the opinion, of the eighteenth-century background of the presentment clause (requiring that a bill be presented to the president for his signature before it can enter as a text into the canon of materials with which lawyers work). There the Court emphasizes a dual purpose for presentment, the first, of course, to allow the president to protect himself and the executive sphere from legislative encroachment, but second and equally important, to check the enactment of "oppressive, improvident, or ill-considered measures." Hamilton's words are used to repeat the thought: "to increase the chances in favor of the community against the passing of bad laws through haste, inadvertence, or design."

The thought that a legislature might enact bad law, for which the legislative and electoral process itself is no cure, is subversive of a positivistic view of law. In this case it did make dissenting justices uncomfortable. But the thought is repeated from time to time in the majority opinion, and extended. It rapidly appears that it is not just bad lawmaking that the authors of the opinion have in mind as the problem. It is legislative lawmaking itself. If what the one house did in its resolution, denying the suspension of deportation of Chadha and six others, was legislation, then, so the dissenters' argument against the majority position went, why wasn't what the *attorney general* did in suspending deportation of Chadha and six others legislation too? The answer in the majority opinion is that the attorney general's decision *had to be made in accordance with standards and criteria, and could not be made for no reason at all*: judicial review of the attorney general's decision would ensure that.

Then came the challenge that, if what the attorney general did was essentially adjudicative and was the same as what the legislature did, why wasn't what the legislature did adjudicative rather than legislative and invalid by reason of separation of powers, so that bicameralism and presentment (applicable, it will be remembered, only to legislation) need not enter the analytic picture at all? This was Justice Powell's view, concurring in the result and suggesting that the decision in the case need not have so broad a sweep as to invalidate legislative vetoes as such. The answer in the majority opinion is that *the House resolution was not adjudication, because it occurred without procedure, deliberation, or substantive standards.*

What then is legislation? The implication, strongly hinted but never fully stated, is that legislation is action that need have no reason and need meet no standards of consistency. That is how we know an act is legislative. And what is being constitutionally enforced, by the majority of the Court, has little to do with democracy as it is usually presented. For if the electorate does not like a legislative veto, in a statute or in statutes generally, then the electorate is in principle in a position to secure the withdrawal of the veto by statute. What is being enforced is rather a check on legislation as such.

In this light it becomes more understandable why the complaint made both inside and outside the Court, that the practical consequence of banning legislative vetoes is to leave greater power in the administrative sphere, is met with such singular equanimity by the majority. The administrative sphere is not arbitrary, at least not by definition arbitrary in the sense that obedience demanded to statements of law is not, in principle, so much to private whim or a system's whimsy, as to a public value. And this view of the administrative sphere was reinforced in a companion decision of the time, *Motor Vehicle Manufac-*

turers Association v. State Farm Mutual, which held arbitrary an agency's withdrawal of a regulation pursuant merely to the desire of the elected president and the president's appointees, without appropriate procedure or substantive justification. Justification and yet more justification is contrasted with arbitrariness and yet more arbitrariness. The justices (if what they say is to be taken as an indication of their true mind, or the legal mind) shy away from a public vision of the political as ultimately authoritative.

VI.16 🐦 *Love and Systems*

A case that does not reach the courts is a case of law in action nonetheless. A state governor in 1978 denied the extradition to another state of a sixty-year-old woman to continue serving a long sentence for perjury in the robbery trial of her lover. If there was in the denial of extradition a paramount consideration, would it have been the concern noted in the governor's explanation, about the effects of prison upon a sixty-year-old? Or, which was also noted, the lack of further criminal activity on her part in the years since she escaped?

Or was it that the governor did not really condemn what she had done? If she had not lied to protect her lover she might have been viewed by all around her, including those ordering her to speak the truth, as a contemptible person. Situations can be imagined in which one's lover, one's child, one's husband or wife, one's dear friend, had tortured, killed, was dangerous, and there was no other way to help him or her but to help close the cage. And at

some point, perhaps, the demands of love can be outweighed, though tragically one cannot say even then that
love disappears—the person may be one's child, whom
one loves whatever. But at any point before that, we can
expect people to protect those whom they love—a descriptive statement: it is common to impeach testimony
by showing love—and we can also say that they ought to
do so—a normative statement. (Here as elsewhere in law
the normative and the descriptive are not separable: if a
person does turn in his beloved, the thought may strike
that that person has revealed he does not really love.)

This is in part a consequence of the awfulness of the
consequences of criminal conviction. But the phenomenon is met with throughout organizational law, in the
army, among children in school, in the underworld. It is
wrong to tattle. Only sometimes it is not.

The proposition that it is wrong to tattle is really star-
tling only to those who struggle seriously with and find
themselves trapped by what they conceive as systems of
rules, which cannot take account of the ineffable in love
and connection. As a descriptive and a normative matter
the proposition is displayed in what we ask of prosecuto-
rial and sentencing discretion—at either end of the doctrinal statement of criminal law—and of extradition or
clemency discretion. Love is taken into account outside
systems. Love threatens systems. If a prosecutor properly
does not prosecute in a situation of this kind, or the judge
properly gives only a nominal sentence, and everyone understands why, we are seeking to have what seems a system, and not have it.

VI.17 🐦 *Complexity and Motive*

Beyond some level of complexity any attempt to solve a problem by reformulating the applicable texts seems inevitably to create another problem, with the frustration that such a created problem not immediately perceived cannot be weighed against the present trouble. What happens when draftsmen and courts recognize this (unconsciously or explicitly) is a shift to motive as a determining factor in judging the legality of conduct. This has been true in antitrust, tax, securities, food and drug law, even in selective service law. And where strict criminal liability is purportedly introduced into complicated regulatory systems divorcing (it is announced) criminal condemnation from *mens rea*, motive is generally admitted to be the test in selecting defendants for criminal rather than civil proceeding, or in subjecting actors to any proceeding at all.

Thus the postulation of law as an external set of constraints so designed that persons may conduct themselves without attention to any value other than their own self-interest—law viewed as a game—is replaced by law envisioned as a set of values or goals to be internalized by individuals. Administrators abandon hope that they can design a system of constraints, rewards, and penalties such that individual calculation, taking into account those constraints, will achieve public good.

A shift to motive is not the end of the matter, for there must be grounds for determining motive, indicating what is to be inquired into and whether that is to be found in a particular case. Once evasion itself is "objectively" determined by the presence of particular factors, the motive test loses its value, and the development that leads back to motive begins again. Evasion objectively defined can be evaded; in the midst of a complex securities regulation designed to relieve uncertainty, by defining conditions in which securities "registration" is not required, is found the plea: "Regulation S is not available with respect to any transaction or series of transactions that, although in technical compliance with these rules, is part of a plan or scheme to evade the registration provisions of the Act. In such cases, registration under the Act is required."

VI.18 & *Play*

In contemplation of law an abandoned house is unlike other property. However clear the law of trespass may seem to be, people do not ordinarily condemn children for finding a way into an abandoned house and playing around in it. They chase the children out, but they do not condemn them. The emptiness of the house is significant in considering how to think legally about the situation.

Emptiness is a consideration independent of any calculus of harm, harm to property, harm to the children themselves, and independent of any appraisal of the intentions of the children. A house is a complex system and in an abandoned house there is no one there in that complex system. Its emptiness invites play and attracts ingenuity, and correspondingly invites and evokes the idea of play in the legal mind. An abandoned house with no one living in it is not just a temptation to be *bad*: the general experience recognized and reflected in law is that it is hard to condemn what one fully understands or can easily contemplate oneself doing. There is an appropriateness in children pitting their wits against its locks and going inside to play. Some may dispute what the claim of the law is in this matter, but who will say what the law is, if we only chase the children out?

Prank and play are regularly separated off in legal thought. Each year for years students at the California Institute of Technology found ways of getting into the system that controlled the scoreboard of the Rose Bowl, and flashed messages about Cal Tech—which has no football team—to the national television audience. They were rather more applauded than condemned. If condemned, there was not much conviction in the condemnation. How comes this behavior to be categorized as prank? Again, the mind of the actor and an evaluation of harm actual or potential are involved. But there is something else independent of them, that aspect of game which most complex systems have and which makes play an appropriate response to them. Large systems indeed are constructed on probabilistic principles that rest in some considerable part on what is appropriately called game theory. The quality of game is in turn associated with a system's emptiness, its standing apart from its creator or creators as a thing and merely a thing.

Thus the difficulty with kids (sometimes adults, but kids particularly) who love to get into computer systems and leave messages such as "Kilroy was here." Legislation has moved toward making their activity criminal, but the reality of the general attitude toward play cannot be legislated away. We know this from bank robbery. The man who robs a bank in a particularly clever way evokes a begrudging admiration if he harms no one physically in the process. And though the applause heard in public is muted, movies and novels on the subject rivet the attention of millions, who identify quite as much with the ingenious gang as with the detectives chasing them. Law student classes who have been asked about their honest attitude toward a bank robber who is immensely clever and sends back the take (perhaps keeping just a little as a reward for his effort) usually find it difficult to condemn him. As in the case of the conscientious objector, they may agree he should have to pay the price the system exacts, and it may be a high price. Paying a price if caught is part of the game. It would not be as good a game, perhaps, if nothing happened when you lost. But the visiting of a sanction upon a bank robber in this situation can hardly be viewed as *punishment*: there is no condemnation in it, or at least not much. Jailers do not condemn, nor the public; nor is the prisoner contrite, nor asked to be. And there is nothing odd in this: losing a game is not an occasion for condemnation.

But where there is a person within the system entered, cleverness evokes just the opposite reaction. The human body is like a house and is a system more complex, but it is not abandoned.

VI.19 ❧ *The Consequences of Words*

Life as art, or text; both life and art as fictional constructions; not real because there is no reality other than givens of a material world which is in itself incomprehensible, all representations of which are historically and culturally contingent; inexpressive because there is no self to express, the self being fiction, appearance thrown up in plays of words—all this collided with the sentence of death passed upon Salman Rushdie. The threatened self suddenly seemed very precious, seemed and then more than seemed: it was very precious. Its loss was more than loss of an illusion. The world lost with retreat into protective custody was a real loss. Words suddenly had consequences. The consequences were loudly judged. Life was no longer language game, it was no longer game of any kind. Actors were playing for real. Those who had been saying that all is fiction revealed they did not believe what they were saying. A great bell tolled outside the classrooms, the cocktail parlors, and the studies. The talk stopped.

Lawyers have been outside the doors all along. They have rather wanted to enter the comfortable closed rooms to play and join the sharp laughter, and they have tried playing a bit out of doors. But the bell tolls as they work, and brings them up short again and again.

Can the talk, when it goes so far, just stop? The people of Israel who were spared had to grind the Golden Calf into a powder and drink it, and watch the slaughtering of their neighbors and companions.

VI.20 ❧ *Terror and Being*

There is a terrible tension in what both lawyers and theologians do, given what tools and methods are put at their disposal for doing it. Always flickering in them is the terror which is the terror of responsibility in face of the unknown. Lawyers and theologians reach for the sovereign, look to the sovereign, speak for the sovereign, something or someone to pay serious attention to, or, to use the liturgical term, to praise. They turn to texts. But the texts to which they turn are selected and are old, necessarily from the past, requiring translation over time and between languages and places, year to year, decade to decade. Why do the words "authentic" and "legitimate" punctuate the history of law and the history of theology? They state the object of the work, of course, but their repetition marks repeated doubt and repeated challenge as the work goes on.

The Arabic for what lawyers and theologians do is far more evocative than the Latin of our "interpretation" or the Greek of our "hermeneutics"—*ijtihād*, which in English is "struggle" or "toil." At each point in speaking and hearing, writing and reading, there is an assertion of responsibility—of *being*. Reading, with translation and restatement for oneself of what is being said, may be speaking for another, but it is also speaking for oneself, as writing, which is speaking for oneself, may also be speaking for another. The culture may be thought to speak through the individual author. It does not speak unless the author speaks. This is as much so in art and literature as in law and religion. But when one reaches for authority in law or religion—to say do this or do that, think this or think that, you ought, you must, we will act if you don't, you will suffer, we will bring suffering to you and take responsibility for it and live with what we have done—what is ultimately being said is not music of the spheres, which says no more than that it is. That is not the ultimate. There must be something more. Love is the word that is sometimes used to express it. There are two senses of order, an order that is form, and an order that is a thrust to do or think. They are connected. They are also different. An order, in the sense of form, is not enough to produce an order to do or think. Modern man may wish to laugh at it now, transcendent love, a universe that is ultimately love, not ultimately form. But if, the way we and the world and the universe are, we cannot do without authority, without saying you ought, you must, we will produce suffering and take responsibility for it, I ought, I must, I must suffer if I do not—and if authority is impossible should this something more not exist—then we have some evidence that what we must believe, is. What we must believe, must be, not because it exists if we believe it exists, but because we exist and have been given the means, by our work, to continue existing.

VI.21 ❧ *Responsibility for the Concrete*

The judge's responsible concern for particulars puts the judge in a special place. The judge helps keep our world real.

Individual cases we call the particulars. Most evident in a trial court but going beyond the trial, a judge's engagement with the concrete, the particular, fights the dissolving of all into the abstract, the statistical, the unreal. In its strange way this responsibility for the concrete, for the tiny things that make all the difference, is what makes possible the writing of general statements of law that are authentic, and that therefore engage readers or listeners whether they be citizens or lawyers.

Then judicial bureaucracy in its various forms attacks this protection against the dissolution of things into process and statistic, whether it be small bureaucracy, separation of responsibility from decision or expression, as happens in delegation, or large bureaucracy eliminating decision itself, dividing up decision in such a way that no one decides, the phenomenon now associated with Kafka and with large administrative agencies. Just because he or she then no longer stands at the gate of the world, and for no other reason than that, the judge might slip from a special place in our affections.

VI.22 ❧ *The Statistical*

"This three-hole punch doesn't work."

"Why not take it back to the store here?"

"I bought it years ago somewhere else."

"It looks new. Why not try?"

"That would be wrong."

"No, no. They expect you to. A certain number of people will bring in these things to them without any real claim, and they have already allowed for that. Why not be one of those?"

"It would be wrong. I didn't buy it from them. I would have to lie."

"But they expect you to lie—you or someone. If no one lies, they get away with more than they expect and take from us all. They have built their expectation into the price. They don't care."

"Of course they care."

"No, they don't: they have it all worked out. If you lie, someone else won't."

"Pooh. There's no connection between me and that other owner of a three-hole punch."

"In their view there is—so why not be the one to win?"

"I won't lie."

"But no one onstage tells a lie. Do you lie when someone assumes you are lying or does not care whether you are lying or not? You're not fooling them—they and you both know it's only a *game, playacting.*"

VI.23 ❧ *Pricing Choices*

Statements that present a mere choice are distinguished in legal analysis from statements that raise some degree of obligation. Suppose a question of parking a car on the sidewalk, posed to a driver looking for a place to park, or to a pedestrian coming upon a car so parked. Anyone would have to do some work before concluding what in an actual situation the law might say about parking on the sidewalk, but even if all were to grant that there was a perfectly clear and understandable formula, a legal statement to be made about sidewalk parking might be treated as channeling or choice presenting, a statement of the kind often found in taxation, where essentially a price is sought to be put on a choice. If, that is, one wants to risk a fine one can occupy the public space for a time—or rather, if one wants to risk a certain amount of money—just as, to take the experience perhaps most common, one can park in a parking spot without putting a coin in the meter if one wants to risk a ticket of a few dollars (or, uncommonly, can smoke marijuana in at least one university town if willing to risk a similar ticket of a few dollars for possession). There is no real blame attached to unmetered parking (or possessing marijuana) or, perhaps, parking across the sidewalk. The question whether to park would be what is sometimes called a "private" one for the individual. The alternative, and contrast, are statements to be taken into the most serious account in the course of making a decision, carrying with them a measure of not only obligation but the mirror image of obligation—blame— for not paying attention to them and taking them into account in an affirmative way.

In some situations legal analysis moves further, to treat sanctions or consequences as probabilistic events, costs of doing business that can be insured against, and (especially insofar as individuals rather than enterprises bear those costs) providing for or allowing indemnification, so that a rather mechanical system of choices and incentives and channels may be set up, again in contrast to a set of statements which are to be listened to and responded to with a sense of obligation. But the mechanical systems so conceived tend to be short-lived, in contemplation and in action, if for no other reason than that, for the well advised, paying the price after the choice is made can become itself a matter of choice, between paying and whatever the alternative to paying might be in the world as it then is.

VI.24 ❧ *The Characterization of Action*

A factory building lies silent, its machinery torn out, its windows shattered, rotting—its usefulness destroyed. Hundreds of people have been idled. They vow undying hatred of those who are responsible for the destruction.

Are those who destroyed it terrorists?

Or are they a board of directors of a corporation?

The *result* of their activity does not tell. And if they are a board of directors, only belief that is connected to everything that emanates from that phrase "board of directors" and runs through the tissue of values and forms of thinking we call corporate law and the law of property can terminate the hatred and stop a move for revenge.

A factory lies silent but its machinery has not been torn out. It is occupied by workers. They are told a judge has ruled that their sit-in "is" a trespass and is "against the law" and they are asked, "What will you do now?" They answer, at their mildest, "What we must do now is to prevent the assets from being stripped so that we can form a cooperative backed by political groups to buy the factory." But they do not give up their occupation.

What is the effect of the legal action brought against them? Everything will hang on that phrase "against the law." What difference does it make, one asks, that the sit-in is "against the law"? The workers must pay damages? If that is all, the statement "against the law" may make no difference, mean nothing for the situation. Donations may pay the damages. There may be no damages because there is yet no buyer for the assets and the delay in sale or stripping is of no consequence. At the most the statement is a statement about time, setting a clock running, and more, much more, must be looked to before one arrives at any definite conclusion about what one ought to do to end the situation, even if one is acting in the utmost good faith toward the law.

VI.25 * *Coercion*

It is sometimes said that threats and force are the hallmark and distinguishing feature of law. The freedom of the market, for instance, is contrasted with the coercive regime of law.

But if you think about it there is no way you can actually force anyone to do anything he or she absolutely refuses to do. Short of drugs and the other devices of what used to be known as brainwashing, the rest of us are helpless against a refusal by one of our fellows. If we insist, he can always insist back. If we say walk down that corridor to your cell, he can refuse and we will have to carry him, doing ourselves what we have ordered him to do. To get our way we offer choices, of pain, incapacitation for something else he may want to do, loss of some thing or person he would like to retain; and these alternatives are then put to criticism, that they are in some way incommensurate, or that the presenting of them is unjustifiable.

The market also only presents choices. Exactly the same questions can be posed about those, since, as with choices presented by other legal institutions, we can do something about them (we think we can do so, else we would not argue about markets and alternatives to markets). Are the choices presented by a market to be measured in what an individual facing them gives up or is incapacitated from or suffers in pain? Are the alternatives presented less incommensurate than nonmarket choices? Are they more justifiable? We can and do discuss these questions, and nothing is advanced by erecting an a priori distinction based upon the presence of coercion. There can be what we call coercion in either, depending upon our answers and conclusions.

Of course an official giving orders can always kill the individual refusing (as markets do not except by starvation). But that rather defeats the purpose of force where the purpose is to force him to do something. A tacit recognition that actually there is always choice where orders are given may possibly be why at base we think the sanction of death so very different from other sanctions, including caging until natural death. Whatever puzzlement some or most of us may have about what happens to us after death or about how to think of another person who is dead, we may agree that death does seem to remove individuals' opportunity to make further choices in the world. The principle of the death penalty is therefore a challenge to the innate freedom of us all, in the most minimal sense in which freedom can be understood: there is a change of relationship between man and man of indubitable kind, rather than debatable degree. (So is there movement away from the market when starvation enters.) This may also be a reason—that choice is eliminated by eliminating the choosing person—why drugs and brainwashing are viewed with such particular horror, rather than as a benign solution to a problem, technological progress bringing us a nice substitute for torture. Indeed drugs, like death, are eventually seen as an admission of defeat, and (revealing our belief in the difference between the appearance of a person and the real) we attribute the act or speech of the brainwashed to *him* or *her* only if we are false to our language and thought, and in calmer moments we absolve the individual of responsibility for what is done or said. We do the same if the individual has been tricked or deceived, except again as we (always half-consciously) deceive ourselves (and we bring in law to supply the meaning of "deception" and evaluate degrees of disclosure, further obscuring any distinction between market and nonmarket forms of ordering).

In organized social life the alternative to attempts at coercion, or the presenting of choices, is an appeal to authority.

VI.26 ☙ *Responsibility for Evil*

Inside the prison lawyer and priest have had similar difficulties. Neither has fared well in presenting prisoners
with solitude as for their own good, or hunger, or hard
labor. Yet when all is said against the self-deception of
lawyers who enter the hell of punishment and participate
in erecting pure forms of the authoritarian, the fact of experience remains that there are in the world abysses of
emotional need, and of malevolence, that can consume
openness and kindness. Human defect itself, original sin,
the beast, presses against the presuppositions that make
caring functionally necessary to the work lawyers do.
Lawyers often think themselves alone with responsibility
for evil in the face of evil, while others wash their hands in
talk. But theology does not filter out evil and tragedy.
Though minister, rabbi, mullah, and priest do not have to
take action in quite the same way a lawyer must, they
think their hands no less involved in the world as it is.

VI.27 ☙ *The Forgetting of Forgiveness:*
An Exercise in the
Identification of the Nonlegal

Torture has been used over much of history and is used in
much of the contemporary world. In an effort to understand its use, it has sometimes been seen as an effort to
destroy the person without killing the body, to use agony
thus guided and in such a way that when the agony is over

the person cannot reconstitute herself—use it to make her do or say things, believe and desire things, think thoughts, which later she will be unable to cope with having done or thought. She will be shattered and forever incoherent, no longer a person.

If that is true, if torture could succeed in that effort, there is a consequence for all, and not only because agony can be experienced outside torture rooms by the civil and the protected and may even be experienced in some form by everyone at some time of life. If that *can* be, if one is so constituted that one can be thus destroyed, then one's substance, what one is, is only a contingency of history, a negative, an omission of an event, the consequence of agony not having happened or not having happened yet, a temporary absence of agony. Safe in one's house and going one's daily round while the police patrol, one exists at the sufferance of the torturer abroad: one's thought, belief, action, desire now are no more authentic and no more one's own than the thought, belief, desire, and action one would discover oneself capable of in agony. And so there is no authenticity, not now, not then. There is only a desire, thought, belief, action that happens to be now, and a desire, thought, belief, action that happens to be then, and one is not connected to either of them, no more now than then. A floating consciousness, a passive recipient of sensation, the "one" in the sentence is the integer "one" in a succession of integers "one" connected in the way integers and Euclidian points are connected, by their utter emptiness and sameness. And a sentence of human language is not different from a sentence of mathematics. What has been experienced as human was always only illusion.

There is underlying all this, the objective of torture so conceived and the evaluation of its success with its general implication, an assumption that may be far from what is actually believed and is against the faith that ultimately is what maintains existence. At the end of *1984*, the reader is led to assume that when Winston cries, "Do it to Julia," Winston is speaking the words. There is an assumption that sincerity of belief, actuality of desire, the thinking of a thought, are equivalent in agony and in the absence of agony. That is what makes the individual later unable to cope with having said, thought, believed, desired, or done the thing that in agony was said, thought, believed, desired, or done. But there may be no such equivalence. Thoughts, beliefs, desires, statements beyond their sounds, and actions that are more than movement, are none of them things that can be so pinned down. The coherence that the person is conceived to be and that is put forward as irretrievably lost is not the coherence of a person—the coherence of a person is not a coherence of such equivalent units but quite beyond particulars and never exhausted in what merely exists, even if each particular in succession were to be taken as a piece of evidence equal in weight.

But there is also throughout this entire speculation, and generally in contemporary nonlegal thinking about the substance of human existence, a forgetting of forgiveness. What is strikingly absent (to the lawyer) from the end of *1984* and its ending thought that the whole person could be permanently destroyed by a "Do it to Julia" response to torture, by a choice of self over love, by the revelation that in fact love fails, is forgiveness. The ending thought depends not just upon the failure of love but upon the absence of forgiveness. The old word for it was grace. In the same way, in so many discussions of Faust, Marguerite is left out. There may of course be, in the exclusion of any offer of forgiveness, a fear of acceptance of forgiveness stemming from a fear of acceptance of any sort, a recognition all too clearly of the fatalism implicit in any true and full acceptance—the incompatible implication of a sense of fate that is parental and not merely the alien happening of a mindless system. But the dependence of the ending thought upon the absence of forgiveness, in *1984* and elsewhere, does point up why it has been thought (for so long that it has become cliché and slipped away) that forgiveness, and perhaps even free forgiveness, underlies the constitution, the reconstitution, the very being of an acting, deciding, desiring, speaking, and believing person.

Forgiveness still has a place in legal thought, not free forgiveness, but true forgiveness for true repentance (both of which are hard enough). There has always been for the modern nonlegal a mystery in lawyers' atavistic incapacity to give up the punitive and to think wholly in terms of prevention, deterrence, and rehabilitation when criminality is raised, and, for the modern nonlegal, a mystery in the repeated discovery that in giving up the punitive, self-control is also given up in acting against the condemned, and respect for the condemned person is given up, and even the very notion that the condemned is a person. But agony, betrayal, self-betrayal, punishment, repentance, and forgiveness present themselves together in human experience as the experience of self, and, equally, as the experience of the presence of persons who are not destroyed before the body is destroyed.

VI.28 ☙ *Internalization*

At the height of the romance of science it used to be said, following Holmes, "Law considers only the external relations of human beings." Wholly inconsistent with legal practice and the evidence of lawyer's language, it was merely a reflection of mathematical thought in which units, like Euclidian points, must be fixed, passive, dead, molecular to fit a world in which all is process. This orientation of mind could not last. It was contrary not only to practice and language, but to the persistent demand that the law be obeyed because it is the law.

VI.29 ☙ *Argument Machines*

The similarity that can be perceived between lawyers and theologians is not between lawyer as hired gun and theologian as apologist. The similarity between lawyers and theologians is between lawyers who presuppose the law in their work and are in fact the source of statements of law in that vastly greater part of human affairs which does not and never could reach a court, and theologians who justify and order and make sense of the belief into which they have entered.

Hired guns are agnostic. They are argument machines. Outside the setting of adversary litigation lawyers are speakers of law. They take oaths to uphold the law. They can be disciplined for teaching false doctrine.

VI.30 ❧ *Deference*

"Here, this is what that is." "Is it so?" In a world of faith that something is there to be known but little direct assurance that it is known, one relies on reasons for believing that a thing is so. One such reason is that another thinks it so. As that reason acquires weight in one's own decision making there is what lawyers call deference to the other. Deference is making another's view a factor, as such, in one's own determination.

No one can escape deferring, not even a final arbiter. Courts most certainly expect deference from others on questions of law; but even on questions of law, courts coming to their own conclusions, taking factors into account in their own decision making on a matter, give deference to others. The practice is reflected in doctrinal formulas and worried over with some explicitness in the branch of lawyers' practice known in the United States as administrative law.

But the actuality of another's belief is critical to such reliance. Deference is to belief, but only to authentic belief in which a whole and responsible person is gathered.

VI.31 ❧ *Formality*

Connected to the legal phenomenon of office is the legal phenomenon of formality. Office and formality are as much problem as phenomenon. Lawyers try to curl their lip at "ritual" while they busy themselves with their own rituals—there is embarrassment, uneasiness, denial everywhere formality is encountered. But formality, or ceremony as it is also called, is the very province of those who toil in law, or in religion. Nonlawyers think lawyers and ecclesiastics the only people for whom formalities have immense or even serious significance.

As phenomenon, formality is a source, and so, as problem, it is a problem that cannot be ignored. Zimbabwe became independent at midnight on a day in April 1980, replacing the colony of Southern Rhodesia. It was announced that a Canadian delegation had gone to Rhodesia beforehand to meet with various ministers-elect, and that this meeting was the opening of relations with Zimbabwe "though of course," it was said, "formal ties could not begin until Zimbabwe came into existence." Fact, actuality, the truth of the matter, were contrasted with formality; illusory entities, *Zimbabwe* or *Rhodesia*, were contrasted with the solid hands of plenipotentiaries and ministers-elect touching. But there was ambivalence. Waiting until the time of Zimbabwe's "coming into existence" was called formality as if to dismiss it and imply that it wasn't there even then, really, in fact. But the formality was kept in the picture.

Why could not this formality of "coming into existence" at a precise time be completely cast aside? A no-nonsense man might say, oh, this is just a reflection of the necessity of some coordination in human affairs. The Canadians can't very well be allowed to start things off when they please. Suppose the Germans did not want to advance the date and scrupulously avoided relations until the midnight hour that day in April. There would be a great deal of wasteful quarreling and confusion. Quarreling and confusion are what these silly ceremonies are designed to prevent. That is their function, like white lines on a road. The no-nonsense man with academic interests might be pushed to say *Zimbabwe*, or *Rhodesia*, is a linguistic phenomenon only, to be used for convenience to refer to a host of other real things to which "it" can be entirely reduced.

But such a wave of the hand toward convenience or efficiency covers over the fact that it is the organization of minds that is being talked about, not just the organization of things or the wording of contracts. It is the introduction of authority that is being talked about. One reason there is force in the formality and actuality in the birth of Zimbabwe is that those ministers-elect to whom the Canadian delegation might speak were not officials until April 1980. It can be heard said that they were already "in fact" officials of Zimbabwe before that time at the end of the twelfth stroke of the midnight chimes, because there would be revolution if they did not take office; and they therefore had power to deal with the future at whatever point that determinative state of political forces came into existence. But this is to exclude entirely from consideration the phenomenon of legitimacy, which would, among other things, figure in the "existence" of a will to revolt. Successors in office may in fact feel less inclined to honor commitments (the very word *honor* is associated with office) "privately" made by ministers-elect before the hour of midnight. The de jure is not categorically separate from the de facto. Legitimacy, so peculiar to legal and religious thinking, is as much phenomenon in the world as problem. It is a force in the world.

VI.32 ❦ *Self-governance*

Some concrete outcome of a decision-making process, some particular decision, makes individuals weep and bleed. To them, and to their mobilization of protest against it or evasion of it, the response from political theory that the decision's legitimacy or authority lies in their own consent to it cannot convince beyond the simplest and most intimate situations. The substance of individual consent to a process of decision making, that may initially attach to and legitimate outcomes, thins as the process expands in scope and lengthens in time; it disappears when among the outcomes of the process is change in the decision-making process itself. And both liberal and post-liberal proposals of legitimation through participation or opportunity for participation founder upon the brevity of life.

There is no self-governance in the easy sense of it. If the measure of what is short and what is long is the span of the individual human life, the time required for change in any complex system or for any countering of change within it is more long than short, whether the system be industrial, natural, political, or intellectual. The effects of what is decided or achieved are not so much felt by the participants—their time is brief, they are aging rapidly, they disappear. The effects are felt by those yet to come who are not there to consent or participate. The benefits of a decision are conferred on others, the losses from it imposed on others. The children in school when desegregation was argued in *Brown* must be long grown up and gone before desegregation is realized; workers exposed to eradicable carcinogens in the workplace will have long retired before eradication of carcinogens can be expected.

What is argued and fought over and traded by those arguing and fighting and trading is less power over themselves than power over others, who cannot be given an opportunity to be present even by lottery. What is created in decision making by participants in the process can never be celebrated as individuals' self-governance—their own however contingent or arbitrary, legitimate whatever it is—for it is not their own lot but others' that is being fashioned.

Knowledge of this is part of knowledge of law and continuously reconfirmed by practice in the actual operations of the organized human world. This is the strength of law, this knowledge. All are trustees, participants and decision makers alike, arguing, deciding, approving, reacting. All is discussion of value, all is drawn forward by value, all identification through time with those who are affected in the future and those who have made decisions in the past is through value. And the central concern of law, atheoretical, pretheoretical, is then connection of value and responsible mind, for value not connected by mind to responsible belief is mirage, nothing, vanishing when questioned or sought.

Thus law is at work before any political theory, and after political theory is finished speaking: nothing is secured by any tracing of power or jurisdiction to a formal source or process, kingly, judicial, legislative, or popular. Against the constant fading of the conditions of authority is what comes from law that pushes toward the personal and a context of decision making in which the personal can be recognized, recognition of the personal being the only entry to the experience of authority.

The judge's promise to administer justice without respect to persons has a silent clause that can be assumed all know from their experience of the world—without respect to persons, it is, who are not persons, not embodiments of responsible mind. Law's promise is respect to persons. There is constant molding of structures for decision making, for challenge to decision making, and for review of decision making, that will permit a presumption of responsible mind to be entertained and the giving and the receiving of true deference to go forward, together with all in the operation of complex systems that depends upon such mutual respect.

The Expression of Responsibility

On the Organizational in

Legal Thought

There is and always has been a distinction between power and authority in the law of organization—in agency, partnership, the law of employment, the law of fiduciary duty, labor law, corporate law. Power is a negative thing, authority a positive. In exploring whether a person participates in control of an enterprise in any way that would make him, her, or it a "partner" rather than a "creditor," or a "general partner" rather than a "limited partner," courts and lawyers ask whether the aspect of control in question is protective, a veto over activities that might unduly harm the investment, or is instead one that may lead to initiation of action by the enterprise. (Shareholders of corporations, for example, traditionally have only a limited veto power, and the management of the business is lodged in a board of directors who delegate decision making to executive officers.)

A veto is a club, and the club is indeed a way not only of stopping others from doing things that they initiate, but of making them initiate things the club wielder wants initiated. The employer's position *over* an employee is linked to the employer's right to fire—to stop a flow of money and respect to the employee—and to countermand what the employee does. Just how precious the right to fire is thought to be is indicated by reaction to various legislative changes in the United States that have allowed factory workers to refuse to obey a foreman's order to do a thing if the order would be in violation of a valid safety regulation, without bringing down upon themselves dismissal for insubordination or disobedience. Allowing employees to protest, to appeal, to seek damages or fines or injunctions or arbitration, or to bargain over rules—any of these remedies against unsafe working conditions was, in the view of employers, quite different from a remedy allowing the worker to disobey an order without fear of being fired. That went to the heart of organized enterprise.

Or so at least it seemed to those giving orders in organizations. But the heart of organization is not struck in this. All that happens is that employers' power is brought more in line with their authority. They may have thought that it was their power—their negative power—that enabled them to cause others to take initiatives into the unknown future for the sake of the joint enterprise. But it was not power, certainly not power alone, but their authority.

It is authority that sees positive orders being carried out, or any work that is beyond "working to rule," a phrase in labor law synonymous with stopping an organization from functioning. With recognition of authority the one who is ordered recognizes the other who is ordering as a source of positive guidance, and insofar as his own initiative and willing cooperation are required to make the enterprise work, he puts his imagination to the task. It is authority, not power, that releases imagination and initiative in the service of the goals of joint enterprise (service, a word drawn from hierarchy containing within it the still active thought that the [servant] is an extension of the [master], joined, not a separate individual any more than an individual arm is separate from an individual's body, and joined such that the [master] is also an extension of the [servant] when the [servant] seeks a goal).

Thus in legal determinations of authority (of whether an official was acting within his charter or beyond or against it in giving the order he did), law is doing what its remedies classified as such cannot do, which is to evoke initiative and willing obedience. For in the train of finding that one has authority and another has a fiduciary duty or duty of loyalty or duty of obedience (all phrases found in the law of organization) comes at least the thought that there should be willing obedience, not just that one may be hurt if he does not obey, as he might have to pay damages if he breaks a contract, but that it is right that he should obey, that carrying forward is the normal thing and not carrying forward is a thought entertained only when something is wrong. Organized life, except on a most rudimentary level, would not be possible otherwise.

VII.2 🔊 *Identity and Property*

"My hand," you say, and you speak somewhat of ownership. This is *my* hand, you would say, if someone suggested taking it for his own. But with your "my" you speak also of identity. The two—ownership, identity—attract one another in the mind. They can be kept apart only with effort, matched by equal effort in explanation of their intended separation to a listener. "My hand" is part of me, one with me. A full belief in incarnation would hold *me* not separate from it any more than "my belief" would be separate from me.

Ownership and identity themselves open out, as well as to one another, and law is an avenue into their further connections in life and action. Suppose a wall with only a hand in front, on the wall, and a voice behind it. "Who's hand is this?" someone asks, and you, if the voice is your voice, reply, "Mine." The hand balls into a fist and bloodies a nose close to it. "Who is responsible for this hand and what it has done?" You might prefer to stay silent, or say, "Not me." But you have associated yourself with it, and the loss represented by the blood—this that someone wishes had not happened—may be translated into another liquid form and flow from you in the workings of the world. The hand's strength is sought by more than one, to help in one or another enterprise. "Who is responsible for this hand?" they ask. "Who is in charge here?" "I am," you say. "I am responsible, I have control of this hand, power over what is mine." And if your identity with this hand is perceived and accepted, there is acquiescence in your determinations. The hand comes to hold a gold coin and someone asks, "Whose gold is this?" "Mine," you answer. "What my hand grasps is mine, for we are not separate, not different"; and like the loss that flowed from you before, the gain into which the gold can be translated will flow to you.

With the taking of the gain you will have traversed the three aspects of ownership with which lawyers work—liability, control, and profit. These are combined also through the term "responsible" which figures so in discourse whenever ownership is pursued. The owner stands behind what is a property of his as behind the wall. He suffers the risks that are realized. He is responsible, he pays rather than someone else paying, and if he does not pay, a question arises whether that which causes the loss is to be perceived as his own and he the owner. Equally with power: if the hand is out of control the one behind the wall is thought not responsible, and not just for purposes of shifting losses, but in perception and in the central sense of human responsibility. With the split of one entity into more than one, with disintegration, with disappearance of a center which aspires and protects and to which the appeal of value is directed in argument and plea, the legal treatment of insanity enters. The event in the world can no longer be traced and connected to value in that direction, and this connection between event and value being law's thrust and work, another direction to another source will be sought. But again, if one who claims ownership has no power or control, and decisions are made by another or by no one, the question arises (as if naturally) whether he is owner. In the case of the hand the question arises when its motion may not be his own. And separated as he is, and immune from blame, the connection of profit to him also falters, simply in itself—profit does not flow on to him because it meets a gap—but also because the search for blame and the search for deserts follow parallel paths and praise and blame and gain and loss converge upon a center were value lives. "Who should receive the reward?" "The one responsible for the good achieved."

It has been the constant dream of legal planners, for clients who come to them, to separate control and profit off, and leave losses behind. And it has been the history of law that the three aspects of ownership are pushed back together, or if they are separated, that ownership fades from perception. This has been the perennial difficulty, for the planner, of limited liability. Ownership begins leaking away, and when control is removed also into the entity that is liable without limitation, which is seen with the growth of business corporations, it becomes difficult to think, however strenuous the attempt, of the entity that is responsible and that bears the risk and initially grasps the good, as anything but owner, or to think of the payments it makes as flows of profit rather than as transfers. And this is pushed by and at the same time reflects the dissolution of an identity—in the mind—between two entities (like hand and head) that can be spoken of differently.

The "my" that looks to identity can run in two directions on the slope of ownership. "My master," "my employer," "my company," says the servant or employee. And the word "possession" subtly blends fusion and control when the one below is a sentient being and says he or she is "possessed" by that which, if it spoke, would point to the sentient being so infused and say "that is my own." But then the aspects of ownership begin their work on the mind. If the possessed are sentient beings, like employees (once called hands) who say "my company," and if they are perceived as at risk and paying in their lives for losses, and if they take gains that are due them, and blame, then to the degree they are part of the entity to which they address their humble "my" and to the degree the sentience of their being is not obscured, decisions on behalf of the entity will be decisions made with them in mind. Then the slope of ownership levels or reverses, and their "my" becomes the active "my" of the owner rather than the passive of the possessed.

VII.3 ☞ *The Merger of Practical and Intellectual in Organizational Law*

A typology of five sorts of social organization is set out by Frank Knight, looked to as founder by the American "Chicago School" of economics (and claimed as source also by opposing schools): (1) organization based upon status and tradition, denominated the caste system; (2) the autocratic or militaristic system (which Knight notes is very much in evidence in modern society, within the family, in the internal organization of business units, and in the internal organization of government itself); (3) anarchism (purely voluntary association, maintained without any giving or taking of orders, or any threat of compulsion or restraint by force); (4) democracy or democratic socialism (a compromise between the autocratic and the anarchistic, the autocrat in democracy being a majority of citizens); and (5) the exchange system (variously referred to as the competitive system, the capitalistic system, or the system of private property and free exchange). The fifth and last of these, the exchange system, is the one he takes to be especially characteristic of modern Western nations. "Its most interesting feature is that it is automatic and unconscious; no one plans or ever planned it out, no one assigns the participants their roles or directs their functions. Each person in such a system seeks his own satisfaction without thought of the structure of society or its interests; and the mere mechanical interaction of such self-seeking units organizes them into an elaborate system and controls and coordinates their activities . . . [with] results which are . . . truly wonderful."

The exchange system is subdivided by Knight into the handicraft system and the free enterprise system. The difference between the two arises from the introduction in the latter of what Knight calls the business unit, or the enterprise. The business unit, which transforms a pure market exchange system into "free enterprise," produces, buys, and sells all commodities in the pure form of free enterprise. The business unit is "made up of individuals (among whom the man who sells to or buys from it may himself be included) but is distinct from these individuals." No individual or small group of individuals can be said to produce anything. The worker owns no thing of economic significance, no means of production, and the worker produces no thing; in free enterprise the worker has only labor or services to sell. Commodities the worker buys from a business unit with the fruits of the labor or services the worker has to sell to a business unit.

Exchange, the market, is not a set of reciprocal relationships between individuals, but between individuals and business units, or between business units themselves.

In addition to eliminating exchange between individuals, introduction of the business unit reintroduces the giving and taking of orders into social organization. Orders are now given and taken within the business unit. What Knight does not go on to note explicitly—he is troubled by it elsewhere—is that the dropping out of individuals from at least one side of the various equations of exchange radically changes the theory of the exchange or capitalistic or private property system. This is the theory of perfect competition, an invisible hand organizing society. What persons do under that theory, as a descriptive matter, and what they must do if the system is to work, is seek their own satisfactions without thought of the interests of others. If the person is a business unit, however, the question inevitably arises: What satisfactions does, should, or must it seek? Its employees' satisfactions? There may at the very least be a conflict between employee interest in employment security and employee interest in immediate income. Its shareholders' satisfactions? But the interests of some shareholders may be in short-term profit and of others in long-term profit; a shareholder may be a group of employees, with its employee interests, or a church, with the interests of a church. Its pensioners' concerns? Its creditors' concerns? The concerns of those whom it physically affects? The concerns of its country of residence or country of origin? There is need for decision, of what the interests of the business unit are. Management may initially decide, but management's decision poses the question whether management in making its decision is seeking the business unit's interests and goals. Someone must "assign participants their roles," and once that is begun, deciding what the unit is, what it seeks, whom it represents, who is a member of it and who is not, what expenditure is to be deemed a cost to be subtracted in calculating profit and what expenditure is to be deemed a distribution of profit after calculation of it, the invisible hand becomes very visible. It is the hand of the law. It takes physical form in the lawyer's hand.

This creates great difficulty for capitalist or private property "systems," which assume that there need be and indeed can be no inquiry into ends or into what actors take into account in coming to a decision. The introduction of the entity causes an intellectual difficulty. It is sometimes called a "crisis of legitimacy," and it is that because, again, the hand is the hand of a lawyer. Lawyers and judges must justify what they do. If they cannot make sense of what they do, they cannot justify it, and if they cannot justify what they do, they tend to become paralyzed at their very core. The system that so depends on them then tends not to work: thus does the intellectual merge, in organizational law, with the practical.

VII.4 ❧ *Disclosure and the Market*

Many believe deception is not intrinsically or conceptually associated with a market. Modern proponents of making the market the source of all organization do not quarrel with the historian Fernand Braudel on this point. But if this is so, that deception is not intrinsic to the operation of a market, it undermines any free market theory that uses economic man as premise and goal of public policy. For law is looked to for protection of economic man from deception—economic man must have more from law than mere protection against the breaking of his contracts and the taking of his property (in his novel *Nihilon* Alan Sillitoe has provided a useful survey of a society where it is the deceiver who is protected rather than the deceived). In law there is no understandable divide between a prohibition of deception and a requirement of candor or full disclosure, as analytic developments in the law of investment securities demonstrate. There is nothing economic theory can do about this. And a requirement of candor dissolves economic man into brother man.

VII.5 ❧ *Abstract Evolution*

Mice in a cage. They are in constant motion, constantly stretching up as if to seek a way out to Freedom. Yet unless you have escaped the full embrace of modernity you will have no great concern for the mice: if they were outside the cage, what would they do but seek the food that is now there for them, and make and feed more mice? Their constant motion is purposeless. Their lives are purposeless—unless survival and increase are misnamed purpose.

Survival and increase, world without end. Quite empty these are. But familiar. These are the objects of man's activity in the eyes of the classical economist or political scientist, of life itself in the eyes of the classical biologist. These comprise indeed the very definition of life in science. Being empty, they can be translated from objectives into consequences and thus link the study of life and man with the study of physical science. It is clever, the way the economic and biological visions fit together. Which came first? Seeing man as seeking only survival and increase, more and more aggrandizement, preferably of an abstraction, more dollars, genes, power, swallowing up, spreading over the whole world if not stopped from without? Or seeing animate nature as without purpose? Is the view taken of animate nature derived from the view of man that economists and political theorists adopted, or is this view taken of man derived from the scientific view? Evolution emerged after economics. "At last," say minds of the mid-nineteenth century, "we have unity." Survival and increase can encompass animate nature as well as social man.

There is so much else affecting perception. But is it not striking how despite all its various windings formal thought should have come to this convergence? And the method of the law is set against this, and always has been.

The lions in their pride play and blink in the sun. The lions are ignored, or there is a drive, a *desire*, to reduce them and eliminate them—to transform them into increase and survival, to empty abstraction. But the lions still play.

VII.6 ❧ *Regress in Legal Calculation*

Lawyers long so to escape the problem of authority and obedience. They are the ones sent off to wrestle with it, because they are lawyers. On their way, from time to time they divert themselves by speculating upon the possibility of making all statements identified as statements of law into mere presentations of choices, with lawyers' own professional concern being only the prices to be put on choices.

They soon stumble over complexity and the limits of language. But they also face a regress. They do not know how to stop. Have you designed and installed an industrial process that is injuring workers? That means you have a choice, between redesigning the process and paying damages. Is there then an obligation to pay damages? No. That is a matter of choice also, a matter of someone saying to you, pay the damages you are ordered to pay—or, no, not ordered: the sum that is offered to you as a choice—or, if you do not pay, you may choose instead to pay the sanction—no, let us not call a "sanction" this double or triple of the old price damages represented, which will be set as the alternative to paying damages.

But there is an alternative to that alternative, on and on. At each stage there will be a proceeding, and at each stage the world will be different. The pursued will always hope his pursuers will tire, or that time will bury their interest in him. He owes them nothing.

At some point speculation halts. There is thought of punishment. But lawyers are more than uncomfortable in stating that a man ought to participate willingly and with imagination and resource in effecting his own punishment, tighten his handcuffs when loose, not touch the extra ration mistakenly put on the prison plate. Lawyers' thought then returns to some obligation at the start, to the authority and the obedience with which inevitably they must wrestle.

VII.7 ✒ *Linguistic Grab*

To say lawyers in law firms are "employees" or "human capital" in a "service industry" is an example of linguistic grab in discussion of law and legal institutions. Even an "associate lawyer" in a law firm who is member of the bar and officer of the court only begins to be described as an "employee." "Employee" comes no more naturally there than it comes naturally to say a priest is an employee of the Roman church or of the pope.

It is for ease, and for the simple delight of appropriation, that something talked about in human language is pressed into the terms of a special vocabulary. Aspects of the experience talked about that are not evoked in the new vocabulary are pared away—some who make linguistic grabs consciously hope that talking long about experience wholly in language that is designed to have no place for various of its aspects will change the experience, which was the hope for Newspeak in *1984*. But with or without any such deliberate plan, what threatens in linguistic grab is precisely its totalitarian character.

Language that limits rather than expanding expression is trivializing. What distinguishes economic analysis (for example) that is serious, by contrast to the trivializing, is something equivalent to self-awareness, which is perceptible to lawyer and lay reader alike. There is full awareness of the temptation even the innocent face to grab for ease and the delight of appropriation. There is also in non-trivializing economic analysis, where law is concerned, some live consciousness of the limit all law-laden disciplines must eventually come up against—the circle they traverse—in understanding the discipline of law, and in making their own contribution to pushing the discipline of law toward self-awareness by illuminating buried or neglected aspects of experience.

VII.8 ❧ *Corporate Crime*

The application of the criminal law to business corporations has one overriding function. It counters, as can nothing else, the temptation to define the purpose of the corporate entity as the maximization of money profit.

Purpose pervades all aspects of the legal analysis of entities. It governs legal decisions on the capacities of individuals, whether when they act they act for the entity. It governs individuals' decisions whether to act when acting for the entity. As a purpose, profit maximization externalizes all value and translates all decision into calculation of advantage, introducing the implacable into an already competitive world and rendering law itself, law that conceives the entity and continues to make it conceivable, an object not just of some manipulation but total manipulation.

Always in the air of thought, a playful postulate of political, economic, and biological theory alike, profit maximization is only of real moment in law in analysis of business corporations, which are not, analytically or as a matter of fact, themselves agents of decision-making individuals. The temptation to profit maximization is handled routinely in the human breast; it appears so rarely in pure form in individuals that its appearance is marked as a sign of disintegration and insanity. The cycle of life and the looming of death are alone usually sufficient to dissolve it. But it can be abstracted out and given to a corporate entity, and the life of the corporate entity can be insulated from the natural cycle of the life of an individual. Thus entry of criminal law; and of a criminal law, moreover, unstained by the bloody rope or the twisted flesh of the prison.

Criminal law is the internalization of value. There is no crime in any set of facts, no matter how much hurt there is in them, unless there is a criminal state of mind. Causing death is common, murder is not; what distinguishes death from murder is mind. The criminal state of mind, raised as a possibility by the applicability of the criminal law, is precisely the externalization of value defined and protected by the criminal law, calculation as to value, manipulation of it, coldness toward it—precisely the state of mind contemplated for the profit-maximizing decision maker.

Prescription drug safety or worker safety are not achieved by simple prohibitions but by ingenious devices and institutional design. The criminal penalties that appear in connection with prescription drugs or worker safety have another function, which is to speak to the agent of the entity who is asking, "What is my duty, how am I to think about actions I may take on behalf of the entity?" and to speak to the lawyer for the entity, advising agents of the entity in the large and in the particular. What is spoken and said is that for the business corporation and agents thereof, as for individuals in other situations in social life, substantive values are ultimately to figure in decision as such and in and for themselves, and are not, ultimately, matters of indifference to be left entirely to the concern of others.

That this needs particularly to be declared in corporate law gives reason for applying the criminal law more broadly to corporations than to individuals. And the reasons for real hesitation in invoking the criminal law—the awful pain of its penalties against the body, the petty tyranny of its application to the weak and poor, the depressive effect of its threats in the psychology of everyday life, which is often named an interference with liberty or with the sense of freedom—have not the same force when the potential defendant is a corporate entity. The vagueness endemic to the criminal law in the specification of what is or is not to be done becomes less a defect, more a protection of its efficacy against a calculating mentality, including that of the litigating lawyer.

Next to this, this declarative and structuring function, the penalties and sanctions criminal law brings to bear are of secondary importance. Criminal law is internal to corporate law, part of the defining and enabling that corporate law and lawyers are engaged in—the instituting of the modern economy, its very peopling. Criminal law does not swoop in from the outside to affect what has already been set in motion. Certainly there is deterrence in some sanctions; but in the absence of pain, and with fines set as for individuals, or set with attention to their effect on individuals who are dependent on the corporation, the consequences of criminal conviction have historically been scoffed at and bundled into cost-benefit formulas. Recent developments, attaching civil liability to criminal conviction and multiplying civil damages by some punitive factor, introducing supervision (as in probation or other semi-incarcerative measures for individuals), and, above all, conditioning corporate continuation in licensed activ-

ities on "fitness" and "character" (to which criminal conviction has always been thought to speak where individuals are involved), have made the actual outcomes of actual
criminal prosecutions factors to be reckoned with by corporate decision makers. And the criminal law can work,
in this sense. Decisions about its scope, appropriateness,
and application are not troubled by any real fear of its im-
potence where corporations are involved.

But each development in the effectiveness of the sanctions that are directed at corporate entities meets the web
of dependencies that surround the corporate entity and
with which the entity itself may be identified. These fila-
ments of connection are usually of such extent that they
cannot be ignored, as the family of the individual convict
is ignored; and increasing sensitivity to systemic effects
generally, economic or ecological, has made the unin-
tended and undesirable side effects of corporate sanctions
factors to be reckoned with by public decision makers. It
is thus in another sense that the criminal law works,
where corporations are involved: before sanctions, addressing the very nature of decision making on behalf of
corporations, speaking to what factors are to be taken into
account and with what weight and what factors are not to
be taken into account, what good faith consists of, what is
authorized and what is not, and touching moreover all
those further organizational and institutional decisions
that determine whether a substantive determination will
be implemented—what is to be taken to another level in
decision-making structures, or what is cause for dissocia-
tion, or what is disclosable and what not, or what is defen-
sible in preventive, protective, and self-protective activity.

Analytically there are other ways to address these questions, and they are addressed at other places in corporate
law. If the interests of those holding securities entitling
them to participate in some way in the equity left on

liquidation (at the end of the corporation's activities) are to be focused upon with special prominence in corporate decision making during corporate life, then there can be exploration in legal argument of what those interests are and how, when they conflict, they are to be weighed or sought. If the universe of such interests is not the sole focus, there can be exploration of what other groups, from employees to customers, are to be admitted into the category of those whose claims are not costs to be minimized, and exploration of how their interests and claims are to be defined. Analytically these interests, groups, or claims are often surrogates for values protected by the criminal law, and might enter the thinking of corporate agents with much the same life and sense of right. But such democratic or communitarian capitalism is yet inchoate and may remain so for as many centuries as the problems of organizational law have so far persisted.

From the earliest time corporations have arguably been subject to the criminal law; certainly through this century they have. In the broadest frame of reference, what is irrational and a stumbling block to those who are sure they know what the corporate entity is may, for the empirical, be critical evidence of the place of entity in the mind and, indeed, the nature of the person created by each individual.

VII.9 ❧ *Organization and Obligation*

Are Ulysses before the Cyclops and the modern corporate briber in different situations? The moral issue is in part empirical, as it may be when one confronts the success of the amoral and waits to see what will happen further. Is the human world in fact organized (not by "rules" but by thought and value), or is it essentially disorganized? If one really loses belief that the world is organized beyond its physical organization, then competition and its consequences must acquire a central place in one's thinking about what one should do (and the relative effectiveness of "law enforcement" becomes a moot point, for law enforcement agencies too have become competitors). Competition, that is entailed in individuality itself: disease and the locust are nothing more, nothing worse than a form of competition among individuations of physical systems. In the absence of anything more connecting one to others than connects one to the virus and the locust, one's stance will be the familiar stance one takes, without guilt, toward the virus and the locust.

VII.10 ❧ *The Individual as an Organization*

The notion of responsibility for what others do extends from what they do at one's behest, which is a simple notion effectively fusing their hands with one's own as a pen in one's hand is treated as an extension of it, to what they do in one's behalf. As to the latter, one has a positive duty to monitor it and intervene in it, and one's omissions become as important as one's commissions. Positive duty then extends on to focus upon the structure and system by which one's multihanded capacities are implemented. If harm occurs with regularity, the person responsible, causally connected to it but connected through the acts of others, is charged with shifting personnel to different positions, or dismissing personnel, or retraining them, or setting up relationships between them that make it possible for them to achieve better results working within their assigned roles, or changing their assigned roles, or ultimately even amending the objects of joint action.

Where many individuals are involved they can rarely operate by behest. They must operate in behalf according to statements, not specific orders, and the simple notion of responsibility, that one commits what another does at one's command (even though that other is an independent human being and not inanimate or brute), fades in importance: the person responsible becomes involved with text and authority, and the hierarchically subordinate reader must at the least approach the reading of guiding statements not with an attitude that effectively denies authority. In general, therefore, responsibility for what is done by others beyond the simple situation can be divided and put at two levels, the level that introduces positive duties and the level that introduces systemic concerns. And the second level, of systemic concerns, can be usefully divided into layers. The arrangement of relations between multiple agents working together and between the agents and oneself is one layer. This merges with, but is separable from, redefinition of the roles or offices or functions of the various agents. This merges with, but again is separable from, the shifting of individuals among roles, functions, or offices, of which dismissal might be viewed as an instance. Finally, there is responsibility for amending or redefining the very goals of one's own responsibility, as one has experience with the possibility of achieving them all.

Much of what is required is examining results and comparing them with objects. There seems to lie in this at first blush a difference between responsibility for what one does personally oneself and responsibility for what one does through others. But the difference does not stand, and this may be thought to raise a difficulty either in personifying individuals or in conceiving organizations as only systems. Perhaps, all of what can be said about responsibility in multi-individual organizations can be translated into the situation of the individual alone. If one could not have predicted what could go wrong, it would seem one can be held truly responsible only for not correcting the system after the wrong has occurred (unless one could have prevented it directly by intervention as it emerged). Individually, we are continuously exploring our own capacities, in child raising, sports activity, domestic arrangements for sanitation or food supply, even friendship. We are not thought responsible for the results except as a consequence of the prior occurrence of results. This is reflected in the formal doctrines and informal notions of one bite of the apple, first offense, and the like. (Where these are not invoked, money alone is usually at stake and it appears possible in large measure to "correct" or wipe out the situation, that is, to stop the future effects of past action.) Although there is a sense in which one is responsible for what one says or does, simply because one says or does it (and it is evidence of who one is), the truth is that one does not know who one is. Who one is unfolds. Furthermore, one can change oneself. The person behind the person who one is, that ever-present second person, is not responsible until after the fact—of who one is—is known.

Indeed, in the case of responsibility for one's own acts, one is very much in the position of obeying oneself, just as, in organizations, individuals are in a position of obeying or following the statements of the person responsible. The functioning of any large system depends upon authority; one must equally have authority for oneself. When one does not, one is disintegrated, irresponsible, and, in others' eyes, dangerous, as is any organization without authority. And as in organizations, authority is not a will that is a force and fact of nature. In organizations it can be seen that the person responsible is no unitary individual; the person responsible in law is the personified organization.

A comparison between the individual and an organization works both ways. One must look carefully at the analogies before one thinks an organization is very different. Such a look might end with a conclusion that we ourselves are systems, but as to that, we can be rather more certain. We know we are not. We know there is a person behind the person that has been revealed in the past, and even behind the person being revealed in the present.

VII.11 ᛣ *Feigned Principals*

Henry VII insisted that all copies of Parliament's act Titulus Regius, the warrant of his predecessor's legitimacy, be destroyed, and that his new Parliament vote to repeal Titulus Regius without reading it.

The repeal of Titulus Regius was never to be taken as a statement of Henry VII only, with Parliament speaking as he might order a pen to make a statement for him. That would not have had the legal effect desired. Whose statement then was it? Mayor Daly in Chicago in the 1960s is said to have insisted that Chicago aldermen receive the text of resolutions only after voting on them. In the constitutional test of the so-called "legislative veto" in the 1980s, the Supreme Court noted—or a clerk writing for the Court noted—that the texts of the veto resolutions overturning the attorney general's administrative decisions had not been made available at the time of the congressional vote.

The feigned principal, ancient and modern, is particularly the lawyer's problem. A feigned principal may be an agent in fact who has no authority because the actual principal has no authority, or the feigned principal may be feigned and not true by reason of its own delegation. Henry's Parliament could be either. Senator Dole of Kansas once disarmingly admitted that neither he nor other members of his Senate Finance Committee wrote or had read a Committee report accompanying a tax bill, which was to be used thereafter in interpretation of the bill. Anyone (and everyone) utters language he does not mean and that is not his whenever he issues as his own a piece of writing he has delegated to another, and often one knows in what specific ways one does not mean it, but does not change it for reasons of time and other claims on one's resources.

Feigned principals are so particularly a lawyer's problem because lawyers do not simply paste statements by feigned principals in scrapbooks as curiosities, on the order of words traced by tufts of moss or by shells washed up on a beach or by branches against a sky. Lawyers grapple with such statements in constant work with the law of agency, contract, and organizations. An individual in an exchange relationship, contracting or engaged in legislation, says what he knows he does not want to say, agrees to language he does not mean, in exchange for another's saying what that other does not want to say and does not mean. An individual is bound by the words of an agent though he has never seen those words when the agent signs a contract or makes an undertaking or waives a claim. An individual is bound as a member of an organization to words he has never seen. The separation of speech from sight, mouth from mind is a common condition of the lawyers' world.

That a separation of speaker and spoken is a common condition does not make lawyers yearn any the less for authenticity.

VII.12 & *Bargaining and Bureaucracy*

It is the text, it is language, that confronts both bargaining and bureaucracy when bargaining and bureaucracy are put at the foundations of social organization. Language is their common problem.

For example, interpolation of words in a text through negotiation without candor pulls a textual situation close to the situation that emerges from the making of "legislative histories" of statutes. In the assembling of the collection of explanatory reports, testimony, and speeches that will accompany the statute to publication and be designated the "legislative history" of the statute, various passages, qualifications, and reasons are added, which one or another lobbyist would like to see included, in the hope that by chance some such "inputs" will survive any review of the final text of the legislative history by those ultimately issuing it and, surviving, will sit there to serve his client's purposes later when his client's lawyer argues to a judge the meaning of the legislation. Lawyers do not think themselves engaged in anything serious when they argue in litigation from such legislative history. They know they are engaged in a game.

The same can be observed in opinions written bureau-cratically by the great administrative agencies. They too contain passages and qualifications that one or another part of the agency has wanted to see included for its own purposes, in the hope, well founded, that one or another such "input" will survive review by the commissioners who sign the opinions.

In ordinary contracts (a contract being the basic in-stance of a text bargained out without candor), it is pri-marily flow of money, somewhat reversible, that is at stake. Not so with statute, regulation, or opinion: there, what is at stake may be of a different order, and not reversible; and, there, the consequences of a manipulative stance on the part of a listener—judge or citizen—in its quality per-fectly matching the knowledgeable lawyer's stance—can expand to a crisis of legitimacy in social organization.

VII.13 ❧ *Proper Names*

We say "Justice White" wrote an opinion. But of what is that "Justice White" a name? Is it the name of a mind? Or is it the name of some rooms (lawyers call them cham-bers)? You can imagine the rooms to which the name "Justice White" might refer. There they are, with a closed door. Suddenly the door opens—or is it opened?—just a crack, and out pops—or is it tossed?—an object. You pick it up. It turns out to be a roll of paper with words on it. The room is dark behind the crack as you stand there holding the roll. Then the door closes again. People do go in and out of the rooms, among them an individual human being who is also known by the name White. But you do not

know what they do, if anything, all those people there inside those rooms. The opinion "issues from the *cham-
bers*," in lawyers' parlance.

What do you do with the object in your hand? Do you
really *read* it? If you do, what faiths, what assumptions,
do you reveal?

VII.14 🔊 *Grecian Urns*

There are ways works of law may be essentially different
from works of art.

One might think that even in a crude imitation of a
work of art there is at least the gross form of the original,
enough of it to discern and be guided by, just as there is in
a poor performance of a score or a script. And one might
think the same to be true in law, in a judicial opinion, for
instance, that is an imitation of what a judge writes put
together by a delegee who does not believe and is not
responsible.

But law may not be a performance, since the script is
changed forever, in what would in law be analogous to
performance, because the elements of the script are living.
Though the mysterious attraction of art, its authority, is a
matter of constant debate, there is at least the possibility
that art is in the settled and smiling. Law never is. In law
there may not be even the theoretical possibility of the
perfect imitation (put aside the problem of method, the
application and attention that must be sustained by a presupposition of authenticity), which there may be thought
to be in art, since in law, as in life and the detection of a
phony person or the phony in a person by a child, *what* is
being imitated is not *there* and settled.

VII.15 ✿ *Functions of Process*

While it is possible one can persuade oneself into delusion by imperceptible stages and eventually forget entirely what one once knew, particularly if one's pain or need is great, we are not alone. We are in a position to check one another. The young who do not face death so immediately are in a position to check the old as they move toward death and become obsessed with it. Literature is such a check, if it is seriously engaged.

This is also what process in legal decision making distinctively contributes, the mutual checking of participant by participant to prevent decision based upon delusion.

VII.16 ✿ *Office*

When one is installed in office one is not passive, receiving only, listening only, being told new things about oneself. Accepting office is an act too, in which one says something about oneself. Accepting office, one does not simply receive power. One asserts responsibility. An adult adopting a child declares willingness to care for the child as well as willingness to receive parental power, and, with both, willingness to be judged according to his or her fulfillment of responsibility. Adoption of a child is not the purchase of a slave. Adoption is inextricably connected with abandonment of an authoritarian position toward other beings. Accepting office to make statements of law is much the same.

Office, that very peculiar phenomenon of law, contributes to the possibility of realizing the presuppositions of authority, of which responsibility is one. In the pragmatics of social organization this is a function of office, its primary function.

VII.17 ❧ *Access to Texts and the Dilemma of Office*

Religious institutions, even viewed most skeptically by the most otherworldly or the most worldly, cannot be thought generated only by the necessity of shelter or revenue. Religious institutions have among their purposes more than increase in revenue or the building of imposing monuments. So do the institutions of law. Ecclesiastical disputes are almost always in part about the design of institutions that will make theology possible. Disputes in constitutional or administrative law are almost always in part about the design of institutions that will make law possible.

For example, the issues associated with diminishing or eliminating a central institution, or retaining it and strengthening its voice, have been the subject of centuries of nonsecular thought which continues now in secular discussions of the establishment of a central point in human society continent by continent or worldwide. Many of the problems of multiple jurisdictions and federalism faced in the European Community, in Canada, or indeed still in the United States may be traced in the history of Protestantism; and Protestantism has always had the Roman church as a backdrop, and a continuing history of Catholicism that makes it at least a matter for wonder whether the presence of a supreme organ in the Roman church has something to do with the vigor of that church and its importance in the thinking of whole populations in the modern world, from South America to Eastern Europe.

But whatever the institutional arrangements, each individual may become an authority where each individual has direct access to the texts—as is the case in law, and as was suddenly made possible in the Catholic church when the Bible was translated from the learned languages into the vernacular. The difference between the literate citizen and the late Justice Hugo Black, who carried a copy of the Constitution in his hip pocket for use in arguments, is then whatever difference there is that arises from office itself.

Individuals with access to texts may be ranged as a body against courts. Or ordained ministers, priests, rabbis, mullahs may face one individual who says that they are wrong and he or she is right, quite as much as courts face the defiant individual who says that she has disobeyed the order of another individual (who may indeed be a judge) but not the command of the law. It is, after all, not just litigants' parochial interest (to use a phrase that mixes the legal and the ecclesiastical), but conviction that they are right and must prevail that drives them on up the appellate hierarchy and, after the highest court has spoken, into relitigation if not barred by any of the various doctrines lawyers use to stop a particular person from continuing to argue a point. It is this, and not just interest, that may lead legislators to seek to pass a statute overruling a decision of the highest court on a point, or to the assembling of councils within churches after hierarchical authorities within the church have spoken.

Against such conviction, undermining it from within, is the phenomenon of office. It has been the fact that councils of the Roman Catholic church are swayed by

what the pope advises them he thinks the text of a doctrine should be, and legislators in Congress are known to
hesitate before they undertake to overrule the Supreme
Court. Quakers handle the effect of office and the weight
due to the statements of those in office in one way, Jews in
another, Presbyterians in yet another. In law the problem
appears daily at the most basic level, namely the attempt
to reserve the practice of law, outside as well as inside the
courtroom, to those who have been admitted to the bar,
and are subject to its discipline, having gone through a
ceremony in which they are personally presented to a
judge sitting in his court.

There are a variety of material or "pragmatic" reasons
for restricting the making of statements of law to the ordained, just as there are a variety of pragmatic reasons for
respecting the conclusions of judges on an issue. Not the
least of them is the methodological implication of the
place of written texts in making authoritative statements
of law, certainly in large societies, which may require
some devoting their full working time to the texts. But
after the pragmatic reasons and countervailing explanations (such as the profitable monopolization of an economic service) are done, there remains in law as in religion a remarkably strenuous emphasis on office, which
produces issues that are resolved without much conscious
understanding of what is guiding or being taken into account in their resolution. Why, for example, should it
matter that it be the commissioned, the elected, the ap-
pointed who makes a decision rather than someone to
whom he or she quietly confides the task? Commissioners of agencies in the United States come very close to
sending their assistants to vote and write for them, as do
judges their clerks and legislators their staffs. We know
more from Kafka what it is in this that troubles—how authority is affected by what some are moved to call in sani-

tized terms "unauthorized delegation"—than we learn from professional discussion of it.

Office remains a phenomenon in the modern world, and of the modern world—it is not an anachronism. But as it has continued part of human experience, it may have become more rather than less a mystery.

VII.18 ✒ *Law and Equity*

There is an imperiousness about lawyers who want to know the true reasons and look for substance rather than form. Better perhaps to have forms, designed to make objectives chosen for "ulterior" or illicit reasons difficult to achieve, and then, in respecting form, to maintain the illusion that the thing done is what it seems to be—as in much corporate practice, particularly the practice of corporate reorganization. Illusion may thus be pressed into the service of freedom from imperial claims.

But this fails. It fails in the way what used to be known as "law" as contrasted with "equity" failed, because we are so clever at manipulating what we put outside ourselves. When rule is piled on rule they become transparent to the manipulator. Thus came "equity." From it much of the usage and structure of our legal thought today is drawn—the law of remedies that are not money remedies, the law of fiduciary duty that actually maintains corporate organization, the law of trusts, the law of nuisance and from nuisance the law of the environment, on and on.

VII.19 ❧ *System, Complexity, Profit*

It is possible that, in law, what is very complex is not understandable by reason of its complexity alone.

This is a consideration somewhat different from the threat to understanding that attends perception of a system rather than a person speaking. A system can be simple but still a system.

And this, perception of system with meaning fading into cause or forms of cause, is in turn different from, though connected to, the problem of understanding a profit maximizer. A person who seems a profit maximizer can for that reason alone lose all credibility, the precondition of understanding—though, in the end, it may be possible to translate any profit maximizer into a system, and even into complexity.

VII.20 ❧ *Restatements of Equality*

Hariton is a "regional municipality" next to the great city of Toronto. What is Hariton? Some new administrative district, with a legal status stamped on a paper in some office and appearing on some map of limited distribution? And what, by contrast, is Toronto?

A teacher tells us to remember that all such entities are "really the people in them, nothing more." But wait: to say that some entity, institution, place is "really the people in it" and nothing more is to say that people "in the entity" are equal, is it not? Is this not implied, and necessary to the sense of the statement? Push further: what more than this is being said? There is nothing simply material, or even fleshly, about what is being referred to. Is not this statement, which looks to be descriptive, an expression of value?

Manifestly, individuals "in the entity" are not equal in a material or fleshly way, or in their arrangement. The teacher knows this. Some are taking goods from others, some have much, some have little, some are old and frail, some muscular and fast. Some are giving orders to others. Not only is there nothing equal in the material, the structural, or the fleshly; "the people in the entity" are not even there in the fleshly sense, because as individuals they come and go, die and are born, go mad and into comas even while the phrase is being uttered. The teacher knows this too.

The statement "a city (or corporation or country) is really the people in it" must be read as a rough pointer to something that is not just a material reality. If a Roman Catholic says, "The church is the Holy Spirit working through a bishop," we must reflect to understand what he means, reflect at the least upon the reverberations of the words "holy spirit" and "bishop." So we must work to understand the meaning of someone's statement that an entity is "really the people in it." At the very least, "an entity is the people in it" is a statement about the importance of equality in dignity as potential source of meaning. And the "really"? It may be not a denial, but an affirmation of the reality of embodied value, an affirmation the "nothing more" that sometimes follows "really" only serves to underline. "Really" almost always has a positive as well as a denying side, and here it may summon what transcends and the living quality of values of which each individual is evidence one to another, which are supra-individual and which govern decisions on behalf of supra-

individual entities—entities that cannot at all be reduced
to an aggregation of bodies: entities that indeed make possible individuals' very sense of themselves as something
other than instruments, hands, fused as slaves are fused.

VII.2 I   & *The Democratic Principle and the Individual Case*

Suppose large numbers of people around us began taking
their own lives saying, just before, that they saw no reason
not to die; that life had no meaning; that they had no
hope; that since the light would eventually be turned off
for them, they might as well go ahead and turn it off now.
You would count this an important fact to be taken into
account in your thinking about yourself, about law.

That large numbers of people do not give up their lives
is equally an important fact, not to be taken for granted or
explained away by restating it as a biological will to live,
the thrust of a system that happens to be a homeostatic
system, to stay intact and processing. That men and
women may live, or die by their own hands, makes their
living a choice, not just a biological fact, and therefore a
piece of evidence from which we may reason about them
and their beliefs.

But "large numbers": in reasoning from numbers there
is only an introducing of democratic thought and an appeal to the naturalness of its premise that, with the same
spirit in all, what the greater number hear said is closer to
what was said, by a political candidate or by the cosmos.
With the very introduction of "large numbers" on a question that has nothing to do with the normal functioning of

a hidden mechanism, reasoning has already proceeded to build on the choice to live. The choice is individual, the evidence appears from each listening and speaking. With large numbers dying of despair on long Siberian marches the absorbing fact is that Eugenia Ginzburg continued to recite Pushkin from memory to her fellow prisoners in the camps and refused to die—she needed step only once out of the line of march: martyrdom, the ultimate expression of belief in action, can be in a choice to live as well as to die. And in reasoning about Ginzburg alone and her beliefs, we also reason from her to our beliefs. The democratic premise returns without numbers, for if it is actually belief about which we reason, and not some other different thing made to masquerade as belief, we cannot stay apart from it and observe it only from the outside.

VII.22 & *Ten Positive Theses on Corporate Law*

1. The objects, functions, and effects of corporate law are, first, the allocation and reallocation of power and participation in power to decide substantive use of the material world, conditions and arrangements of life and work, and impacts of such use and arrangements; second, the allocation and reallocation of wealth, streams of wealth, and loss and risk of loss; third, the creation of authority in organized activity and the maintenance of organization.

2. Power and wealth are separable in corporate law, as they are in nonlegal analysis (and, by contrast, may not be in the law of property).

3. Power and wealth, though separable, are evidently connected, power reallocating streams of wealth to itself, wealth purchasing power.

4. In attaining its objects, performing its functions, and bringing about its effects, corporate law populates language and to some extent the world with entities beyond the material or the individually human.

5. The principal analytic concerns of corporate law are the *entity* and the *factor of decision*. The two are more than merely associated. The recognition of entity guides the choice and weighting of factors of decision. The choice and weighting of factors of decision specify the entity recognized.

6. In judging the decisions of individuals exercising authority derived from corporate law, the choice and weighting of interests that become factors of decision is secondary: there is no known correct outcome of decision making with which to compare decisions made, and the interests to be weighed proceed from the recognition of entity. Primary is the recognition of entity.

7. Limitation of the liability that would otherwise flow from private law analysis—the limitation that is a characteristic feature of modern industrial and commercial organization—is largely the recognition and separation of entities.

8. The field of law closest to corporate law under current taxonomies is administrative law.

9. Corporate law has its origins in and maintains the force of the worlds of slavery, the tribe, and what is often summed up in the word "feudal." But so central is it to modern thought and practice that it cannot be thought mere atavism or survival.

10. Corporate law is not to be understood or explained in the terms of other forms of social organization, the contractual, for example, or those, so characteristic of the

twentieth century, that are based upon terror. But the structural strength of corporate law, in what are doubtless very changed circumstances, may perhaps be explained in terms other than its own. An instance is the substitution, for master, owner, lord, chief, or king (principals all of them), of entities perceptibly connected to the immediate interests of great percentages of members of society. In a world thought to be more egalitarian, the agents now governed by corporate law are those who might individually have been principals in premodern eras.

VII.23 ▶ *Eight Negative Theses on Corporate Law*

1. Corporate law is not a branch of the law of property, or contract, or tort. It is not a combination of them, nor reducible to them.

2. The search for ownership (in analysis) and its restoration (in remedy) are the hallmarks of the law of property. The search for consent or agreement (in analysis) and the molding or remolding of arrangements to the agreed-upon (in remedy) are the hallmarks of the law of contract. The search for positive harm (in analysis) and compensation for loss (in remedy) are the hallmarks of the law of tort. These together concern what is known as "private law." But these are not the concerns of corporate law, analytic or remedial. Corporate law is not private law.

3. Analysis of problems in corporate law, or discussion of their resolution, is not and cannot be pursued through the language of rights. Analysis in the language of rights cannot be viewed as analysis at the basic level, at the

irreducible, the most general (or the most specific). For rights, there must be entities to which rights can be attached, possessing or bearing rights. In corporate law the entity is in question and is the focus of argument. Where the entity is in question, a search for rights is distraction.

4. In view of the large part of legal discourse historically and presently given over to corporate matters, the language of rights cannot be viewed as the lingua franca of lawyers.

5. Little that is of importance in corporate law is defined, by statute or otherwise. Corporate law cannot be viewed as consisting of or analogous to a set of rules or commands.

6. Given the large place corporate law occupies in legal discourse and practice, law cannot be viewed as consisting essentially of or as essentially analogous to a set of rules or commands.

7. Profit maximization as a standard of decision making or a mode of analysis is rarely seen in corporate law, including the law of business corporations. Where it seems to appear it is often negated by the general law of crime.

8. Corporate law analysis proceeds toward a positive that is made more palpable by being set always against the possibility of a negative: the analytic methods of corporate law are fashioned to maintain a way that does not slip to slavery at one side or disintegration at the other. Slavery resides in an absence, absence of distinction between the enslaving and the enslaved, and between slave and slave—at the extreme slavery is the whole fungibility of individuals, sometimes articulated in absence of distinction between the product of one individual and the product of another, which are instead attributed to factors of production. Reference to "ownership" when speaking of slavery does not quite capture slavery in its analytic manifestations, particularly when ownership of "time" or

"imagination" is claimed. So analysis in corporate law is ontological work, work with entities. On the other side, disintegration resides also in absence, an absence of trust—which does pull what is within one individual together with what is within another—and an absence of agency, of one ever truly doing something for another, either on behalf of or for the sake of another. At the extreme, in the utter absence of trust and agency, all is war, all achievement is limited to the strength of a human arm. So again corporate law turns back to work with entities.

VII.24 ❧ *The Ideal of Limited Law*

The liberty dreamt of by John Stuart Mill—to act as one wills, subject only to the constraint that one not harm others or limit them in their own action—is wholly illusory, though still taught, and repeated by students. Every action harms or limits others, and to say it does not is simply to manipulate a definition of harm or to ignore the truth of causation. The ideal of a limited law is flawed at its base. It presumes a natural order into which there can be "intervention," when in fact there is no such natural order, no area of liberty that might be constrained or not according to whether decisions of law are applicable.

VII.25   ❧   *Due Process*

The connection between due process and equality is revealed whenever deliberate arbitrariness is observed.

Arbitrariness is a choice form of the assertion of superiority and subordination. Disclosure of thought, and justification and consistency, all required in due process, deny this means of assertion and deny also the assertion. Equality, which is a matter of faith, does not follow this denial of inequality. But the ground is prepared for it.

VII.26   ❧   *The Premise of Equality*

Does human equality rest on the given constitution of the state? Then with equality come the methods and the presuppositions of law, which are neither individualistic nor relativistic, which point to unity and which use hierarchy. Does equality come simply as part of a structure of thought, inherited from Jerusalem, Rome, Mecca? Then what sustains this equality—covenant, incarnation, prophetic text—must come with it or it must dissolve away.

Is equality natural, resting on observation of the facts? Some individuals are slyer, cleverer, physically stronger, smarter, more courageous, more ruthless, more charismatic—often vastly so. Some are more devoted to family, or more capable of long-term strategy and waiting. Equality has to push hard and constantly against the facts.

That an identification of humanity with existing human individuals conceived as interchangeable units—a mathematical equality—may alone be consistent with modernism's deep premise, what is is what is and all is system, is not enough to maintain human equality. This is not the premise of human equality, not its meaning, and not its source. Mathematical equality produces no action. Nor is it enough that such identification may be the only way, in empirical science, to maintain a methodological line between the present material world and the denied that is beyond it.

Radical egalitarianism—that everyone has something good about him or her, only it is different—has its own appeal. Anyone with more than one child knows the pull of it, even the truth of it. Radical egalitarianism is a form of love of all, the parent writ large, fully as much as it is a form of envy of all. Belief in equality may actually permit one to perceive true equalities that one would not perceive without belief (which will be called empirically true when belief and truth are joined). But the Christian church which begins with each the child of God has never solved law's problem, of speaking to a life that requires of human beings more than celebration of the goods of life in all the forms in which they are found. Some human beings give more beauty, some are wiser, harder working, more serious, more trustworthy. Hope is followed by celebration of the realization of hope.

Adults never cease to be children each worthy of celebration; but in a world that must be half-created they cannot cease being adults also. Law spans these two truths. If lawyers cannot make them one truth, at the least lawyers can continue holding them together so neither of them is denied.

SECTION ❧ VIII

Beyond Words

On the Temporal in

Legal Thought

The transcendent produces such agony now, that we want to deny it. Why? Is the reason frustration, that we cannot understand despite our yearning to understand and so we try to avoid the trial altogether? Not this only. "Frustration" is too mild. There is fear too, fear of pain, being torn apart.

The principal way of avoiding the transcendent has been to conceive or define thought as representational. Words or images come to mind. They appear, we are something of a recipient or observer of them. Their appearance raises the question of their source, since their source is not in our choice. The answer to the question of source is that it is the material external world, of which these words and images are representations. They are then tested and used to negotiate survival and increase in the world. Whatever is not encompassed in the representational—"theories," or "ideas," which also appear and raise a question of source—is to be treated as forms of spontaneous variation, random accidental products of putting representations together much as unicorns are made. These are then (again in a blending of circuitry and evolution) confirmed or refuted, preserved or destroyed, by the environment they enter, that external material world which is being represented in the representational part of thought.

Transcendence is banished. Circuits from what is, to what is, to what is replace the mysterium tremendum. But such an answer to the question of source, this conception, this definition of thought, is not true to experience. The world is full of oddnesses and incongruities, and this is not the least of them, this departure from the empirical taken by so many whose chief pride is their empiricism. Words enter the mind, yes, but, an instant before, something else enters, which one must clothe in words or images to retain it as one must move quickly to capture a dream. Since we must ourselves move to translate this that must be translated into images or words by our activity, the image or word that is the translation is not merely a given, traceable back to the external world, a given in the way the external world is a given and representations of it are derivative givens. The circuit going round and round is broken. The answer to the question of source— the "world"—is not available, except as protection or avoidance. The question of source is put again.

As for those parts of thought that are acknowledged not to be representational, conceptions, theories, ideas, fancies, they are not things, like a feather of another color, or a different eye socket, which the outer environment will foster or not for the time being. Even if they were to appear immediately in the form of words, words must have meaning—which cannot be produced by any mechanical juxtaposition—if they are to be paid attention to and retained.

From the beginning of efforts to express the experience of thought and all that makes mind and intent, there has been a link between creation—in philosophy, affairs of state, politics, or art—and possession or divine madness. The madness is fearful, a tearing apart, the Dionysian, a close connection with the gods, individuated, it may be, in the form of a mediating daemon (whence the "daemonic" still in our language). The creation, the words or images or even actions taken, was then what was worth full and repeated attention. It evoked attention, it rewarded attention. It was that in which meaning was found and which moved listeners to their own creation.

Now at the end of the twentieth century we must characterize the source anew. For Karl Barth the source is a person who seeks us out and whom no amount of effort on our part can find.

For others the source is natural law or cosmic order going beyond the law and cosmos physicists dream of, and meaning and beauty consist in harmony or correspondence with it. But such law, that one listens to and obeys, and obeys by reproducing it in one's own life and person, imitating it as it were, is not dead system. That is why *law* is summoned to expression, law, not regularity, why, if the notion of order is used, it is cosmic order that is summoned and not mere order. Law in this characterization of source cannot be scientific law, hypothesis for testing and prediction. Scientific law can claim no obedience; indeed, it is there to be challenged in every possible way and with every resource of ingenuity. As to it there is no morality whatever, no call to obey or imitate. The reference in natural law or cosmic order is human law and human order, and human law and human order are constructed by activity, on presuppositions that what is constructed is not simply the creature of the constructor or worker but is nonetheless constructed.

If the God of Karl Barth is replaced by such law, person reappears in the belief, the commitment to presuppositions, that must accompany the continuation of activity, the continuation of very existence. So when we pause and consciously experience our minds, like good empiricists or ideal scientists, we come again to one of those joinders that are the opposite of the antinomies which have occupied man's thought to the point of exhaustion. Here the combination is that of the passive and the active: the pull or the push within the mind, as to which you are passive, open yourself to, do not make happen, only avoid interfering with its happening; and the decision, which is active even though pushed or pulled, to do something toward wholeness; the combination being variously described as grace calling to free man, conscience calling to fallen man, the authentic calling to the inauthentic.

VIII.2 ❧ *Authenticity in Music and in Law*

In music "authentic performance" assumes that the performer has kept the notes as the composer wrote them (stopping short of the problem of the composer's own revisions). It has come also to refer to continuing to play instruments designed like those upon which the composer would have heard the notes played, or, as is sometimes more boldly said, the instruments for which the composer wrote the notes.

But there remains a difference between changing the notes and varying the performance. In sensing that difference we imply to ourselves that a voice can dream beyond the instruments of the day. The instruments did not change on their own. One can assert that a choice between the sounds of an old instrument and the sounds of a modern instrument is simply a preference and preference is simply a matter of individual taste culturally and historically determined and there is no more to it than that. But one need not take that position. One must choose to take that position. There is something more to it.

The voice that speaks through a modern instrument is not the original voice, in the sense that it is the same

voice (any more than Shakespeare spoken without Eliza-
bethan accent and pronunciation is the same). It is a voice
merged with our own. But we cannot say that because the
voice is not the same in this sense, we then do not hear
the voice or it is not the voice of the composer that we
hear. A composer does dream beyond the instruments of
the day. What is heard by the composer from the orchestra
at the moment of composition? From what angle does the
composer hear, how far back? Did he possibly hear the
clarinet and the cello (if he *heard* them at all) as we today
listening to recordings are able to hear them through mi-
crophones set about? Or—to come at the question of authentic performance from the opposite direction—though
we may remain comfortable with music performed on
new instruments, we may nonetheless be interested in
facts uncovered by historians and instruments recon-
structed by them; but the reason we will be interested, or
have more than a mere antiquarian curiosity, is that these
facts about the past, what the composer would have heard
through his eardrum rather than his mind's ear, reveal
something about him. The sound may express something.

But the sound can express only what we can understand. If expression and understanding were not involved,
we would not in the least be interested in the sound of
all-gut strings that lose their tune while they are being
played. What is, again, not at stake is authenticity in the
sense of mere sameness, which, in the legal world, would
be authoritarianism.

The problem of authenticity in law moves a step beyond authentic performance in music. For if we say we do
not change the words of a constitution any more than we
would change the notes of a Beethoven symphony, we see
also that we do not perform the words as notes, by repeating them. Repeating the words of a constitution does not
produce music, even bad or wooden music. There is no

intermediate position in the objective world—the script or notes as written—to keep hold of in our search for what is expressed. Nor do words reach the suggestion of the unchanging that some painting and some music seem to reach. If words fail, they fail. Theirs is not a beauty, there, to be heard or seen, repeated over and over.

We cannot of course ignore the words, as if they were not at all like notes. The words are attended to most closely. Change a word and you cut a link to anything that matters. But our interest is focused entirely on what is being expressed. And in law we must believe that the voice dreams not only beyond the instruments of the day, but beyond the very words of the day, which, though like notes, are no more than instruments.

VIII.3 ☞ *Community*

There is always a steadying going on in the joining of writer and reader, as in the joining of composer and listener.

Read one day a work inspires; another day it doesn't. It has unplumbed riches; it is a construction with air behind it. Put it aside for a month or a year and it is almost new; or its magic is never recovered. Or the reverse: read once, it is obvious; read a second time it enthralls. Here it is a querulous noise in the ear; then a snatch, heard by chance, dances in the mind. It changes with our eye or ear or mind.

Or does it only seem to change? Is it a drug, a molecule with the same structure but a different fit according to the condition of our receptors? Inert, a system of marks and sounds? That would be it staying the same, with us the changeable part of the conjunction. But when the thought occurs that it only seems to change, the thought is not of this. The thought is of something that is beyond ourselves and our reactions but also beyond the words and sounds that are seen or not seen, heard or not heard, highlighted or not, interrelationships among which are perceived or not. That something beyond is not the same like the shapes of the words are the same (this becomes evident in law when there is constant restatement and the script, the score, what is read and played and seen and heard, itself changes with restatement). "Remains the same" is a phrase of crude contrast evoked by the thought that the work is a mere reflection of our state and changes with us. But the work is alive, itself expression of something beyond itself that is not forms nor in forms, neither in the work's forms nor in further forms.

Any sense of a work, on which sense something will turn, must be actively pursued. Meaning does declare itself, but still memory must enter, there must be testimony, to arrive at a judicious sense of a work—or of a person, or of any concrete reality. The testimony of memory must enter, and reflection upon memory, including, when one is working entirely within oneself, the memory of the direct touch of meaning. The steadying that goes on in the meeting of guided vessel and turbulent water, the seeking of the quiet point of sameness, recalls something of the necessity of driving with will and application toward right perception of what is not in us and not a projection of or a correlation with us, but which is itself not still. Yet the allusion implies a conquering, a learning about forces and a reduction of them to the will, which has little to do with the life of the mind and nothing to do with meaning. The conjunction is of spirit with spirit; the observation, the testimony of memory, the sense achieved, is of what is itself searching, reading, listening; and the proof of having gotten it, seen it as it is and not as it seems, is as much in one's own living as in any summation in shapes and sounds, words, notes, stones, paint.

Judicious, of sense; right, in perception: these terms, used in speaking of concrete reality, are drawn over from law. What law's method does is eliminate even the form of the work that might be thought to remain the same. That the reader is constructing and joining that which is living beyond is assumed, unnoticed while the work continues—as it is assumed, unnoticed, when looking again and again into the eyes of any person with whom one lives, except of course the eyes of a calculating enemy. There is in law no resting on the text, as readers, players, and audience can rest on *The Tempest*. There is restatement, not just of the roles but of the words of the roles. Law is more like life than art, and despite all its trappings less daunting than art; for art, restating into life what is heard—reviving and building—nonetheless wants a circle woven around it thrice: to deny to its readers, through closure, the possibility of doing what it has just demonstrated the possibility of doing.

The steadying seen and experienced in law is seen and experienced not only in any approach to the texts from which a statement of law is to be drawn, but in any approach to the facts from which a statement of facts is to be drawn, and in any approach to a decision. The condition for the steadying, the balance, the construction, is that there is something beyond, or beyond or yet again beyond; otherwise the effort could not be made. One steadies and constructs one's sense of things with a sense of community of spirit with oneself at the different times one tries, and with a sense of community of spirit with others who also state law and appraise facts and make decisions and whose statements and appraisals one reads and weighs. So law's authority has its base in community, in the jury, the judges, the lawyers, each of them responsible. So it is, in part, that the past is part of law's authority.

VIII.4 ❧ *Easy Cases*

Finding a case easy is something of an agreement with oneself, as finding it not easy is a reflection of argument with oneself. There is, of course, frequently agreement about a case, agreement with oneself, or with others. But agreement is a fact of history. There is no necessity that agreement rather than argument should occur or continue.

VIII.5 ❧ *Novelty*

Under any assertion that a text acquires new meaning as it ages, meaning which because it is new is not the author's meaning, lie three immediate assumptions, about the author of a text, about the language of a text, and about the reader of a text. These three assumptions are accompanied by a minor fourth, an assumption about the one making the assertion. Calling a meaning new implies that the author did not see it. Easy agreement that the author did not see it is made possible only by a physical notion of consciousness, as a thing which is there or is not there, time-bound in a finite skull. An assertion that a text can have an unmeant meaning assumes a mechanical view of language. Language is a machine that works without authors. Associated with the first assumption about the author and the author's limitations and about mind and the nature of mind, this second assumption about language denies constant newness in language, the metaphorical, the newness that is associated with its substance. The third assumption, about the reader, is that a reader looks at a text in isolation and is not always looking to other texts in reading any one of them. The minor fourth is the assumption evident in assertion itself, that a disassociation of author from text does not apply to the writer proposing such disassociation.

VIII.6 ❧ *Due Process in Music*

There is music from an earlier era of amateur performance, written for the pleasure of playing it. A pattern is repeated, in the voice of another instrument, less for expression, or for the beauty of repetition, than to give each performer his due. To the extent this is the case one cannot ask what the piece or part means, even musically. Yet it can be listened to attentively, as well as played, for in listening there can be playing in imagination, and a vicarious pleasure in having a turn, discovering that one will not be left out, that one can add one's own foot to the dance.

VIII.7 ❧ *Reproduction*

Many remark upon the importance of saying a thing in one's own words to make it live. Even some teachers urge this. Any such injunction leads to the question whether what is being said, when it is said in one's own words and lives, is the same as what was said before.

Of course it is not exactly the same, in the sense that both could be reduced to or reproduced in some other formulation. It does not seem even the same in the sense that both are members of a class and differ only in particulars, as any particular thing differs from any other—that is, that it is "abstractly" the same but not concretely so. It is the same only in the sense in which two living beings (or entities) are related to each other; or, perhaps better, in the sense in which one living being is related to itself later in time.

And, of course, the thing said in a living way must be understood in a living way. Wilhelm Dilthey speaking a century ago might have been speaking to lawyers today: "Mankind, if apprehended only by perception and perceptual knowledge, would be for us a physical fact, and as such it would be accessible only to natural-scientific knowledge. It becomes an object for the human studies only in so far as human states are consciously lived, in so far as they find expression in living utterances, and in so far as these expressions are understood."

VIII.8 ❧ *The Arrangement of Marks*

Outside epic, or poem cycle, poems are not prepared to fit a book of poems. A book of poems emerges (a poem cycle may also emerge) rather than having been initially conceived in outline. The mind rather than a preconceived form with an outer line tends to dictate the arrival of the individual poem. When an opportunity for collection comes to the poet, and for publication other than in journals and magazines, the poet generally does not scoop up scattered sheets randomly or take poems one after another out of journals chronologically bound.

The poet arranges the poems, taking time over it though perhaps unable (if interrupted and asked) to say just why one fits better in one place rather than another. Pascal arranged some of his pensées on strings before he died, and he left others ordered as if ready to go on strings. A third pile was assembled from what was found jumbled or filed as he had written them. Pascal's published *Pensées* can be read at random. So can poems in a book of poems be read at random, and they often are. But if these lines, sentences, paragraphs, or works being read have been put in an order, one loses something by ignoring the form of their order, as at the extreme one loses in listening to a musical composition by listening to bits of it at random, or in taking apart a composition a composer put together over years gradually working in new material around old, and listening to the pieces in a sequence indicated by the dates of the watermarks on the various manuscript pages.

What is that something lost? It is not controlling. It is further evidence. It is not the person lost—just as language is in some sense transparent with person behind

and beyond if language has meaning and is not the clicking of dry sticks, person is in some sense transparent also,
not capturable into form and fixed, there. If an implied
text of which individual pieces are fragments unifies the
fragments, this implied text is not finished; and imagining
that it is finished, as Wordsworth might suggest with his
cathedral nave to which all his individually finished
works were chapels, shrinks it so that as an image it can
no longer begin to fit the person.

So the same drive that would take one to an ordering of
the third pile of Pascal's pensées, an ordering proceeding
without knowledge of an order he imposed, allows one to
rearrange the pensées he did order on strings and those he
had almost ready to be strung. The drive that takes one to
an order in the sentences and statements of an individual
friend that, recorded, would be fixed simply in chronological order, carries one also to consider the meaning of what
is said in the course of a narrative or story, and in considering what is said in any way other than repeating its
marks and sounds as a machine might repeat them again
and again, meaninglessly, one rearranges what was presented in the order dictated by the story. What was presented may have come a bit as if alphabetized, the story
locating one and leading one to read something before
something else—or say something before something
else—but that order not itself identical to the meaning of
what is said any more than the alphabetical ordering of a
series of statements, remarks, or sentences would be even
part of their meaning read as a whole. One rearranges
what is presented into one's own arrangement, just as one
arranges and rearranges the fragments, pieces, and parts
that go into one's own statements expressing one's meaning over minutes or over a life, trying sometimes to make
them worlds in themselves explorable in themselves, but
knowing that if their form became essential they would

lose their meaning and would be only repeatable, repeatable, repeatable, and that once put forth worlds become fragments to be arranged and rearranged.

VIII.9 ✺ *The Repetition of Unresolved Themes*

Ambivalence and ambiguity are like the blending of the bass and treble notes in music. And also like the bass and treble notes in music are the constant themes in thought and writing, which cannot be translated into one another and so often seem at odds because of their intractable difference, and that in their constantness make us feel there is nothing new under the sun.

In music we do not complain about striking together two notes separated far from each other, and as different as the low is from the high. Nor do we complain about the recurrence of a note, nor feel limited by the availability of only a few notes that have also been available to all before us.

VIII.10 ✺ *Daily Process*

Men and women seem to live in a conflict between substance and process. It is felt in the commonplace pull between achievement and life and family. But life and family float above the details of living; and achievement, once one is into the achieving of it, becomes a process itself, each substantial accomplishment fading into the past and losing its meaning and importance, and finished objects, in the eye of their creator, coming undone to seem only the details and pieces of an ongoing, unfinished development, the substance of which does not differ from the substance floating above the process of family, love, travel, friendship, sport, and the conviviality of commercial games, which fill a life—or the cherished part of it.

VIII.II 🐦 *The Evidence of Writing*

You know a person over time. You know yourself over time. If you are writing, rather than speaking intimately face to face, you do not rush to bare yourself. Any writing is distillation of vacillations, resolution of doubts, linking of intermittent perceptions you know you have some days and times and have not on others. Writing is much an act of remembering, though remaining throughout open to displacement of memory by what is newly seen. Even at the point of first composition, words that come to mind are held for judgment—the moments of being possessed, in which writing seems automatic bypassing mind as angers bypass mind in the afflicted, only postpone judgment. The very act of writing, of capturing, discarding, correcting, improving, points to what writing is writing about. Writing is not conveyance of an inner state, but of something of which the inner state at any time is evidence sometimes more and better, sometimes less and worse. What do you truly feel? Reveal yourself. Say it. Ah, what do I truly feel? That is the question, and time will tell.

VIII.12 ✿ *The Object of Utopian Politics*

Look and listen to the slow movement of the *Suite Saint-Saëns* by the Joffrey: conceive that what the music and dance are conveying, capturing, describing, encapsulating, creating, is a form of day, or afternoon, with shape, full, sufficient to itself, the emotions and the senses in play, the self found but the other not other, a day that for centuries only a few could have: civilization itself: the object of life: with which productivity is inconsistent, since one must withdraw and shift rhythms to be productive. Have such days ever been your own object? Have you ever had them?

VIII.13 ✿ *Change in the Meaning of the Spoken*

The meaning of something one says, which is formed in some objective sense ("objective," insofar as there is no issue raised about the evidence left of what the form is or was), which is put into form, into marks, shapes, words: does that meaning change, beyond what was intended at the time of utterance or delivery or letting go?

An impossible question? The very notion of change brings to mind something fixed at one time, and something fixed at another, which then can be compared to determine whether change has occurred. "Know thyself," we hear suggested to us for our own good. We hardly know ourselves. What we say is evidence for us as well as for others. We can hardly fix that first point, to begin determining whether change has occurred.

But there are forms of expression other than shapes or sounds. A child is a living expression, a parent's own meaning formed as best a parent can. And, if general experience is acknowledged, a child is surprising. One recognizes oneself in son or daughter, but one does not control one's child. The child speaks to others, is to others—one speaks and is to others in and through the child—and at the end of one's life one can imagine not disavowing what one has seen, although one could not have predicted what one has seen and was not in a position to adopt what one has seen, at the time of one's effort to put meaning into form, because one could not then have specified it sufficiently for adoption. Has one's meaning changed? It might be said so. But then "change" will not carry with it its implication about what *meaning* must be—fixed here, fixed there, held hold of and compared—if meaning "changes."

VIII.14 ✿ *Death and Spirit*

Art may be thought to be generated by knowledge of death, a wishful speculation of a final harmony with nature. Religion like art may be thought only a response to death, an obsessive justifying of nature's way with us. Art and religion are only death playing upon consciousness, epiphenomena of death. But *death*, to which art and religion are thus reduced, is a very human notion, which escapes nature unless nature is humane. Without spirit, there is never *death*; there is only migration and reformation of matter.

VIII.15 ❧ *Reading the Word "We" Appearing in Print*

You or I write "we" in a book addressed to the world. The word in the text stays the same as the book gets older. As time goes on you or I become less evidently part of any embodied "we" to whom the book is speaking. If the book is read and accepted to some extent by a reader then (who might jot a "yes" in a margin), the "we" in the book will then refer to the reader and his or her contemporaries, not to you an individual and me an individual, who will then be forebears of the reader along with millions of other forebears. And what you or I say in the book will have to be restated by those born after your death and my death and the deaths of our youngest friends, through quotation or otherwise, for the "we" in the book will not be made merely through joining something that already exists in the world.

VIII.16 ❧ *Ancient Texts*

Once into its spirit you may be inclined to finish something you know to have been dashed down by its composer between eleven and twelve midnight and not touched again. At least you may listen differently, ignoring an awkwardness here and stretching out a line there as you listen, in effect dropping from and adding to the thing itself.

Though not adding to or dropping from its spirit; until its spirit is taken over and becomes your spirit; and perhaps not even then.

If this is so—that the inclination to stretch and ignore, add and drop, is strengthened, and hesitations to do so are lessened, as the time of initial composition seems shorter—then observe that a long time looking and listening, extending to years, centuries, and millennia, will make the time of composition of any work comparatively shorter and shorter.

(Will you be arrested in your finishing if you are struck directly by a sense of consummate genius at work in that late short hour of composition? Not arrested and certainly not imprisoned. You will be slowed—your faith that an awkwardness is not an awkwardness will continue longer.)

VIII.17 ☜ *Quotation in Law and the Rearrangement of Fragments*

The Chinese classics, now more than two millennia old, were first collected in book form. They were written without punctuation on sheets that were not numbered. The sheets were bound together by thongs. The thongs decayed. The sheets fell and scattered. Their particular physical order was lost—as the particular physical order of the stones of King's College Chapel has not been lost, during their continual physical replacement. In looking to them and commenting on them over centuries Chinese commentators rearranged them in various sequences.

The sheets with their sentences and sayings once were arranged in fact. That was passed down and believed, and there was the continuing material evidence of the holes for the thongs. If it were thought that this initial arrangement was without significance or point, random perhaps, like leaves on the ground or rocks on the beach, then a commentator's rearrangement of the piles into which they might be gathered after they fell would be unjudgeable and, equally, would have no force beyond the force of his own writing. His arrangement of the units of writing on the sheets would be much like his, or our, rearrangement of the individual words that might come to us arranged alphabetically if we took down a book collecting previously used individual words that we might use (or quote, since they have been used by others before) instead of making up new marks, shapes, or sounds to arrange.

But if it had been urged that the initial arrangement was significant and, further, that the commentator's arrangement gave particular reason to pay attention to the commentator's writing appearing amidst all the contemporary writing that competed for attention, then the commentator's arrangement would be put forth as a product of a search for the sentences' and sayings' proper order. The commentator then was scholar participating in the scholarly or hermeneutical effort to secure a correct text in the sense of reproducing the historical fact of the initial arrangement, even if the initial arrangement were itself only that point in a composition where there had been a giving up and a cessation of arranging and rearranging and the composition was thus said to be "finished" only in that sense. But drawing the scholarly effort on was and still is an assumption, implicit or announced, that the historical fact was not only material fact, like the arrangement at some point of rocks on a beach or leaves on the ground, but rather (again if it were to give reason to pay attention) establishment of what a mind did from which the sayings came as marks. If there were no physical evidence to rely upon as physical evidence is relied upon in the arrangement of a sequence of fossils—no tracings across thong holes or mutually torn corners—the rearrangement of the piles must then be what a mind would have produced, and (again in the absence of physical evidence) this rearrangement blends with the rearrangement that occurs even in the presence of a historically correct text because of universal knowledge that what minds do in action is flawed.

A rearrangement that is not a product of a search for mind is a product of ulterior purpose, strategic or political, or a product produced by social or economic forces. Whether or not the initial order was a product of mind, the rearrangement is separated from it.

Contemporary legal writing consists heavily of quotations and commentary not absolutely different in kind from the Chinese. Parts of statutes and sentences from earlier opinions are arranged—"As the Congress says"; "As this Court said over a century ago"; "What we said at the end of the First World War is just as pertinent today." It is an open possibility that commentary might be written entirely in quotations. There was a long Western tradition of theological writing, seeking authoritative statement, in the Byzantine genre known as the florilegium, which was an arrangement of quotations from prior authoritative texts that made the commentator's point, a new point in the sense of living and his own, without his adding words and sentences, the juxtapositions and omissions he made becoming active in the expression, rather as juxtaposition and omission are active in poetic or musical expression. (Jaroslav Pelikan has urged the similarity in form between the florilegium and the legal opinion.) The quotation or fragment of a prior statement loses meaning taken out of context, like a single word. A fragment "Because these greengages are green" on a slip of paper fluttering down to one's feet might mean almost anything, perhaps anything. Putting in punctuation and sentence form does not help appreciably: "These greengages are green." might similarly mean almost anything. Expand the number of words, phrases, sentences, and paragraphs and one moves toward a "work" to work with, though always at risk because out of context, as the meaning of a single word or a single letter is at risk out of context—that is the problem of the detail and the whole, the whole itself being a detail. All his works, Wordsworth said, were chapels to the unbuilt nave of a cathedral.

But the risk of meaninglessness recedes, and meaning lost from loss of context is not lost, if the fragments, the parts, the lifted quotations, are replaced in a context that is connected to the old. Insofar as they are marks emanating from a mind and their rearrangement is a product of search for that mind as the commentator searches for his own, they are still expressive. We are engaged in doing the same with the fragments of a person whom we are trying to understand, the quotations remembered, presented to us as a life presents statements to us, initially chronologically ordered, and sometimes more than chronologically ordered into works or in sequences with an underlying order not merely chronological but always leaving us with more than enough to do if we seek to understand and incorporate our understanding in our own action and speech.

What is critical is approach, attitude. If the search is for a mind, one's sense of which is evidenced, marked, by one's arrangement of the marks left behind in the expression of that mind, then the arrangement one makes oneself may be looked to for its meaning, or one's meaning, or the meaning of the one whose marks one is arranging. If the search is not for a mind, one is playing a game, and one's arrangement is a secret joke. When the joke is uncovered by someone upon whom it is played, there is no further looking to the arrangement for any meaning or perhaps even any looking to the marks themselves (insofar as they have enough detail to begin to be looked at in themselves as works). The intention of the arranger is to gain some object that he knows (and his listener now knows he knows) his listener would rather not have him gain, and his arrangement of the marks offers the listener no reason to change the thought or action that has been or might be arrived at without attention to and without regard to the utterances of the speaker (regard introducing the element of respect, which is very nearly implied, in any event, in attention itself). The speaker's utterances, if they cannot otherwise claim attention, lose their force, the force that the force of law has, their power to move. They have no authority, and are not held in regard, kept in attention as thought and action proceed, which thought and action inevitably will.

VIII.18 🍃 *The Language of Belief*

How can a willingness to change one's mind or belief be consistent with any belief? Ask yourself *what* you believe, and then look at what you say. In seeking to define what we believe we enter into notions that open out into the future, not into closed systems. The very terms of our descriptions of what we believe, our nounlike terms, have the quality of verbs as well as nouns. There is movement in them.

A true description of what you believed earlier can have in it the seeds of reconciliation with what you believe now. Despite what we may have been taught in elementary school, distinctions between noun and verb do not hold: in the very statement of what you believe at a particular point you are carried forward from that time toward the realization of a hope. And though that hope may not be realized or be possible to realize in your individual life, still you cannot divorce yourself from its realization. The general run of people putting belief into words may sense this with less difficulty than the disciplined professional, whose discipline is likely to be enamored with the possibility of substituting mathematics for human language.

In the United States large numbers of the general run (those whose use of language provides the material for professional study of language) listen with every evidence of understanding to Christian and Jewish theologians and ministers explicating the name of God, and one cannot help but be struck by the standard observation in biblical commentary that when Jehovah replies to Moses' insistence on a *name* to take back to Israel, the Hebrew of his reply—"I am that I am, that is who I am, tell them I am sent you"—has a quality not just of being but of becoming. The translation into English using our static English "be," "am," "is," is read as the ancient Hebrew, and without much difficulty, suggesting not only much about translation and its affinities with the act of reading itself, but a capacity within to understand the thought of the ancient Hebrew.

We are not limited by our nouns and verbs, as an artificial intelligence would be. Or, to say the same, the apparent meaning of words and their actual meaning are not the same, as the objectivist would have them be: our nouns, like our verb "to be," only appear to be static. In much Western theology this openness and movement in human language is connected in an explicit way with person; the ultimate object of knowledge and belief, toward which our descriptive terms so full of movement move, is within the world of theology a person. In worlds of thought that today deny knowing anything of theology, the object of knowledge and belief is not different.

VIII.19 🦋 *Cosmology and Time*

Who is the person who grows from incontinent baby without memory to aged incontinent without memory, changing and self-changed, beautiful and complete at twelve as at thirty, handsome at forty, wise at sixty? It does not matter, if our whole life outer and inner exists forever as a memory in a greater mind, and eternity is time ultimately quick, to which the decades point, that when they have come and gone are seen not to have been long at all but a moment only if they have contained even a modicum of the experience of love.

So paradise that is eternal love is not entirely beyond comprehension. So imprisonment is the cruelest of punishments, displaying a human understanding of the nature of time, and of hell—time ultimately slow, loveless.

Boredom is not accounted for in any material view of the universe. It cannot be, because it is the experience of the person in time and over time, whose future is his own and not some other's; and the person is denied. Denied partly for fear of boredom, it may be: boredom is banished when the person is banished, and any cost to banish boredom may be thought not too great a cost. For boredom is hell on earth and its very possibility makes eternity a horror, time itself a punishment.

Punishment for what? For not loving—if the capacity for love can be nurtured, if it is at all a matter of will after insight; if the capacity for love cannot be nurtured through insight and will, there is only pain, not punishment.

But a time of love flashes by in retrospect even if love is marked when it is present, and an eternity touched by love will be as short as a lover's meeting.

Boredom itself, with us but not accounted for, speaks of hope as well as the person. Boredom is not merely a craving for novelty, innate and merely innate, like hunger. Boredom is not just curiosity untickled. A diet of novelty can become boring. Boredom is more, a craving for meaning as well as the new, the new having its value because of hope there will be meaning not experienced before—and meaning that will not pale, not because it will last unchanging forever, but because of what it does to time in us.

PRESENT MEANING

I say to you.
        You said to me.
I say to you—
        What you said to me.
Only said, never say?
        Only was, never is.
        Here now, only you—
With me.
What we say—
        Always behind us,
        You, me,
In the silence,
        The present silence,
Existing beyond words,
        Always beyond words,
In the clear silence,
        The moving stillness—

A Note on Form ❧ _____

These studies in eight sections, ending here, pursue particularly the presence of law and its significance for questions of actual belief. They may be picked up separately, as time and occasion allow; they are listed each by title and page after the general Contents. Arranged under their several headings these studies together may be taken as a phenomenology of law, argued in the only way experience so connected to action and to identity will not be lost in the presentation. They are meant for those whose attention to the features of human law may be a pastime as well as those for whom it is a profession, and for any whose work or interest turns to the problem of reading ourselves and to the actualities of the modern mind.

Law connects language to person, and person to action, through a form of thought that is not reducible to any other. The legal form of thought is not waning—rather the reverse. It may yet move to take a place beside the forms of thought of other disciplines that are self-reflective, as something to be reckoned with, in its own terms, in coming to any general understanding of the working of the world.

References and
Acknowledgments ☞

References and acknowledgments are keyed to fragment numbers.

Epigraph

"And twofold Always. May God us keep / From Single vision & Newton's sleep!" See *The Letters of William Blake with Related Documents*, 3d ed., ed. Geoffrey Keynes (Oxford: Clarendon Press, 1980), pp. 43–46; and *The Portable Blake*, ed. with introduction by Alfred Kazin (New York: Penguin Books, 1976), p. 210. *Jerusalem*: see *The Portable Blake*, pp. 32, 412. On Newton, see Richard S. Westfall, *The Life of Isaac Newton* (Cambridge: Cambridge University Press, 1993); John Maynard Keynes, *Essays in Biography*, ed. Geoffrey Keynes (New York: W. W. Norton, 1963), pp. 310–23; Richard H. Popkin, *The Third Force in Seventeenth Century Thought* (Leiden: E. J. Brill, 1992), pp. 172–202.

I. Introductory

3. Gustave Flaubert, *Madame Bovary*, trans. Allen Russell (Harmondsworth: Penguin Books, 1971), p. 301.

7. Racter, *The Policeman's Beard Is Half Constructed*, ed. William Chamberlain (New York: Warner Books, 1984) (unpaginated).

10. Owen Barfield, *Poetic Diction: A Study in Meaning* (London: Faber and Gwyer, 1928; reprint, with a foreword by Howard Nemerov, Middletown, Conn.: Wesleyan University Press, 1984).

13. Timberlake Wertenbaker, *Our Country's Good* (London: Methuen, 1988); Thomas Keneally, *The Playmaker* (London: Hodder and Stoughton, 1988).

17. Joyce Carol Oates, "Actress," *Michigan Quarterly Review* 30, no. 4 (Fall 1991): 659, 661.

19. See, e.g., Edward O. Wilson, *On Human Nature* (Cambridge, Mass.: Harvard University Press, 1978). Cf. Guy Routh, *The Origin of Economic Ideas* (New York: Vintage Books, 1977).

20. William Blackstone, *Commentaries on the Laws of England*, 21st ed., vol. 1 (New York: Harper and Brothers, 1854), "Section II. Of the Nature of Laws in General," p. 38; see also pp. 44–46. On "law," and "legal," cf., e.g., Michael A. Arbib, *In Search of the Person: Philosophical Explorations in Cognitive Science* (Amherst, Mass: University of Massachusetts Press, 1985), p. 32. Roy Harris, *The Language Machine* (Ithaca, N.Y.: Cornell University Press, 1987), pp. 136–37, comments upon A. M. Turing's reference to "authority" in "Computing Machinery and Intelligence" (1950), in *Minds and Machines*, ed. Alan Ross Anderson (Englewood Cliffs, N.J.: Prentice-Hall, 1964), p. 8.

25. Lytton Strachey, *Eminent Victorians* (Garden City, N.Y.: Garden City Publishing Co., 1928), pp. 192–93.

26. I am indebted to Kenneth J. DeWoskin for this translation of the *Spring and Autumn Annals* and the *Gongyang Commentary*, and for discussion, over many years, of Chinese language and practice and the questions presented to the Western mind by non-Western experience. For a review of the place of the mathematical form of thought within scientific disciplines at the beginning of the century, see D'Arcy Wentworth Thompson, *On Growth and Form* (1917), abridged ed., ed. with an introduction by John Tyler Bonner (Cambridge: Cambridge University Press, 1975), pp. 1–14 (biology and mathematics). For a mid-century example of its application to mind, see John von Neumann, *The Computer and the Brain* (New Haven: Yale University Press, 1958) (but see von Neumann's hesitation on the question of language, pp. 80–82). For examples of its generalization within and beyond scientific disciplines, leading to the cosmological speculation and proposals of the end of the century, see Herbert A. Simon, *The Sciences of the Artificial*, 2d ed. (Cambridge,

Mass.: MIT Press, 1982), pp. 10, 27, 63–66, 157–59; Stephen W. Hawking, *A Brief History of Time: From the Big Bang to Black Holes*, with an introduction by Carl Sagan (New York: Bantam Books, 1988) (and see, in this connection, Hawking's rendering of words into "pieces of information" that can be counted and compared with units of "heat," p. 152); John R. Searle, *The Rediscovery of the Mind* (Cambridge, Mass.: MIT Press, 1992), pp. 85–93.

27. Stanley Cavell, "The Avoidance of Love: A Reading of King Lear," in *Must we mean what we say? A Book of Essays* (Cambridge: Cambridge University Press, 1976). John Keats, *Ode on Melancholy*, in *New Oxford Book of English Verse*, ed. Helen Gardner (Oxford: Oxford University Press, 1972), pp. 610–11.

29. I am indebted to Luis O. Gómez for his expositions of aspects of Buddhism. See, e.g., Luis O. Gómez, "Buddhist Views of Language," in *The Encyclopedia of Religion*, ed. Mircea Eliade (New York: Macmillan, 1987), 8: 446–51.

30. Freeman Dyson, *Infinite in All Directions* (New York: Harper & Row, 1988), pp. 99, 100, 107, 99, 108, 109, 104, 119, 115, 118, 118, 118, 110; see also Freeman Dyson, *Disturbing the Universe* (New York: Harper & Row, 1979), e.g., pp. 92–93. William James, *The Varieties of Religious Experience: A Study in Human Nature*, ed. and with foreword by Martin E. Marty (New York: Viking Penguin, 1985). Michael Polanyi, *Personal Knowledge: Towards a Post-Critical Philosophy* (Chicago: University of Chicago Press, 1958; paperback ed., 1962). Steven Weinberg, *The First Three Minutes: A Modern View of the Origin of the Universe*, 2d pbk. ed. with afterword (New York: Basic Books, 1993), p. 154.

33. Franz Kafka, *The Trial*, trans. Willa and Edwin Muir (Harmondsworth: Penguin Books, 1963), pp. 251, 18, 245, 23, 34, 10, 245, 251, 246, 7, 19, 21–30, 12, 18, 33.

II. Language

2. Theory of everything: see, e.g., John D. Barrow, *Theories of Everything: The Quest for Ultimate Explanation* (Oxford: Clar-

endon Press, 1991); Steven Weinberg, *Dreams of a Final Theory: The Search for the Fundamental Laws of Nature* (New York: Pantheon, 1993). Compare Roger Penrose, *The Emperor's New Mind: Concerning Computers, Minds, and the Laws of Physics* (Oxford: Oxford University Press, 1989).

3. Compare, e.g., Oliver Sacks, *Seeing Voices: A Journey into the World of the Deaf* (Berkeley: University of California Press, 1989), pp. 85–103 (on sign language). I am indebted to Richard D. Friedman for discussion of the use of diagrams in place of language.

9. The doctor's eye: see Frank Lynn Meshberger, M.D., "An Interpretation of Michelangelo's *Creation of Adam* Based on Neuroanatomy," *Journal of the American Medical Association* 264, no. 14 (October 10, 1990): 1837.

14. On *dabar*, see Milner S. Ball, *The Word and the Law* (Chicago: University of Chicago Press, 1993), pp. 110–12, 117–20.

17. Mole and Rat: Kenneth Grahame, *The Wind in the Willows*, 38th ed. (London: Methuen & Co., 1931). Finger of God: Exodus 31:18.

19. See, e.g., A. D. Nock, *Conversion: The Old and the New in Religion from Alexander the Great to Augustine of Hippo* (London: Oxford University Press, 1965).

21. See, e.g., Richard D. Alexander, *Darwinism and Human Affairs* (Seattle: University of Washington Press, 1982); *The Adapted Mind: Evolutionary Psychology and the Generation of Culture*, ed. Jerome H. Barkow, Leda Cosmides, and John Tooby (New York: Oxford University Press, 1992), pp. 555–600. Cf. Ivan Moravec, *Mind Children: The Future of Robot and Human Intelligence* (Cambridge, Mass.: Harvard University Press, 1988).

26. L. N. Tolstoy, *War and Peace*, trans. Rosemary Edmonds (Harmondsworth: Penguin Books, 1971).

27. A. M. Turing, "Computing Machinery and Intelligence" (1950), in *Minds and Machines*, ed. Alan Ross Anderson (Englewood Cliffs, N.J.: Prentice-Hall, 1964), pp. 4–30.

30. I am indebted to Robben W. Fleming for discussion of the situation of the arbitrator.

31. See James Joyce, *Ulysses: The Corrected Text*, ed. Hans

Walter Gabler with Wolfhard Steppe and Claus Melchior, with preface by Richard Ellmann and afterword by Hans Walter Gabler (New York: Vintage Books, 1986).

33. For inquiry into translation, by three to whom I am indebted for discussion of the phenomenon and the experience, see James Boyd White, *Justice as Translation: An Essay in Cultural and Legal Criticism* (Chicago: University of Chicago Press, 1990); Alton L. Becker, *Beyond Translation: Essays toward a Modern Philology* (Ann Arbor: University of Michigan Press, forthcoming); David Noel Freedman, "Editing the Editors: Translation and Elucidation of the Text of the Bible," in *Palimpsest: Editorial Theory in the Humanities*, ed. George Bornstein and Ralph G. Williams (Ann Arbor: University of Michigan Press, 1993), pp. 227–56. For discussion of metaphor that does not seek to escape metaphor, see Owen Barfield, *Poetic Diction: A Study in Meaning* (London: Faber and Gwyer, 1928; reprint, with a foreword by Howard Nemerov, Middletown, Conn.: Wesleyan University Press, 1984).

III. Logic

2. David Sutton, *Settlements* (Calstock, Cornwall, Eng.: Peterloo Poets, 1991), pp. 15, 24.

6. On Michelangelo, see *New York Times*, 25 May 1991. On Joyce, see, e.g., Hans Walter Gabler, "Afterword," in James Joyce, *Ulysses: The Corrected Text*, ed. Hans Walter Gabler with Wolfhard Steppe and Claus Melchior, with preface by Richard Ellmann (New York: Vintage Books, 1986), pp. 647–50.

10. Lawyers too are misled, or mislead themselves. See, as an example of the traditional account, the definition of "legal justice" (set forth not as expression, but as definition) in Roberto Mangabeira Unger, *Knowledge and Politics* (New York: Free Press, 1975; pbk. ed. 1976), p. 89.

14. Oliver Wendell Holmes, *The Common Law*, ed. Mark DeWolfe Howe (Cambridge, Mass.: Harvard University Press, 1963), p. 33. "Question rarely asked": but see John T. Noonan, Jr., "The Alliance of Law and History," in *Persons and Masks of*

the Law: Cardozo, Holmes, Jefferson, and Wythe as Makers of the Masks (New York: Farrar, Straus and Giroux, 1976), pp. 152–67. On the authoritarian "as if" and illusion's possibilities, and as an exercise in listening to the whole of what lawyers say in gauging lawyers' belief, see Steven D. Smith, "Idolatry in Constitutional Interpretation," *Virginia Law Review* 79, no. 3 (April 1993): 583. *Dred Scott v. Sandford*, 60 U.S. (19 How.) 393 (1857). Common law prosecution: see, e.g., *People v. O'Neil*, 194 Ill. App. 3d 79 (1990) (homicide); *People v. Pymm*, 561 N.Y.S. 2d 687 (Ct. App. 1990) (assault). Refuse Act of 1899, ch. 425, 30 Stat. 1121, sec. 13, 16 (1899) (codified as amended at 33 U.S.C. sec. 407, 410 [1988]): on what is termed the revival of the Refuse Act, before passage of the Clean Water Acts of the 1970s, and its decline thereafter, see William H. Rodgers, Jr., *Environmental Law* (St. Paul: West, 1986), 2:11–17, 162–80.

18. *Max Weber on Law in Economy and Society*, ed. Max Rheinstein, trans. Edward Shils and Max Rheinstein (Cambridge, Mass.: Harvard University Press, 1954), pp. 201–2. For discussion, see Anthony T. Kronman, *Max Weber* (Stanford: Stanford University Press, 1983), pp. 87–92. On "mathematics as language," see Saul A. Kripke, *Wittgenstein on Rules and Private Language: An Elementary Exposition* (Oxford: Basil Blackwell, 1982), p. 7.

19. José Ortega y Gasset, quoted in Bruno Bettelheim, *Freud and Man's Soul* (New York: Vintage Books, 1984), p. 54.

23. *Mens rea*: the mind of the accused, one of the general elements of a crime to be argued and proved, reference to which is maintained in latinate form in legal discussion in English, without closure in its various definitions. John Stuart Mill, *Autobiography* (London: Oxford University Press, 1924), p. 113: "At this my heart sank within me: the whole foundation on which my life was constructed fell down. All my happiness was to have been found in the continual pursuit of this end . . . I seemed to have nothing left to live for."

24. Irwin Ross, "How Lawless Are Big Companies?" *Fortune* (December 1, 1980): 57.

25. Hans Küng: see Hans Küng, *Infallible? An Inquiry*, trans.

Edward Quinn (Garden City, N.Y.: Doubleday, 1983). Karl Barth: see Karl Barth, *Final Testimonies*, ed. Eberhard Busch, trans. Geoffrey W. Bromiley (Grand Rapids, Mich.: William B. Eerdmans, 1977).

28. John Keats, "Letter to George and Georgiana Keats, February 24, 1819," in *Complete Works of John Keats*, ed. H. Buxton Forman (Glasgow: Gowars & Gray, 1901), 5:37.

31. Aldo Leopold also uses the wolf and the mountain in *A Sand County Almanac and Sketches Here and There* (New York: Oxford University Press, 1968), pp. 129–33.

32. Fyodor Dostoyevsky, *The Brothers Karamazov*, trans. Constance Garnett (New York: Vintage Books, 1950). Karl Marx, Preface to First Edition, *Capital*, trans. Eden and Cedar Paul, with introduction by G.D.H. Cole (London: J. M. Dent, 1974), p. l.

35. On the golden section, and the golden proportion and golden rectangle, see H. E. Huntley, *The Divine Proportion: A Study in Mathematical Beauty* (New York: Dover Publications, 1970), pp. 23–34, 60–65.

36. Charles Darwin, *Autobiography*, ed. Nora Barlow (New York: Harcourt Brace, 1959), pp. 138–39. Wilder Penfield, *The Mystery of the Mind: A Critical Study of Consciousness and the Human Brain* (Princeton: Princeton University Press,1975). Erwin Schrödinger, *What Is Life? and Other Scientific Essays* (Garden City, N.Y.: Doubleday, 1956). Michael Polanyi, *Personal Knowledge: Toward a Post-Critical Philosophy* (Chicago: University of Chicago Press, 1958; pbk. ed. 1962).

37. On Foucault, see Hervé Guibert, *To the Friend Who Did Not Save My Life*, trans. Linda Coverdale (New York: Macmillan, 1991), pp. 21–22. See also James Miller, *The Passion of Michel Foucault* (New York: Simon & Schuster, 1992). Cf. Catherine A. MacKinnon, "Does Sexuality Have a History?" *Michigan Quarterly Review* 30, no. 1 (Winter 1991): 10 n. 7. On subjection, see Michel Foucault, "The Subject and Power," in *Art After Modernism: Rethinking Representation*, ed. Brian Wallis (New York: New Museum of Contemporary Art, 1984), pp. 417–32; "Two Lectures," in *Power/Knowledge: Selected Interviews*

and Other Writings, 1972–1977, ed. Colin Gordon (New York: Pantheon, 1980), pp. 78–79, 98; "What Is an Author?" in *The Foucault Reader*, ed. Paul Rabinow (New York: Pantheon, 1984), pp. 101, 117–20. On cyclically destructive subjectivity, see,e.g., Elias Canetti, *Crowds and Power*, trans. Carol Stewart (New York: Farrar Straus and Giroux, 1984). Cf. Robert A. Burt, *Taking Care of Strangers: The Rule of Law in Doctor-Patient Relations* (New York: Free Press, 1979).

38. On coldness and the gambler's stance, see, e.g., Detlev F. Vagts, "Legal Opinions In Quantitative Terms: The Lawyer As Haruspex Or Bookie?" *The Business Lawyer* 34, no. 2 (January 1979): 421, 424, 425 n. 12, 427; *United States v. Hartford-Empire Co.*, 46 F. Supp. 541, 606 (N.D. Ohio, 1942). On abuse and artificiality, see, e.g., J.J.B. Skinner, "Introduction," in International Bar Association, *Tax Avoidance, Tax Evasion* (London: Sweet & Maxwell, 1982), pp. 1–8.

43. Form criticism: see, e.g., Edgar V. McKnight, *What Is Form Criticism?* (Philadelphia: Fortress Press, 1969), 12, 15, 17, 37, 42, 51, 55; Helmut Koester, *Introduction to the New Testament* (Berlin: Walter de Gruyter, 1982), 2:59–70; Helmut Koester, "Writings and the Spirit: Authority and Politics in Ancient Christianity," *Harvard Theological Review* 84, no. 4 (1991): 353–72. Cargo cults: see, e.g., I. C. Jarvie, *The Revolution in Anthropology*, with foreword by Ernest Gellner (London: Routledge & Kegan Paul, 1964).

IV. Person

5. Noam Chomsky, *Syntactic Structures* (The Hague: Mouton & Co., 1957), p. 15. Andrew Marvell, *The Garden*, in *New Oxford Book of English Verse*, ed. Helen Gardner (Oxford: Oxford University Press, 1972), pp. 335–37.

6. Friedrich Nietzsche, *The Will to Power: An Attempted Transvaluation of All Values*, sections 548, 481–92, trans. Anthony M. Ludovici, in *The Complete Works of Friedrich Nietzsche*, ed. Oscar Levy (New York: Russell & Russell, 1964), 15:54,

12–20. Cf. Pierre Schlag, "The Problem of the Subject," *Texas Law Review* 69, no. 7 (June 1991): 1627.

7. View of man behind cognitive science: see, e.g., Herbert A. Simon, *The Sciences of the Artificial,* 2d ed. (Cambridge, Mass.: London: MIT Press, 1982); Philip N. Johnson-Laird, *The Computer and the Mind: An Introduction to Cognitive Science* (Cambridge, Mass.: Harvard University Press, 1988). For the possibly different approach of cognitive ethology, see Donald R. Griffin, *Animal Thinking* (Cambridge, Mass.: Harvard University Press, 1984). John Macquarrie: see *God-Talk: An Examination of the Language and Logic of Theology* (London: SCM Press, 1967), p. 176.

15. Physiochemical: the addition of twentieth-century features, such as indeterminacy in quantum mechanics, or acceptance of Gödel's theorem, does not alter the stance as it is taken, either in lay discussion, or in discussion within the terms of a discipline. For an example of anticipation of the stance (tied as it must be to a view of language), see Thomas Hobbes, "Of Sense," "Of Speech," "Of Reason, and Science," in *Leviathan,* ed. with introduction by C. B. MacPherson (Harmondsworth: Penguin Books, 1984), pp. 85–87, 100–110, 110–18 (and for departure from the view of language declared, see, e.g., "Of Civill Lawes," pp. 321–28, or indeed the book, *Leviathan*).

27. The child centered: cf. Stephen R. L. Clark, *Civil Peace and Sacred Order: Limits and Renewals I* (Oxford: Clarendon Press, 1989), pp. 57–60.

30. Cf. "there is no sense . . ." in G. J. Warnock, *The Object of Morality* (London: Methuen, 1971), p. 84, quoted in Charles Fried, *Right and Wrong* (Cambridge, Mass.: Harvard University Press, 1978), p. 61.

31. Plato, "The Apology," "Crito," in *Dialogues of Plato,* trans. W.H.D. Rouse (New York: New American Library, 1956), pp. 423–59. I am indebted to James Boyd White for discussion and his readings of the *Dialogues.* See, e.g., *Heracles Bow: Essays on the Rhetoric and Poetics of the Law* (Madison: University of Wisconsin Press, 1985), pp. 215–37.

32. See also Joseph Vining, "The Mysterious Example of the

Legislature" and "The Democratic Connection," in *The Authoritative and the Authoritarian*, pbk. ed. (Chicago: University of Chicago Press, 1988), pp. 110–41. For an example of late twentieth-century questioning among lawyers of the special status of statutes, see Guido Calabresi, *A Common Law for the Age of Statutes* (Cambridge, Mass.: Harvard University Press, 1982).

34. On evolutionary contingency, see, e.g., D'Arcy Wentworth Thompson, *On Growth and Form* (1917), abridged ed., ed. with introduction by John Tyler Bonner (Cambridge: Cambridge University Press, 1975), pp. 200–201; Stephen Jay Gould, *Wonderful Life: The Burgess Shale and the Nature of History* (London: Hutchinson Radius, 1990). Cf. Richard Rorty, "Mind as Ineffable," in *Mind in Nature: Nobel Conference VII*, ed. Richard Q. Elvee (New York: Harper & Row, 1982), pp. 60–95.

36. On combinatorial thinking, see, e.g., François Jacob, *The Logic of Life: A History of Heredity*, trans. Betty E. Spilman (New York: Viking Penguin, 1989).

39. "And twofold Always. May God us keep / From Single vision & Newton's sleep!" *With happiness stretch'd across the hills* (1802), in *The Letters of William Blake with Related Documents*, 3d ed., ed. Geoffrey Keynes (Oxford: Clarendon Press, 1980), pp. 43–46; and *The Portable Blake*, ed. with introduction by Alfred Kazin (New York: Penguin Books, 1976), p. 210. See also References to Epigraph, above.

V. Action

3. *Calder v. Bull*, 3 U.S. (3 Dall.) 386 (1798). *Marbury v. Madison*, 5 U.S. (1 Cranch) 137 (1803). G.R.D., "Introduction to the Old Testament," pp. xvii–xviii; C.H.D., "Introduction to the New Testament," pp. v–viii, *The New English Bible, with the Apocrypha*, 2d ed. (New York: Cambridge University Press, 1970). Sherman Antitrust Act, ch. 647, 26 Stat. 209 (1890) (codified as amended at 15 U.S.C. sec. 1 *et seq.* (1988)).

4. On imitation, see Mercia Eliade, *The Sacred and the Profane: The Nature of Religion* (New York: Harcourt Brace Jovanovich, 1959).

5. On the unquestionable, see Roy A. Rappaport, *Ecology, Meaning, and Religion* (Richmond, Calif.: North Atlantic Books, 1979).

6. On usury generally, see John T. Noonan, Jr., *The Scholastic Analysis of Usery* (Cambridge, Mass.: Harvard University Press, 1957). For a description of an example of modern Islamic practice, see Paul Gosling, "Mortgage Made for the Muslim Buyer," *Independent on Sunday*, 14 October 1990. The thrust of practice is toward joinder of profit and risk of loss of time or money; the resistance is to their separation. On mergers, see, e.g., Robert C. Clark, *Corporate Law* (Boston: Little, Brown, 1986), pp. 443–61; Alfred F. Conard, *Corporations in Perspective* (Mineola, N.Y.: Foundation Press, 1976), pp. 215–23, 240–45; *Farris v. Glen Alden Corporation*, 393 Pa. 427, 143 A.2d 25 (1958).

12. *Monty Python and the Holy Grail* (Python Pictures and EMI, 1974).

15. "Then whets and combs its silver wings, / And, till prepared for longer flight, / Waves in its plumes the various light." Andrew Marvell, *The Garden*, in *New Oxford Book of English Verse*, ed. Helen Gardner (Oxford: Oxford University Press, 1972), pp. 335–37. On the "name of God," see *The Interpreter's Dictionary of the Bible*, ed. George Arthur Buttrick et al. (New York: Abingdon Press, 1962), 2:409–11.

16. Robert Hayden, *Monet's "Waterlilies,"* in *Collected Poems*, ed. Frederick Glaysher (New York: Liveright, 1985), p. 101.

VI. Force

1. Treatment of Hindu texts: see, e.g., the arguments between Brian K. Smith and Wendy Doniger set out in their Introduction to *The Laws of Manu*, trans. Wendy Doniger with Brian K. Smith (London: Penguin Books, 1991), pp. xv–lxi.

2. Friedrich Nietzsche, *The Anti-Christ* (New York: Arno Press and the New York Times, 1972), pp. 51–52. For a single work surveying efforts in social philosophy and social science to

escape, without acknowledgment of the person, or law, from nineteenth-century positivism, see Richard J. Bernstein, *Beyond Objectivism and Relativism: Science, Hermeneutics, and Praxis* (Philadelphia: University of Pennsylvania Press, 1983). For an introduction in a single volume to parallel discussions in literary criticism, see the collection of papers in *Against Theory: Literary Studies and the New Pragmatism*, ed. W.J.T. Mitchell (Chicago: University of Chicago Press, 1985); see also Joseph Vining, "Generalization in Interpretive Theory," in *Law and the Order of Culture*, ed. Robert Post (Berkeley: University of California Press, 1991), pp. 1–12. For a background example (and an example also of usage of the term "science"), see Hans Reichenbach, *The Rise of Scientific Philosophy* (Berkeley: University of California Press, 1951, pbk. ed. 1958). For introduction to and discussion of efforts to bring positivism to American discussion of legal practice, see Philip Soper, *A Theory of Law* (Cambridge, Mass.: Harvard University Press, 1984).

5. *USAir* (June 1989): 53.

10. For a partial objection to the characterization of mathematical thought both inside and outside the professional discipline of mathematics, and to the implications of its characterization, see Imre Lakatos, *Proofs and Refutations: The Logic of Mathematical Discovery*, ed. John Worral and Elie Zahar (Cambridge: Cambridge University Press, 1976), pp. 1–5. On the thought of mathematicians, compare G. H. Hardy, *A Mathematician's Apology* (1940), with a foreword by C. P. Snow (Cambridge: Cambridge University Press, 1982), pp. 121–30, with Roger Penrose, *The Emperor's New Mind: Concerning Computers, Minds, and the Laws of Physics* (Oxford: Oxford University Press, 1989), pp. 417–18, noting use by Penrose of the words "bow down" and "authority"; but see also p. 447, "There is as much mystery and beauty as one might wish in the precise Platonic mathematical world," following the placing of "some" before "profound advances in the understanding of mind." I am indebted particularly to Alton L. Becker for discussion of inquiries in anthropology. On the dissolution of science into history, see, e.g., Thomas S. Kuhn, *The Structure of Scientific Revolutions* (Chicago: University of Chicago Press, 1962); George Le-

vine, *Darwin and the Novelists: Patterns of Science in Victorian Fiction* (Cambridge, Mass.: Harvard University Press, 1988) (and pp. 235–37, 271–72, on Darwin's response to the prospect of internalization of theory: e.g., a theory of evolution a product of evolution; definition of mind as product of evolution, the product of a mind that is a product of evolution).

11. John Grossman, "Exploring the Slot Market," *American Way* (November 1983): 173.

15. *Immigration and Naturalization Service v. Chadha*, 462 U.S. 919 (1983); *Motor Vehicle Manufacturers Association of the United States, Inc. v. State Farm Mutual Automobile Insurance Company*, 463 U.S. 29 (1983).

17. Regulation S—Rules Governing Offers and Sales Made Outside the United States without Registration under the Securities Act of 1933, preliminary note 2 preceding 17 C.F.R. § 230.901 (1992).

19. On Salman Rushdie, see Salman Rushdie, "In Good Faith," "Is Nothing Sacred?" and "One Thousand Days in a Balloon," in *Imaginary Homelands: Essays and Criticism, 1981–1991* (New York: Penguin Books, 1991), pp. 393–439; Ali A. Mazrui, "Is *The Satanic Verses* a Satanic Novel?: Moral Dilemmas of the Rushdie Affair," *Michigan Quarterly Review* 28, no. 3 (Summer 1989): 347–71; *The Rushdie Letters: Freedom to Speak, Freedom to Write*, ed. Steve MacDonogh (Lincoln: University of Nebraska Press, 1993). Drinking the Golden Calf: Exodus 32:20, 27–28.

20. See Bernard G. Weiss, "Interpretation in Islamic Law: The Theory of *Ijtihād*," *American Journal of Comparative Law* 26, no. 2 (spring 1978): 199, 207–10, 212; "The Long Journey Toward God's Law: The Venture of *Usul Al-Fiqh*," unpublished paper (January 20, 1988). Cf. Bernard Lewis, *The Political Language of Islam* (Chicago: University of Chicago Press, 1988), p. 129 n. 11; Fazlur Rahman, *Islam and Modernity: Transformation of an Intellectual Tradition* (Chicago: University of Chicago Press, 1982), pp. 7–8, 107–8.

23. On parking meters and possession of marijuana, see Ann Arbor, Michigan, City Charter, 16.2.(b) (1974). On taxation, see Learned Hand's statement in *Helvering v. Gregory*, 69 F.2d 809,

810 (2d Cir. 1934), memorized by generations of American lawyers ("Any one may so arrange his affairs that his taxes shall be as low as possible . . .").

27. George Orwell, *1984* (New York: Harcourt Brace Jovanovich, 1949). Cf., e.g., Elaine Scarry, *The Body in Pain: The Making and Unmaking of the World* (New York: Oxford University Press, 1985); Richard Rorty, *Contingency, irony, and solidarity* (Cambridge: Cambridge University Press, 1989), pp. 172–87. Faust: e.g., Johann Wolfgang von Goethe, *Faust: Part One*, trans. Bayard Taylor, ed. Stuart Atkins, (New York: Collier Books, 1963), pp. 190–312.

28. Holmes: For Holmes's proposition that law "in the broadest sense" is a phenomenon that "like everything else" is in "fixed quantitative relations" to "its antecedents and consequents," "connected" in its "general aspects" with "the universe" and "the universal law," see O. W. Holmes, "The Path of the Law," *Harvard Law Review* 10, no. 8 (March 25, 1897): 465, 478.

31. Zimbabwe and Rhodesia: see *The Statesman's Year-Book 1993–1994*, ed. Brian Hunter (New York: St. Martin's Press, 1993), p. 1634.

32. *Brown v. Board of Education of Topeka*, 347 U.S. 483 (1954). Judge's promise: see, e.g., ch. 646, 62 Stat. 907 (1948), codified as amended at 28 U.S.C. sec. 453 (Supp. II, 1990).

VII. Organization

1. Joinder: some horse and dog trainers know this joinder where the individuals *above* and *below* are not both human beings. See Vicki Hearne, *Adam's Task: Calling Animals by Name* (New York: Vintage, 1987). Protection of employee disobedience: see, e.g., *Whirlpool Corporation v. Marshall*, 445 U.S. 1 (1980).

3. Frank H. Knight, *The Economic Organization* (New York: Augustus M. Kelly, 1951), pp. 23–30. On Knight, see Rutledge Vining, *On Appraising the Performance of an Economic System* (Cambridge: Cambridge University Press, 1984). I am indebted to Rutledge Vining, not least for the nature of his inquiries.

4. Fernand Braudel, *Afterthoughts on Material Civilization and Capitalism*, trans. Patricia M. Ranum (Baltimore: Johns Hopkins University Press, 1977). Alan Sillitoe, *Travels in Nihilon* (London: W. H. Allen, 1971).

7. Human capital: see, e.g., Ronald J. Gilson and Robert H. Mnookin, "Coming of Age in a Corporate Law Firm: The Economics of Associate Career Patterns," *Stanford Law Review* 41, no. 3 (February 1989): 567, 570. For an introductory account of the linguistic problem in economics, see Paul Anthony Samuelson, *Foundations of Economic Analysis*, with a new foreword (New York: Atheneum, 1967), pp. iii, vii–xiii.

9. Ulysses before the Cyclops: Homer, *The Odyssey*, trans. E. V. Rieu (Harmondsworth: Penguin Books, 1959), pp. 139–54.

11. On Titulus Regius, see Mortimer Levine, *Tudor Dynastic Problems, 1460–1571* (London: George Allen & Unwin, 1973), pp. 35–36, 140: "So that all things said and remembered in the said bill and act thereof may be for ever out of remembrance and also forgot." (The incident is used by Josephine Tey in her detective mystery, *The Daughter of Time* [New York: Berkley Medallion, 1970], pp. 103–9, 135). On veto resolutions, see *Immigration and Naturalization Service v. Chadha*, 462 U.S. 919 (1983). On committee reports, see the colloquy in *Congressional Record*, 97th Cong., 2d sess., 1982, vol. 128, pt. 12, pp. 16,918–919 (July 19, 1982).

14. On the gross form of an original discernable in a crude imitation, see Rudolf Arnheim, "On Duplication," in *The Forger's Art: Forgery and the Philosophy of Art*, ed. Denis Dutton (Berkeley: University of California Press, 1983), p. 237.

17. For work on the mystery of office in the creation of authority through language, and as an example of disciplinary affinity, see Gersham G. Scholem, "Religious Authority and Mysticism," in *On the Kabbalah and Its Symbolism*, trans. Ralph Manheim (London: Routledge and Kegan Paul, 1965), pp. 5–31.

20. There is a "Halton Hills," a regional municipality, outside Toronto. There is no "Hariton."

21. Eugenia Ginzburg, *Journey into the Whirlwind*, trans. Paul Stevenson and Max Hayward (New York: Harcourt, Brace & World, 1967), pp. 292–96; *Within the Whirlwind*, trans. Ian

Boland with an introduction by Heinrich Böll (London: Collins and Harville, 1981).

24. See, e.g., John Stuart Mill, "On Liberty," in *On Liberty, Representative Government, The Subjection of Women: Three Essays* (London: Oxford University Press, 1954), pp. 1–141.

VIII. Time

1. On the extension of natural selection to thought, see, as an early example, William James, quoted in Robert J. Richards, *Darwin and the Emergence of Evolutionary Theories of Mind and Behavior* (Chicago: University of Chicago Press, 1987), pp. 426–50, and in Nicholas Humphrey, *Consciousness Regained: Chapters in the Development of Mind* (Oxford: Oxford University Press, 1984), p. 178. But see Jacques Barzun, *A Stroll with William James* (New York: Harper & Row, 1983). For a contemporary example, see Herbert A. Simon, *The Sciences of the Artificial*, 2d ed. (Cambridge, Mass.: MIT Press, 1982). Mysterium tremendum: the phrase is from Rudolf Otto, *The Idea of the Holy: An Inquiry into the non-rational factor in the idea of the divine and its relation to the rational*, trans. John W. Harvey (London: Oxford University Press, 1958). Karl Barth, *The Epistle to the Romans*, 6th ed., trans. Edwyn C. Hoskins (London: Oxford University Press, 1965). For an appeal to cosmic order that is contemporary and is an appeal rather than an analysis (of, for example, Coleridge or Goethe), see Rudolf Arnheim, "Visual Aesthetics," in *The Encyclopedia of Religion*, ed. Mircea Eliade (New York: Macmillan, 1987), pp. 47–51.

3. William Shakespeare, *The Tempest*, ed. Northrop Frye (Baltimore, Md.: Penguin Books, 1970).

7. Wilhelm Dilthey, *The Construction of the Historical World in the Human Studies* (1910), in H. A. Hodges, *Wilhelm Dilthey: An Introduction* (London: Routledge & Kegan Paul, 1949), p. 142, quoted in John Macquarrie, *Existentialism* (Harmondsworth: Penguin Books, 1973), p. 222. Dilthey continues with a discussion of the scope of the evidence upon which understanding is based.

8. Alban Krailsheimer, *Pascal* (Oxford: Oxford University Press, 1980), pp. 41–43; Pascal, *Pensées*, trans. with introduction by A. J. Krailsheimer (Harmondsworth: Penguin Books, 1981), pp. 18–20. William Wordsworth, *The Excursion 1814* (Oxford: Woodstock Books, 1991), preface, p. ix. On determining composition over time by dating manuscript paper, see Alan Tyson, *Mozart: Studies of the Autograph Scores* (Cambridge, Mass.: Harvard University Press, 1987).

17. On the florilegium, see Jaroslav Pelikan, *The Vindication of Tradition* (New Haven, Conn.: Yale University Press, 1984), pp. 73–77. I am indebted to Kenneth DeWoskin for the example from the Chinese.

18. On "I Am," see, e.g., "God, Names of" in *The Interpreter's Dictionary of the Bible*, ed. George Arthur Buttrick et al. (New York: Abingdon Press, 1962), 2:409–11; Brevard S. Childs, *The Book of Exodus: A Critical, Theological Commentary* (Philadelphia: Westminster Press, 1974), pp. 69, 71.

Index ✖ _____

265; legal, 282, 311, 324; and
pattern, 247; political, 252, 281;
reduction to, 30, 31, 41, 148,
184, 248, 276; and substance,
255, 342–43. *See also* system
profit: and control, 319; flow of,
289, 319–20; in law of property,
288
profit maximization: and corporate law, 322; and criminal
law, 298; in economic theory,
291; and law, 292, 298; as proposed purpose, 35, 131, 293,
294–95, 298; and quantification of desire, 244; and system,
316; in writing, 243. *See also*
maximizing
progress, 176
pronouns, reading of, 6, 9, 92, 143,
175, 179, 184, 236, 346
property, 287–90, 321; and emptiness, 260, 262; and identity,
287; as static, 22. *See also*
agency; control; liability; profit
propitiation, 127
psychoanalysis, 190
psychology, 10–11, 42, 148, 213
punishment, 262, 272, 300; belief
in way of, 125, 152, 134; limit
to, 154–55, 275, 296; and madness, 47; and person, 154–55,
208, 275; and time, 353
punitive damages, 152, 300
purpose, 42, 140, 222; and agency,
298; and care, 207; and cause,
294; creation of, 190; entity and,
104, 292–93, 298; and hypocrisy, 68; and respect, 294

quantification: of desire, 244; of
disclosure, 83; dissolution of, in
reading, 167; of justice, 188; of
person, 39; reading of, 318–19;
restatement and, 339; of value,
299
quantum mechanics, 367n.15

Queen of England, 172–73
question beginning legal analysis,
101–2, 113, 151, 251
quotation, 14, 97, 191, 232, 348,
349–51; as repetition, 57; and restatement, 339, 346
quotation marks, reading of, 8

race, 112, 196, 236
Racter, 7–8
randomness, 7, 68, 329, 340–42,
347–51; and self-reference, 101,
103, 138, 233
reading, 70, 96, 218, 335; as evidence, 310; explanation and,
149; of joint writing, 84; as
praise, 153; presuppositions of,
8, 80–82, 149, 310, 336; and rereading, 219, 334–36, 337, 349–
51; as speaking for oneself, 264;
translation compared, 31, 217;
of whole, 55, 63, 156, 159, 249,
338, 350; and writing, 6, 56, 96,
159–60, 217, 219, 346–47
reality: and action, 9, 11–12, 13–
14, 141, 232; of another, 169–70;
and authenticity, 46, 234; of
cases, in law, 124, 265; and creation, 141, 264–65; and deference, 104–5; and definition, 10,
54; of desire, 245; as freedom,
126, 195, 235; and indifference,
201; loss of, 124, 139, 176; physical, 213; and randomness, 137;
and responsibility, 176; of voice,
116
Refuse Act of 1899, 117
relativism: and action, 13–14, 229;
aesthetic, 18, 142, 230, 236; appeal of, 325; and individuality,
136; and novelty, 176; and vision of the world, 13. *See also*
cultural relativism
reliance, 117–18
religion: institutions of, 312; invariant texts in, 223–24; and